Welcome to the Daily Live Trading Clinic (DLTC) Journal. I created this journal to help traders of the DLTC system better exercise focus and discipline as they execute and track their trades each day. It is unlike any other trading journal, and you if happen to get your hands it.

Congratulation.

This book is dedicated to the co-designer of the DLTC, Mr James Thompkins, for teaching me and hundreds of people this skill that opened the door to economic freedom. We love you Mr. T.

This book was created by Miss Danielle Dowie, DLTC trader from the class of 2023.
Copyright disclaimer

WRITE DOWN YOUR GOALS

Creating SMART Goals

SMART goals are specific, measurable, achievable, relevant, and time-bound. They provide clear milestones and an end point to aim for. When setting goals in trading, ensure they adhere to the SMART criteria to increase the likelihood of success.

EXAMPLE OF A SMART GOAL IN TRADING

SPECIFIC: I want to increase my trading account balance by 20% using the DLTC system.

_____

_____

_____

MEASURABLE: I will measure my account balance weekly to track progress.

_____

_____

_____

ACHIEVABLE: I will achieve this by making consistent trades that follow the DLTC system rules.

_____

_____

_____

RELEVANT: This goal will help me become a more disciplined and profitable trader.

_____

_____

_____

TIME-BOUND: I aim to achieve this goal within the next 6 months.

_____

_____

_____

GOAL OUTLINE

BIG GOAL: Define your overarching trading goal.

_____

_____

_____

EXAMPLE: Increase trading account balance by 20% in 6 months.

MONTHLY MILESTONES: Break down your big goal into smaller monthly targets that will lead you towards your big goal.

_____

_____

_____

EXAMPLE: Increase account balance by 3.33% each month.

WEEKLY OBJECTIVES: Set specific objectives for each week that contribute to your monthly milestones.

_____

_____

_____

EXAMPLE: Execute at least 5 trades following the DLTC system.

DAILY ACTIONABLE STEPS: Identify daily tasks that will help you meet your weekly objectives.

_____

_____

_____

EXAMPLE: Review market conditions for 30 minutes and identify 2 potential trades.

TRADER'S CHECKLIST

ALL INSTRUMENTS:

1. Enter trade as soon as you confirm two or more entry signals

2. Exit trade as soon as you enter profit

3. Ten (10%) percent risk management exercised

HARD SHARES/CRYPTO:

1. Day chart momentum is bullish

2. Hourly chart momentum is bullish

3. 5 min chart momentum is bullish

OPTIONS:

1. Contract was as close to the money as your trading powder allows

2. Open Interest exceeds 3,000

3. Volume exceeds 3,000

FOREX:

1. Trading Pair

2. Leverage Minimum leverage used

3. Lot Size

CRYPTO:

1. Bitcoin is bullish

ENTRY SIGNALS

Review Entry Signals before the trading session begins. As a DLTC trader you should be familiar with the following entry signals. It helps to review these signals before each trading session begins. Embrace the repetition; it is a small price to pay for freedom.

Call (Bul)	Entry Signal		Put (Bear)
Golden Crossover			**Death Crossover**
Two Green Candles closes ABOVE both 5 and 9 day moving averages.			Two Red Candles closes BELOW both 5 and 9 day moving averages.
MACD Main line crosses above signal line far BELOW the midline.			MACD Signal line crosses above MACD line far ABOVE the midline.
MACD Convergence			**MACD Divergence**
Bollinger Band sees candles close BELOW the lower Bollinger Band 3X			Bollinger Band sees candles close ABOVE the upper Bollinger Band 3X
RSI Oversold- Below 30 Extremely Oversold – Below 10			Overbought – Above 70 Extremely Overbought – Above 90
RSI Convergence – RSI making higher lows while stock price is making lower lows			RSI Divergence – RSI making lower highs while stock price is making higher highs
DMI- the D+ converges and breaks above the D- (positive divergence)			DMI- the D- converges and breaks above the D+ (negative divergence)
ADX starts picking up			**ADX starts picking up**
Stochastic- Oversold: When %K or %D falls below a certain threshold (typically 30), it suggests that the asset may be oversold, indicating a potential buying opportunity.			Stochastic- Overbought: When %K or %D rises above a certain threshold (typically 70), it suggests that the asset may be overbought, indicating a potential selling opportunity.

DATE:_____   ACCOUNT BALANCE:_____

TRADING POWDER:_____   MAXIMUM RISK AMOUNT PER TRADE:_____

DAILY GOAL: _____

MARKET ANALYSIS

Check the momentum of the market based on Key Indices, Commodities, and ETFs.

Type of Market Day	Key Indices and Commodities					
	S&P 500	Dow 30	Nasdaq	Russell 2000	Crude Oil	Gold
GREEN						
RED						

INDICATORS OVERVIEW

	Ticker Symbol																	
Indicators	5M	15M	30M	1HR	4HR	1D	5M	15M	30M	1HR	4HR	1D	5M	15M	30M	1HR	4HR	1D
Moving Averages																		
5 day																		
9 day																		
50 day																		
100 day																		
200 day																		
Bollinger Bands																		
Upper Band																		
Lower Band																		
DMI																		
Bullish																		
Bearish																		
MACD																		
Bullish																		
Bearish																		
RSI																		
Overbought																		
Oversold																		
Stochastic																		
Overbought																		
Oversold																		

Company Ticker	Chart Momentum																
	5 MIN			15 MIN			30 MIN			1 HR			4 HR			1 DAY		

Instrument(s) Traded	Hard Shares		Options		Forex		Crypto		
Trade #	Entry Time	Exit Time	Time Elapsed	Buy/Call Sell/Put	Entry Price	Exit Price	Quantity	Profit/Loss	Total
1									
2									
3									
4									
5									
6									
7									
8									
9									
10									

Total Trades	Winning Trades	Losing Trades	Win Rate %
Notes			

DATE:_____   ACCOUNT BALANCE:_____

TRADING POWDER:_____   MAXIMUM RISK AMOUNT PER TRADE:_____

DAILY GOAL: _____

MARKET ANALYSIS

Check the momentum of the market based on Key Indices, Commodities, and ETFs.

Type of Market Day	Key Indices and Commodities					
	S&P 500	Dow 30	Nasdaq	Russell 2000	Crude Oil	Gold
GREEN						
RED						

INDICATORS OVERVIEW

	Ticker Symbol																	
Indicators	5M	15M	30M	1HR	4HR	1D	5M	15M	30M	1HR	4HR	1D	5M	15M	30M	1HR	4HR	1D
Moving Averages																		
5 day																		
9 day																		
50 day																		
100 day																		
200 day																		
Bollinger Bands																		
Upper Band																		
Lower Band																		
DMI																		
Bullish																		
Bearish																		
MACD																		
Bullish																		
Bearish																		
RSI																		
Overbought																		
Oversold																		
Stochastic																		
Overbought																		
Oversold																		

Company Ticker	Chart Momentum																	
	5 MIN			15 MIN			30 MIN			1 HR			4 HR			1 DAY		

Instrument(s) Traded	Hard Shares		Options		Forex		Crypto		
Trade #	Entry Time	Exit Time	Time Elapsed	Buy/Call Sell/Put	Entry Price	Exit Price	Quantity	Profit/Loss	Total
1									
2									
3									
4									
5									
6									
7									
8									
9									
10									

Total Trades	Winning Trades	Losing Trades	Win Rate %

Notes

DATE:_____   ACCOUNT BALANCE:_____

TRADING POWDER:_____   MAXIMUM RISK AMOUNT PER TRADE:_____

DAILY GOAL: _____

MARKET ANALYSIS

Check the momentum of the market based on Key Indices, Commodities, and ETFs.

Type of Market Day	Key Indices and Commodities					
	S&P 500	Dow 30	Nasdaq	Russell 2000	Crude Oil	Gold
GREEN						
RED						

INDICATORS OVERVIEW

| | Ticker Symbol | | | | | | | | | | | | | | | | | |
| | | | | | | | | | | | | | | | | | | |
Indicators	5M	15M	30M	1HR	4HR	1D	5M	15M	30M	1HR	4HR	1D	5M	15M	30M	1HR	4HR	1D
Moving Averages																		
5 day																		
9 day																		
50 day																		
100 day																		
200 day																		
Bollinger Bands																		
Upper Band																		
Lower Band																		
DMI																		
Bullish																		
Bearish																		
MACD																		
Bullish																		
Bearish																		
RSI																		
Overbought																		
Oversold																		
Stochastic																		
Overbought																		
Oversold																		

Company Ticker	Chart Momentum																
	5 MIN			15 MIN			30 MIN			1 HR			4 HR			1 DAY		

Instrument(s) Traded	Hard Shares		Options		Forex		Crypto		
Trade #	Entry Time	Exit Time	Time Elapsed	Buy/Call Sell/Put	Entry Price	Exit Price	Quantity	Profit/Loss	Total
1									
2									
3									
4									
5									
6									
7									
8									
9									
10									

Total Trades	Winning Trades	Losing Trades	Win Rate %

Notes

DATE:_____   ACCOUNT BALANCE:_____

TRADING POWDER:_____   MAXIMUM RISK AMOUNT PER TRADE:_____

DAILY GOAL: _____

MARKET ANALYSIS

Check the momentum of the market based on Key Indices, Commodities, and ETFs.

Type of Market Day	Key Indices and Commodities					
	S&P 500	Dow 30	Nasdaq	Russell 2000	Crude Oil	Gold
GREEN						
RED						

INDICATORS OVERVIEW

	Ticker Symbol																	
Indicators	5M	15M	30M	1HR	4HR	1D	5M	15M	30M	1HR	4HR	1D	5M	15M	30M	1HR	4HR	1D
Moving Averages																		
5 day																		
9 day																		
50 day																		
100 day																		
200 day																		
Bollinger Bands																		
Upper Band																		
Lower Band																		
DMI																		
Bullish																		
Bearish																		
MACD																		
Bullish																		
Bearish																		
RSI																		
Overbought																		
Oversold																		
Stochastic																		
Overbought																		
Oversold																		

Company Ticker	Chart Momentum																
	5 MIN			15 MIN			30 MIN			1 HR			4 HR			1 DAY		

Instrument(s) Traded	Hard Shares		Options		Forex		Crypto		
Trade #	Entry Time	Exit Time	Time Elapsed	Buy/Call Sell/Put	Entry Price	Exit Price	Quantity	Profit/Loss	Total
1									
2									
3									
4									
5									
6									
7									
8									
9									
10									

Total Trades	Winning Trades	Losing Trades	Win Rate %

Notes

DATE:_____   ACCOUNT BALANCE:_____

TRADING POWDER:_____   MAXIMUM RISK AMOUNT PER TRADE:_____

DAILY GOAL: _____

MARKET ANALYSIS

Check the momentum of the market based on Key Indices, Commodities, and ETFs.

Type of Market Day	Key Indices and Commodities					
	S&P 500	Dow 30	Nasdaq	Russell 2000	Crude Oil	Gold
GREEN						
RED						

INDICATORS OVERVIEW

	Ticker Symbol																	
Indicators	5M	15M	30M	1HR	4HR	1D	5M	15M	30M	1HR	4HR	1D	5M	15M	30M	1HR	4HR	1D
Moving Averages																		
5 day																		
9 day																		
50 day																		
100 day																		
200 day																		
Bollinger Bands																		
Upper Band																		
Lower Band																		
DMI																		
Bullish																		
Bearish																		
MACD																		
Bullish																		
Bearish																		
RSI																		
Overbought																		
Oversold																		
Stochastic																		
Overbought																		
Oversold																		

Company Ticker	Chart Momentum					
	5 MIN	15 MIN	30 MIN	1 HR	4 HR	1 DAY

Instrument(s) Traded	Hard Shares		Options		Forex		Crypto		
Trade #	Entry Time	Exit Time	Time Elapsed	Buy/Call Sell/Put	Entry Price	Exit Price	Quantity	Profit/Loss	Total
1									
2									
3									
4									
5									
6									
7									
8									
9									
10									

Total Trades	Winning Trades	Losing Trades	Win Rate %

Notes

DATE:_____   ACCOUNT BALANCE:_____

TRADING POWDER:_____   MAXIMUM RISK AMOUNT PER TRADE:_____

DAILY GOAL: _____

MARKET ANALYSIS

Check the momentum of the market based on Key Indices, Commodities, and ETFs.

Type of Market Day	Key Indices and Commodities					
	S&P 500	Dow 30	Nasdaq	Russell 2000	Crude Oil	Gold
GREEN						
RED						

INDICATORS OVERVIEW

	Ticker Symbol																	
Indicators	5M	15M	30M	1HR	4HR	1D	5M	15M	30M	1HR	4HR	1D	5M	15M	30M	1HR	4HR	1D
Moving Averages																		
5 day																		
9 day																		
50 day																		
100 day																		
200 day																		
Bollinger Bands																		
Upper Band																		
Lower Band																		
DMI																		
Bullish																		
Bearish																		
MACD																		
Bullish																		
Bearish																		
RSI																		
Overbought																		
Oversold																		
Stochastic																		
Overbought																		
Oversold																		

Company Ticker	Chart Momentum												
	5 MIN		15 MIN		30 MIN		1 HR		4 HR		1 DAY		

Instrument(s) Traded	Hard Shares		Options		Forex		Crypto		
Trade #	Entry Time	Exit Time	Time Elapsed	Buy/Call Sell/Put	Entry Price	Exit Price	Quantity	Profit/Loss	Total
1									
2									
3									
4									
5									
6									
7									
8									
9									
10									

Total Trades	Winning Trades	Losing Trades	Win Rate %

Notes

DATE:_____ ACCOUNT BALANCE:_____

TRADING POWDER:_____ MAXIMUM RISK AMOUNT PER TRADE:_____

DAILY GOAL: _____

MARKET ANALYSIS

Check the momentum of the market based on Key Indices, Commodities, and ETFs.

Type of Market Day	Key Indices and Commodities					
	S&P 500	Dow 30	Nasdaq	Russell 2000	Crude Oil	Gold
GREEN						
RED						

INDICATORS OVERVIEW

	Ticker Symbol																	
Indicators	5M	15M	30M	1HR	4HR	1D	5M	15M	30M	1HR	4HR	1D	5M	15M	30M	1HR	4HR	1D
Moving Averages																		
5 day																		
9 day																		
50 day																		
100 day																		
200 day																		
Bollinger Bands																		
Upper Band																		
Lower Band																		
DMI																		
Bullish																		
Bearish																		
MACD																		
Bullish																		
Bearish																		
RSI																		
Overbought																		
Oversold																		
Stochastic																		
Overbought																		
Oversold																		

Company Ticker	Chart Momentum																
	5 MIN			15 MIN			30 MIN			1 HR			4 HR			1 DAY		

Instrument(s) Traded	Hard Shares		Options		Forex		Crypto		
Trade #	Entry Time	Exit Time	Time Elapsed	Buy/Call Sell/Put	Entry Price	Exit Price	Quantity	Profit/Loss	Total
1									
2									
3									
4									
5									
6									
7									
8									
9									
10									

Total Trades	Winning Trades	Losing Trades	Win Rate %

Notes

DATE:_____   ACCOUNT BALANCE:_____

TRADING POWDER:_____   MAXIMUM RISK AMOUNT PER TRADE:_____

DAILY GOAL: _____

MARKET ANALYSIS

Check the momentum of the market based on Key Indices, Commodities, and ETFs.

Type of Market Day	Key Indices and Commodities					
	S&P 500	Dow 30	Nasdaq	Russell 2000	Crude Oil	Gold
GREEN						
RED						

INDICATORS OVERVIEW

	Ticker Symbol																	
Indicators	5M	15M	30M	1HR	4HR	1D	5M	15M	30M	1HR	4HR	1D	5M	15M	30M	1HR	4HR	1D
Moving Averages																		
5 day																		
9 day																		
50 day																		
100 day																		
200 day																		
Bollinger Bands																		
Upper Band																		
Lower Band																		
DMI																		
Bullish																		
Bearish																		
MACD																		
Bullish																		
Bearish																		
RSI																		
Overbought																		
Oversold																		
Stochastic																		
Overbought																		
Oversold																		

Company Ticker	Chart Momentum											
	5 MIN		15 MIN		30 MIN		1 HR		4 HR		1 DAY	

Instrument(s) Traded	Hard Shares		Options		Forex		Crypto		
Trade #	Entry Time	Exit Time	Time Elapsed	Buy/Call Sell/Put	Entry Price	Exit Price	Quantity	Profit/Loss	Total
1									
2									
3									
4									
5									
6									
7									
8									
9									
10									

Total Trades	Winning Trades	Losing Trades	Win Rate %

Notes

DATE:_____   ACCOUNT BALANCE:_____

TRADING POWDER:_____   MAXIMUM RISK AMOUNT PER TRADE:_____

DAILY GOAL: _____

MARKET ANALYSIS

Check the momentum of the market based on Key Indices, Commodities, and ETFs.

Type of Market Day	Key Indices and Commodities					
	S&P 500	Dow 30	Nasdaq	Russell 2000	Crude Oil	Gold
GREEN						
RED						

INDICATORS OVERVIEW

	Ticker Symbol																	
Indicators	5M	15M	30M	1HR	4HR	1D	5M	15M	30M	1HR	4HR	1D	5M	15M	30M	1HR	4HR	1D
Moving Averages																		
5 day																		
9 day																		
50 day																		
100 day																		
200 day																		
Bollinger Bands																		
Upper Band																		
Lower Band																		
DMI																		
Bullish																		
Bearish																		
MACD																		
Bullish																		
Bearish																		
RSI																		
Overbought																		
Oversold																		
Stochastic																		
Overbought																		
Oversold																		

Company Ticker	Chart Momentum												
	5 MIN		15 MIN		30 MIN		1 HR		4 HR		1 DAY		

Instrument(s) Traded	Hard Shares		Options		Forex		Crypto		
Trade #	Entry Time	Exit Time	Time Elapsed	Buy/Call Sell/Put	Entry Price	Exit Price	Quantity	Profit/Loss	Total
1									
2									
3									
4									
5									
6									
7									
8									
9									
10									

Total Trades	Winning Trades	Losing Trades	Win Rate %

Notes

DATE:_____   ACCOUNT BALANCE:_____

TRADING POWDER:_____   MAXIMUM RISK AMOUNT PER TRADE:_____

DAILY GOAL: _____

MARKET ANALYSIS

Check the momentum of the market based on Key Indices, Commodities, and ETFs.

Type of Market Day	Key Indices and Commodities					
	S&P 500	Dow 30	Nasdaq	Russell 2000	Crude Oil	Gold
GREEN						
RED						

INDICATORS OVERVIEW

| | Ticker Symbol | | | | | | | | | | | | | | | | | |
| | | | | | | | | | | | | | | | | | | |
Indicators	5M	15M	30M	1HR	4HR	1D	5M	15M	30M	1HR	4HR	1D	5M	15M	30M	1HR	4HR	1D
Moving Averages																		
5 day																		
9 day																		
50 day																		
100 day																		
200 day																		
Bollinger Bands																		
Upper Band																		
Lower Band																		
DMI																		
Bullish																		
Bearish																		
MACD																		
Bullish																		
Bearish																		
RSI																		
Overbought																		
Oversold																		
Stochastic																		
Overbought																		
Oversold																		

Company Ticker	Chart Momentum											
	5 MIN		15 MIN		30 MIN		1 HR		4 HR		1 DAY	

Instrument(s) Traded	Hard Shares		Options		Forex		Crypto		
Trade #	Entry Time	Exit Time	Time Elapsed	Buy/Call Sell/Put	Entry Price	Exit Price	Quantity	Profit/Loss	Total
1									
2									
3									
4									
5									
6									
7									
8									
9									
10									

Total Trades	Winning Trades	Losing Trades	Win Rate %

Notes

DATE:_____   ACCOUNT BALANCE:_____

TRADING POWDER:_____   MAXIMUM RISK AMOUNT PER TRADE:_____

DAILY GOAL:_____

MARKET ANALYSIS

Check the momentum of the market based on Key Indices, Commodities, and ETFs.

Type of Market Day	Key Indices and Commodities					
	S&P 500	Dow 30	Nasdaq	Russell 2000	Crude Oil	Gold
GREEN						
RED						

INDICATORS OVERVIEW

	Ticker Symbol																	
Indicators	5M	15M	30M	1HR	4HR	1D	5M	15M	30M	1HR	4HR	1D	5M	15M	30M	1HR	4HR	1D
Moving Averages																		
5 day																		
9 day																		
50 day																		
100 day																		
200 day																		
Bollinger Bands																		
Upper Band																		
Lower Band																		
DMI																		
Bullish																		
Bearish																		
MACD																		
Bullish																		
Bearish																		
RSI																		
Overbought																		
Oversold																		
Stochastic																		
Overbought																		
Oversold																		

Company Ticker	Chart Momentum																	
	5 MIN			15 MIN			30 MIN			1 HR			4 HR			1 DAY		

Instrument(s) Traded	Hard Shares		Options		Forex		Crypto		
Trade #	Entry Time	Exit Time	Time Elapsed	Buy/Call Sell/Put	Entry Price	Exit Price	Quantity	Profit/Loss	Total
1									
2									
3									
4									
5									
6									
7									
8									
9									
10									

Total Trades	Winning Trades	Losing Trades	Win Rate %

Notes

DATE:_____   ACCOUNT BALANCE:_____

TRADING POWDER:_____   MAXIMUM RISK AMOUNT PER TRADE:_____

DAILY GOAL: _____

MARKET ANALYSIS

Check the momentum of the market based on Key Indices, Commodities, and ETFs.

Type of Market Day	Key Indices and Commodities					
	S&P 500	Dow 30	Nasdaq	Russell 2000	Crude Oil	Gold
GREEN						
RED						

INDICATORS OVERVIEW

	Ticker Symbol																	
Indicators	5M	15M	30M	1HR	4HR	1D	5M	15M	30M	1HR	4HR	1D	5M	15M	30M	1HR	4HR	1D
Moving Averages																		
5 day																		
9 day																		
50 day																		
100 day																		
200 day																		
Bollinger Bands																		
Upper Band																		
Lower Band																		
DMI																		
Bullish																		
Bearish																		
MACD																		
Bullish																		
Bearish																		
RSI																		
Overbought																		
Oversold																		
Stochastic																		
Overbought																		
Oversold																		

Company Ticker	Chart Momentum																
	5 MIN			15 MIN			30 MIN			1 HR			4 HR			1 DAY		

Instrument(s) Traded	Hard Shares		Options		Forex		Crypto		
Trade #	Entry Time	Exit Time	Time Elapsed	Buy/Call Sell/Put	Entry Price	Exit Price	Quantity	Profit/Loss	Total
1									
2									
3									
4									
5									
6									
7									
8									
9									
10									

Total Trades	Winning Trades	Losing Trades	Win Rate %

Notes

DATE:_____   ACCOUNT BALANCE:_____

TRADING POWDER:_____   MAXIMUM RISK AMOUNT PER TRADE:_____

DAILY GOAL: _____

MARKET ANALYSIS

Check the momentum of the market based on Key Indices, Commodities, and ETFs.

Type of Market Day	Key Indices and Commodities					
	S&P 500	Dow 30	Nasdaq	Russell 2000	Crude Oil	Gold
GREEN						
RED						

INDICATORS OVERVIEW

| | Ticker Symbol | | | | | | | | | | | | | | | | | |
| | | | | | | | | | | | | | | | | | | |
Indicators	5M	15M	30M	1HR	4HR	1D	5M	15M	30M	1HR	4HR	1D	5M	15M	30M	1HR	4HR	1D
Moving Averages																		
5 day																		
9 day																		
50 day																		
100 day																		
200 day																		
Bollinger Bands																		
Upper Band																		
Lower Band																		
DMI																		
Bullish																		
Bearish																		
MACD																		
Bullish																		
Bearish																		
RSI																		
Overbought																		
Oversold																		
Stochastic																		
Overbought																		
Oversold																		

Company Ticker	Chart Momentum											
	5 MIN		15 MIN		30 MIN		1 HR		4 HR		1 DAY	

Instrument(s) Traded	Hard Shares		Options		Forex		Crypto		
Trade #	Entry Time	Exit Time	Time Elapsed	Buy/Call Sell/Put	Entry Price	Exit Price	Quantity	Profit/Loss	Total
1									
2									
3									
4									
5									
6									
7									
8									
9									
10									

Total Trades	Winning Trades	Losing Trades	Win Rate %

Notes

DATE:_____   ACCOUNT BALANCE:_____

TRADING POWDER:_____   MAXIMUM RISK AMOUNT PER TRADE:_____

DAILY GOAL: _____

MARKET ANALYSIS

Check the momentum of the market based on Key Indices, Commodities, and ETFs.

Type of Market Day	Key Indices and Commodities					
	S&P 500	Dow 30	Nasdaq	Russell 2000	Crude Oil	Gold
GREEN						
RED						

INDICATORS OVERVIEW

	Ticker Symbol																	
Indicators	5M	15M	30M	1HR	4HR	1D	5M	15M	30M	1HR	4HR	1D	5M	15M	30M	1HR	4HR	1D
Moving Averages																		
5 day																		
9 day																		
50 day																		
100 day																		
200 day																		
Bollinger Bands																		
Upper Band																		
Lower Band																		
DMI																		
Bullish																		
Bearish																		
MACD																		
Bullish																		
Bearish																		
RSI																		
Overbought																		
Oversold																		
Stochastic																		
Overbought																		
Oversold																		

Company Ticker	Chart Momentum																	
	5 MIN			15 MIN			30 MIN			1 HR			4 HR			1 DAY		

Instrument(s) Traded	Hard Shares		Options		Forex		Crypto		
Trade #	Entry Time	Exit Time	Time Elapsed	Buy/Call Sell/Put	Entry Price	Exit Price	Quantity	Profit/Loss	Total
1									
2									
3									
4									
5									
6									
7									
8									
9									
10									

Total Trades	Winning Trades	Losing Trades	Win Rate %

Notes

DATE:_____   ACCOUNT BALANCE:_____

TRADING POWDER:_____   MAXIMUM RISK AMOUNT PER TRADE:_____

DAILY GOAL:_____

MARKET ANALYSIS

Check the momentum of the market based on Key Indices, Commodities, and ETFs.

Type of Market Day	Key Indices and Commodities					
	S&P 500	Dow 30	Nasdaq	Russell 2000	Crude Oil	Gold
GREEN						
RED						

INDICATORS OVERVIEW

	Ticker Symbol																	
Indicators	5M	15M	30M	1HR	4HR	1D	5M	15M	30M	1HR	4HR	1D	5M	15M	30M	1HR	4HR	1D
Moving Averages																		
5 day																		
9 day																		
50 day																		
100 day																		
200 day																		
Bollinger Bands																		
Upper Band																		
Lower Band																		
DMI																		
Bullish																		
Bearish																		
MACD																		
Bullish																		
Bearish																		
RSI																		
Overbought																		
Oversold																		
Stochastic																		
Overbought																		
Oversold																		

Company Ticker	Chart Momentum																
	5 MIN			15 MIN			30 MIN			1 HR			4 HR			1 DAY		

Instrument(s) Traded	Hard Shares		Options		Forex		Crypto		
Trade #	Entry Time	Exit Time	Time Elapsed	Buy/Call Sell/Put	Entry Price	Exit Price	Quantity	Profit/Loss	Total
1									
2									
3									
4									
5									
6									
7									
8									
9									
10									

Total Trades	Winning Trades	Losing Trades	Win Rate %

Notes

DATE:_____   ACCOUNT BALANCE:_____

TRADING POWDER:_____   MAXIMUM RISK AMOUNT PER TRADE:_____

DAILY GOAL: _____

MARKET ANALYSIS

Check the momentum of the market based on Key Indices, Commodities, and ETFs.

Type of Market Day	Key Indices and Commodities					
	S&P 500	Dow 30	Nasdaq	Russell 2000	Crude Oil	Gold
GREEN						
RED						

INDICATORS OVERVIEW

| | Ticker Symbol | | | | | | | | | | | | | | | | | |
| | | | | | | | | | | | | | | | | | |
Indicators	5M	15M	30M	1HR	4HR	1D	5M	15M	30M	1HR	4HR	1D	5M	15M	30M	1HR	4HR	1D
Moving Averages																		
5 day																		
9 day																		
50 day																		
100 day																		
200 day																		
Bollinger Bands																		
Upper Band																		
Lower Band																		
DMI																		
Bullish																		
Bearish																		
MACD																		
Bullish																		
Bearish																		
RSI																		
Overbought																		
Oversold																		
Stochastic																		
Overbought																		
Oversold																		

Company Ticker	Chart Momentum												
	5 MIN		15 MIN		30 MIN		1 HR		4 HR		1 DAY		

Instrument(s) Traded	Hard Shares		Options		Forex		Crypto		
Trade #	Entry Time	Exit Time	Time Elapsed	Buy/Call Sell/Put	Entry Price	Exit Price	Quantity	Profit/Loss	Total
1									
2									
3									
4									
5									
6									
7									
8									
9									
10									

Total Trades	Winning Trades	Losing Trades	Win Rate %

Notes

DATE:_____   ACCOUNT BALANCE:_____

TRADING POWDER:_____   MAXIMUM RISK AMOUNT PER TRADE:_____

DAILY GOAL: _____

MARKET ANALYSIS

Check the momentum of the market based on Key Indices, Commodities, and ETFs.

Type of Market Day	Key Indices and Commodities					
	S&P 500	Dow 30	Nasdaq	Russell 2000	Crude Oil	Gold
GREEN						
RED						

INDICATORS OVERVIEW

	Ticker Symbol																	
Indicators	5M	15M	30M	1HR	4HR	1D	5M	15M	30M	1HR	4HR	1D	5M	15M	30M	1HR	4HR	1D
Moving Averages																		
5 day																		
9 day																		
50 day																		
100 day																		
200 day																		
Bollinger Bands																		
Upper Band																		
Lower Band																		
DMI																		
Bullish																		
Bearish																		
MACD																		
Bullish																		
Bearish																		
RSI																		
Overbought																		
Oversold																		
Stochastic																		
Overbought																		
Oversold																		

Company Ticker	Chart Momentum																
	5 MIN			15 MIN			30 MIN			1 HR			4 HR			1 DAY		

Instrument(s) Traded	Hard Shares		Options		Forex		Crypto		
Trade #	Entry Time	Exit Time	Time Elapsed	Buy/Call Sell/Put	Entry Price	Exit Price	Quantity	Profit/Loss	Total
1									
2									
3									
4									
5									
6									
7									
8									
9									
10									

Total Trades	Winning Trades	Losing Trades	Win Rate %

Notes

DATE:_____   ACCOUNT BALANCE:_____

TRADING POWDER:_____   MAXIMUM RISK AMOUNT PER TRADE:_____

DAILY GOAL: _____

MARKET ANALYSIS

Check the momentum of the market based on Key Indices, Commodities, and ETFs.

Type of Market Day	Key Indices and Commodities					
	S&P 500	Dow 30	Nasdaq	Russell 2000	Crude Oil	Gold
GREEN						
RED						

INDICATORS OVERVIEW

	Ticker Symbol																	
Indicators	5M	15M	30M	1HR	4HR	1D	5M	15M	30M	1HR	4HR	1D	5M	15M	30M	1HR	4HR	1D
Moving Averages																		
5 day																		
9 day																		
50 day																		
100 day																		
200 day																		
Bollinger Bands																		
Upper Band																		
Lower Band																		
DMI																		
Bullish																		
Bearish																		
MACD																		
Bullish																		
Bearish																		
RSI																		
Overbought																		
Oversold																		
Stochastic																		
Overbought																		
Oversold																		

Company Ticker	Chart Momentum																
	5 MIN			15 MIN			30 MIN			1 HR			4 HR			1 DAY		

Instrument(s) Traded	Hard Shares		Options		Forex		Crypto		
Trade #	Entry Time	Exit Time	Time Elapsed	Buy/Call Sell/Put	Entry Price	Exit Price	Quantity	Profit/Loss	Total
1									
2									
3									
4									
5									
6									
7									
8									
9									
10									

Total Trades	Winning Trades	Losing Trades	Win Rate %

Notes

DATE:_____   ACCOUNT BALANCE:_____

TRADING POWDER:_____   MAXIMUM RISK AMOUNT PER TRADE:_____

DAILY GOAL: _____

MARKET ANALYSIS

Check the momentum of the market based on Key Indices, Commodities, and ETFs.

Type of Market Day	Key Indices and Commodities					
	S&P 500	Dow 30	Nasdaq	Russell 2000	Crude Oil	Gold
GREEN						
RED						

INDICATORS OVERVIEW

	Ticker Symbol																	
Indicators	5M	15M	30M	1HR	4HR	1D	5M	15M	30M	1HR	4HR	1D	5M	15M	30M	1HR	4HR	1D
Moving Averages																		
5 day																		
9 day																		
50 day																		
100 day																		
200 day																		
Bollinger Bands																		
Upper Band																		
Lower Band																		
DMI																		
Bullish																		
Bearish																		
MACD																		
Bullish																		
Bearish																		
RSI																		
Overbought																		
Oversold																		
Stochastic																		
Overbought																		
Oversold																		

Company Ticker	Chart Momentum																
	5 MIN			15 MIN			30 MIN			1 HR			4 HR			1 DAY		

Instrument(s) Traded	Hard Shares		Options		Forex		Crypto		
Trade #	Entry Time	Exit Time	Time Elapsed	Buy/Call Sell/Put	Entry Price	Exit Price	Quantity	Profit/Loss	Total
1									
2									
3									
4									
5									
6									
7									
8									
9									
10									

Total Trades	Winning Trades	Losing Trades	Win Rate %

Notes

DATE:_____   ACCOUNT BALANCE:_____

TRADING POWDER:_____   MAXIMUM RISK AMOUNT PER TRADE:_____

DAILY GOAL: _____

MARKET ANALYSIS

Check the momentum of the market based on Key Indices, Commodities, and ETFs.

Type of Market Day	Key Indices and Commodities					
	S&P 500	Dow 30	Nasdaq	Russell 2000	Crude Oil	Gold
GREEN						
RED						

INDICATORS OVERVIEW

	Ticker Symbol																	
Indicators	5M	15M	30M	1HR	4HR	1D	5M	15M	30M	1HR	4HR	1D	5M	15M	30M	1HR	4HR	1D
Moving Averages																		
5 day																		
9 day																		
50 day																		
100 day																		
200 day																		
Bollinger Bands																		
Upper Band																		
Lower Band																		
DMI																		
Bullish																		
Bearish																		
MACD																		
Bullish																		
Bearish																		
RSI																		
Overbought																		
Oversold																		
Stochastic																		
Overbought																		
Oversold																		

Company Ticker	Chart Momentum																
	5 MIN			15 MIN			30 MIN			1 HR			4 HR			1 DAY		

Instrument(s) Traded	Hard Shares		Options		Forex		Crypto		
Trade #	Entry Time	Exit Time	Time Elapsed	Buy/Call Sell/Put	Entry Price	Exit Price	Quantity	Profit/Loss	Total
1									
2									
3									
4									
5									
6									
7									
8									
9									
10									

Total Trades	Winning Trades	Losing Trades	Win Rate %

Notes

DATE:_____   ACCOUNT BALANCE:_____

TRADING POWDER:_____   MAXIMUM RISK AMOUNT PER TRADE:_____

DAILY GOAL: _____

MARKET ANALYSIS

Check the momentum of the market based on Key Indices, Commodities, and ETFs.

Type of Market Day	Key Indices and Commodities					
	S&P 500	Dow 30	Nasdaq	Russell 2000	Crude Oil	Gold
GREEN						
RED						

INDICATORS OVERVIEW

	Ticker Symbol																	
Indicators	5M	15M	30M	1HR	4HR	1D	5M	15M	30M	1HR	4HR	1D	5M	15M	30M	1HR	4HR	1D
Moving Averages																		
5 day																		
9 day																		
50 day																		
100 day																		
200 day																		
Bollinger Bands																		
Upper Band																		
Lower Band																		
DMI																		
Bullish																		
Bearish																		
MACD																		
Bullish																		
Bearish																		
RSI																		
Overbought																		
Oversold																		
Stochastic																		
Overbought																		
Oversold																		

Company Ticker	Chart Momentum											
	5 MIN		15 MIN		30 MIN		1 HR		4 HR		1 DAY	

Instrument(s) Traded	Hard Shares		Options		Forex		Crypto		
Trade #	Entry Time	Exit Time	Time Elapsed	Buy/Call Sell/Put	Entry Price	Exit Price	Quantity	Profit/Loss	Total
1									
2									
3									
4									
5									
6									
7									
8									
9									
10									

Total Trades	Winning Trades	Losing Trades	Win Rate %

Notes

DATE:_____   ACCOUNT BALANCE:_____

TRADING POWDER:_____   MAXIMUM RISK AMOUNT PER TRADE:_____

DAILY GOAL: _____

MARKET ANALYSIS

Check the momentum of the market based on Key Indices, Commodities, and ETFs.

Type of Market Day	Key Indices and Commodities					
	S&P 500	Dow 30	Nasdaq	Russell 2000	Crude Oil	Gold
GREEN						
RED						

INDICATORS OVERVIEW

	Ticker Symbol																	
Indicators	5M	15M	30M	1HR	4HR	1D	5M	15M	30M	1HR	4HR	1D	5M	15M	30M	1HR	4HR	1D
Moving Averages																		
5 day																		
9 day																		
50 day																		
100 day																		
200 day																		
Bollinger Bands																		
Upper Band																		
Lower Band																		
DMI																		
Bullish																		
Bearish																		
MACD																		
Bullish																		
Bearish																		
RSI																		
Overbought																		
Oversold																		
Stochastic																		
Overbought																		
Oversold																		

Company Ticker	Chart Momentum																
	5 MIN			15 MIN			30 MIN			1 HR			4 HR			1 DAY		

Instrument(s) Traded	Hard Shares		Options		Forex		Crypto		
Trade #	Entry Time	Exit Time	Time Elapsed	Buy/Call Sell/Put	Entry Price	Exit Price	Quantity	Profit/Loss	Total
1									
2									
3									
4									
5									
6									
7									
8									
9									
10									

Total Trades	Winning Trades	Losing Trades	Win Rate %

Notes

DATE:_____ ACCOUNT BALANCE:_____

TRADING POWDER:_____ MAXIMUM RISK AMOUNT PER TRADE:_____

DAILY GOAL: _____

MARKET ANALYSIS

Check the momentum of the market based on Key Indices, Commodities, and ETFs.

Type of Market Day	Key Indices and Commodities					
	S&P 500	Dow 30	Nasdaq	Russell 2000	Crude Oil	Gold
GREEN						
RED						

INDICATORS OVERVIEW

	Ticker Symbol																	
Indicators	5M	15M	30M	1HR	4HR	1D	5M	15M	30M	1HR	4HR	1D	5M	15M	30M	1HR	4HR	1D
Moving Averages																		
5 day																		
9 day																		
50 day																		
100 day																		
200 day																		
Bollinger Bands																		
Upper Band																		
Lower Band																		
DMI																		
Bullish																		
Bearish																		
MACD																		
Bullish																		
Bearish																		
RSI																		
Overbought																		
Oversold																		
Stochastic																		
Overbought																		
Oversold																		

Company Ticker	Chart Momentum																
	5 MIN			15 MIN			30 MIN			1 HR			4 HR			1 DAY		

Instrument(s) Traded	Hard Shares		Options		Forex		Crypto		
Trade #	Entry Time	Exit Time	Time Elapsed	Buy/Call Sell/Put	Entry Price	Exit Price	Quantity	Profit/Loss	Total
1									
2									
3									
4									
5									
6									
7									
8									
9									
10									

Total Trades	Winning Trades	Losing Trades	Win Rate %

Notes

DATE:_____   ACCOUNT BALANCE:_____

TRADING POWDER:_____   MAXIMUM RISK AMOUNT PER TRADE:_____

DAILY GOAL: _____

MARKET ANALYSIS

Check the momentum of the market based on Key Indices, Commodities, and ETFs.

Type of Market Day	Key Indices and Commodities					
	S&P 500	Dow 30	Nasdaq	Russell 2000	Crude Oil	Gold
GREEN						
RED						

INDICATORS OVERVIEW

	Ticker Symbol																	
Indicators	5M	15M	30M	1HR	4HR	1D	5M	15M	30M	1HR	4HR	1D	5M	15M	30M	1HR	4HR	1D
Moving Averages																		
5 day																		
9 day																		
50 day																		
100 day																		
200 day																		
Bollinger Bands																		
Upper Band																		
Lower Band																		
DMI																		
Bullish																		
Bearish																		
MACD																		
Bullish																		
Bearish																		
RSI																		
Overbought																		
Oversold																		
Stochastic																		
Overbought																		
Oversold																		

Company Ticker	Chart Momentum												
	5 MIN		15 MIN		30 MIN		1 HR		4 HR		1 DAY		

Instrument(s) Traded	Hard Shares		Options		Forex		Crypto		
Trade #	Entry Time	Exit Time	Time Elapsed	Buy/Call Sell/Put	Entry Price	Exit Price	Quantity	Profit/Loss	Total
1									
2									
3									
4									
5									
6									
7									
8									
9									
10									

Total Trades	Winning Trades	Losing Trades	Win Rate %

Notes

DATE:_____   **ACCOUNT BALANCE:**_____

TRADING POWDER:_____   **MAXIMUM RISK AMOUNT PER TRADE:**_____

DAILY GOAL: _____

MARKET ANALYSIS

Check the momentum of the market based on Key Indices, Commodities, and ETFs.

Type of Market Day	Key Indices and Commodities					
	S&P 500	Dow 30	Nasdaq	Russell 2000	Crude Oil	Gold
GREEN						
RED						

INDICATORS OVERVIEW

| | Ticker Symbol | | | | | | | | | | | | | | | | | |
| | | | | | | | | | | | | | | | | | |
Indicators	5M	15M	30M	1HR	4HR	1D	5M	15M	30M	1HR	4HR	1D	5M	15M	30M	1HR	4HR	1D
Moving Averages																		
5 day																		
9 day																		
50 day																		
100 day																		
200 day																		
Bollinger Bands																		
Upper Band																		
Lower Band																		
DMI																		
Bullish																		
Bearish																		
MACD																		
Bullish																		
Bearish																		
RSI																		
Overbought																		
Oversold																		
Stochastic																		
Overbought																		
Oversold																		

Company Ticker	Chart Momentum												
	5 MIN			15 MIN			30 MIN			1 HR		4 HR	1 DAY

Instrument(s) Traded	Hard Shares		Options		Forex		Crypto		
Trade #	Entry Time	Exit Time	Time Elapsed	Buy/Call Sell/Put	Entry Price	Exit Price	Quantity	Profit/Loss	Total
1									
2									
3									
4									
5									
6									
7									
8									
9									
10									

Total Trades	Winning Trades	Losing Trades	Win Rate %

Notes

DATE:_____   ACCOUNT BALANCE:_____

TRADING POWDER:_____   MAXIMUM RISK AMOUNT PER TRADE:_____

DAILY GOAL: _____

MARKET ANALYSIS

Check the momentum of the market based on Key Indices, Commodities, and ETFs.

Type of Market Day	Key Indices and Commodities					
	S&P 500	Dow 30	Nasdaq	Russell 2000	Crude Oil	Gold
GREEN						
RED						

INDICATORS OVERVIEW

	Ticker Symbol																	
Indicators	5M	15M	30M	1HR	4HR	1D	5M	15M	30M	1HR	4HR	1D	5M	15M	30M	1HR	4HR	1D
Moving Averages																		
5 day																		
9 day																		
50 day																		
100 day																		
200 day																		
Bollinger Bands																		
Upper Band																		
Lower Band																		
DMI																		
Bullish																		
Bearish																		
MACD																		
Bullish																		
Bearish																		
RSI																		
Overbought																		
Oversold																		
Stochastic																		
Overbought																		
Oversold																		

Company Ticker	Chart Momentum											
	5 MIN		15 MIN		30 MIN		1 HR		4 HR		1 DAY	

Instrument(s) Traded	Hard Shares		Options		Forex		Crypto		
Trade #	Entry Time	Exit Time	Time Elapsed	Buy/Call Sell/Put	Entry Price	Exit Price	Quantity	Profit/Loss	Total
1									
2									
3									
4									
5									
6									
7									
8									
9									
10									

Total Trades	Winning Trades	Losing Trades	Win Rate %

Notes

DATE:_____   ACCOUNT BALANCE:_____

TRADING POWDER:_____   MAXIMUM RISK AMOUNT PER TRADE:_____

DAILY GOAL: _____

MARKET ANALYSIS

Check the momentum of the market based on Key Indices, Commodities, and ETFs.

Type of Market Day	Key Indices and Commodities					
	S&P 500	Dow 30	Nasdaq	Russell 2000	Crude Oil	Gold
GREEN						
RED						

INDICATORS OVERVIEW

	Ticker Symbol																	
Indicators	5M	15M	30M	1HR	4HR	1D	5M	15M	30M	1HR	4HR	1D	5M	15M	30M	1HR	4HR	1D
Moving Averages																		
5 day																		
9 day																		
50 day																		
100 day																		
200 day																		
Bollinger Bands																		
Upper Band																		
Lower Band																		
DMI																		
Bullish																		
Bearish																		
MACD																		
Bullish																		
Bearish																		
RSI																		
Overbought																		
Oversold																		
Stochastic																		
Overbought																		
Oversold																		

Company Ticker	Chart Momentum																	
	5 MIN			15 MIN			30 MIN			1 HR			4 HR			1 DAY		

Instrument(s) Traded	Hard Shares		Options		Forex		Crypto		
Trade #	Entry Time	Exit Time	Time Elapsed	Buy/Call Sell/Put	Entry Price	Exit Price	Quantity	Profit/Loss	Total
1									
2									
3									
4									
5									
6									
7									
8									
9									
10									

Total Trades	Winning Trades	Losing Trades	Win Rate %

Notes

DATE:_____   ACCOUNT BALANCE:_____

TRADING POWDER:_____   MAXIMUM RISK AMOUNT PER TRADE:_____

DAILY GOAL: _____

MARKET ANALYSIS

Check the momentum of the market based on Key Indices, Commodities, and ETFs.

Type of Market Day	Key Indices and Commodities					
	S&P 500	Dow 30	Nasdaq	Russell 2000	Crude Oil	Gold
GREEN						
RED						

INDICATORS OVERVIEW

	Ticker Symbol																	
Indicators	5M	15M	30M	1HR	4HR	1D	5M	15M	30M	1HR	4HR	1D	5M	15M	30M	1HR	4HR	1D
Moving Averages																		
5 day																		
9 day																		
50 day																		
100 day																		
200 day																		
Bollinger Bands																		
Upper Band																		
Lower Band																		
DMI																		
Bullish																		
Bearish																		
MACD																		
Bullish																		
Bearish																		
RSI																		
Overbought																		
Oversold																		
Stochastic																		
Overbought																		
Oversold																		

Company Ticker	Chart Momentum											
	5 MIN		15 MIN		30 MIN		1 HR		4 HR		1 DAY	

Instrument(s) Traded	Hard Shares		Options		Forex		Crypto			
Trade #	Entry Time	Exit Time	Time Elapsed	Buy/Call Sell/Put	Entry Price	Exit Price	Quantity	Profit/Loss	Total
1									
2									
3									
4									
5									
6									
7									
8									
9									
10									

Total Trades	Winning Trades	Losing Trades	Win Rate %
Notes			

DATE:_____   ACCOUNT BALANCE:_____

TRADING POWDER:_____   MAXIMUM RISK AMOUNT PER TRADE:_____

DAILY GOAL: _____

MARKET ANALYSIS

Check the momentum of the market based on Key Indices, Commodities, and ETFs.

Type of Market Day	Key Indices and Commodities					
	S&P 500	Dow 30	Nasdaq	Russell 2000	Crude Oil	Gold
GREEN						
RED						

INDICATORS OVERVIEW

	Ticker Symbol																	
Indicators	5M	15M	30M	1HR	4HR	1D	5M	15M	30M	1HR	4HR	1D	5M	15M	30M	1HR	4HR	1D
Moving Averages																		
5 day																		
9 day																		
50 day																		
100 day																		
200 day																		
Bollinger Bands																		
Upper Band																		
Lower Band																		
DMI																		
Bullish																		
Bearish																		
MACD																		
Bullish																		
Bearish																		
RSI																		
Overbought																		
Oversold																		
Stochastic																		
Overbought																		
Oversold																		

Company Ticker	Chart Momentum													
	5 MIN		15 MIN		30 MIN		1 HR		4 HR		1 DAY			

Instrument(s) Traded	Hard Shares		Options		Forex		Crypto		
Trade #	Entry Time	Exit Time	Time Elapsed	Buy/Call Sell/Put	Entry Price	Exit Price	Quantity	Profit/Loss	Total
1									
2									
3									
4									
5									
6									
7									
8									
9									
10									

Total Trades	Winning Trades	Losing Trades	Win Rate %

Notes

DATE:_____   ACCOUNT BALANCE:_____

TRADING POWDER:_____   MAXIMUM RISK AMOUNT PER TRADE:_____

DAILY GOAL: _____

MARKET ANALYSIS

Check the momentum of the market based on Key Indices, Commodities, and ETFs.

Type of Market Day	Key Indices and Commodities					
	S&P 500	Dow 30	Nasdaq	Russell 2000	Crude Oil	Gold
GREEN						
RED						

INDICATORS OVERVIEW

	Ticker Symbol																	
Indicators	5M	15M	30M	1HR	4HR	1D	5M	15M	30M	1HR	4HR	1D	5M	15M	30M	1HR	4HR	1D
Moving Averages																		
5 day																		
9 day																		
50 day																		
100 day																		
200 day																		
Bollinger Bands																		
Upper Band																		
Lower Band																		
DMI																		
Bullish																		
Bearish																		
MACD																		
Bullish																		
Bearish																		
RSI																		
Overbought																		
Oversold																		
Stochastic																		
Overbought																		
Oversold																		

Company Ticker	Chart Momentum											
	5 MIN		15 MIN		30 MIN		1 HR		4 HR		1 DAY	

Instrument(s) Traded	Hard Shares		Options		Forex		Crypto			
Trade #	Entry Time	Exit Time	Time Elapsed	Buy/Call Sell/Put	Entry Price	Exit Price	Quantity	Profit/Loss	Total
1									
2									
3									
4									
5									
6									
7									
8									
9									
10									

Total Trades	Winning Trades	Losing Trades	Win Rate %

Notes

DATE:_____   ACCOUNT BALANCE:_____

TRADING POWDER:_____   MAXIMUM RISK AMOUNT PER TRADE:_____

DAILY GOAL: _____

MARKET ANALYSIS

Check the momentum of the market based on Key Indices, Commodities, and ETFs.

Type of Market Day	Key Indices and Commodities					
	S&P 500	Dow 30	Nasdaq	Russell 2000	Crude Oil	Gold
GREEN						
RED						

INDICATORS OVERVIEW

	Ticker Symbol																	
Indicators	5M	15M	30M	1HR	4HR	1D	5M	15M	30M	1HR	4HR	1D	5M	15M	30M	1HR	4HR	1D
Moving Averages																		
5 day																		
9 day																		
50 day																		
100 day																		
200 day																		
Bollinger Bands																		
Upper Band																		
Lower Band																		
DMI																		
Bullish																		
Bearish																		
MACD																		
Bullish																		
Bearish																		
RSI																		
Overbought																		
Oversold																		
Stochastic																		
Overbought																		
Oversold																		

Company Ticker	Chart Momentum																
	5 MIN			15 MIN			30 MIN			1 HR			4 HR			1 DAY		

Instrument(s) Traded	Hard Shares		Options		Forex		Crypto		
Trade #	Entry Time	Exit Time	Time Elapsed	Buy/Call Sell/Put	Entry Price	Exit Price	Quantity	Profit/Loss	Total
1									
2									
3									
4									
5									
6									
7									
8									
9									
10									

Total Trades	Winning Trades	Losing Trades	Win Rate %

Notes

DATE:_____   ACCOUNT BALANCE:_____

TRADING POWDER:_____   MAXIMUM RISK AMOUNT PER TRADE:_____

DAILY GOAL: _____

MARKET ANALYSIS

Check the momentum of the market based on Key Indices, Commodities, and ETFs.

Type of Market Day	Key Indices and Commodities					
	S&P 500	Dow 30	Nasdaq	Russell 2000	Crude Oil	Gold
GREEN						
RED						

INDICATORS OVERVIEW

	Ticker Symbol																	
Indicators	5M	15M	30M	1HR	4HR	1D	5M	15M	30M	1HR	4HR	1D	5M	15M	30M	1HR	4HR	1D
Moving Averages																		
5 day																		
9 day																		
50 day																		
100 day																		
200 day																		
Bollinger Bands																		
Upper Band																		
Lower Band																		
DMI																		
Bullish																		
Bearish																		
MACD																		
Bullish																		
Bearish																		
RSI																		
Overbought																		
Oversold																		
Stochastic																		
Overbought																		
Oversold																		

Company Ticker	Chart Momentum												
	5 MIN		15 MIN		30 MIN		1 HR		4 HR		1 DAY		

Instrument(s) Traded	Hard Shares		Options		Forex		Crypto			
Trade #	Entry Time	Exit Time	Time Elapsed	Buy/Call Sell/Put	Entry Price	Exit Price	Quantity	Profit/Loss	Total
1									
2									
3									
4									
5									
6									
7									
8									
9									
10									

Total Trades	Winning Trades	Losing Trades	Win Rate %

Notes

DATE:_____   ACCOUNT BALANCE:_____

TRADING POWDER:_____   MAXIMUM RISK AMOUNT PER TRADE:_____

DAILY GOAL: _____

MARKET ANALYSIS

Check the momentum of the market based on Key Indices, Commodities, and ETFs.

Type of Market Day	Key Indices and Commodities					
	S&P 500	Dow 30	Nasdaq	Russell 2000	Crude Oil	Gold
GREEN						
RED						

INDICATORS OVERVIEW

	Ticker Symbol																	
Indicators	5M	15M	30M	1HR	4HR	1D	5M	15M	30M	1HR	4HR	1D	5M	15M	30M	1HR	4HR	1D
Moving Averages																		
5 day																		
9 day																		
50 day																		
100 day																		
200 day																		
Bollinger Bands																		
Upper Band																		
Lower Band																		
DMI																		
Bullish																		
Bearish																		
MACD																		
Bullish																		
Bearish																		
RSI																		
Overbought																		
Oversold																		
Stochastic																		
Overbought																		
Oversold																		

Company Ticker	Chart Momentum											
	5 MIN		15 MIN		30 MIN		1 HR		4 HR		1 DAY	

Instrument(s) Traded	Hard Shares		Options		Forex		Crypto		
Trade #	Entry Time	Exit Time	Time Elapsed	Buy/Call Sell/Put	Entry Price	Exit Price	Quantity	Profit/Loss	Total
1									
2									
3									
4									
5									
6									
7									
8									
9									
10									

Total Trades	Winning Trades	Losing Trades	Win Rate %

Notes

DATE:_____ ACCOUNT BALANCE:_____

TRADING POWDER:_____ MAXIMUM RISK AMOUNT PER TRADE:_____

DAILY GOAL: _____

MARKET ANALYSIS

Check the momentum of the market based on Key Indices, Commodities, and ETFs.

Type of Market Day	Key Indices and Commodities					
	S&P 500	Dow 30	Nasdaq	Russell 2000	Crude Oil	Gold
GREEN						
RED						

INDICATORS OVERVIEW

	Ticker Symbol																	
Indicators	5M	15M	30M	1HR	4HR	1D	5M	15M	30M	1HR	4HR	1D	5M	15M	30M	1HR	4HR	1D
Moving Averages																		
5 day																		
9 day																		
50 day																		
100 day																		
200 day																		
Bollinger Bands																		
Upper Band																		
Lower Band																		
DMI																		
Bullish																		
Bearish																		
MACD																		
Bullish																		
Bearish																		
RSI																		
Overbought																		
Oversold																		
Stochastic																		
Overbought																		
Oversold																		

Company Ticker	Chart Momentum																
	5 MIN			15 MIN			30 MIN			1 HR			4 HR			1 DAY		

Instrument(s) Traded	Hard Shares		Options		Forex		Crypto		
Trade #	Entry Time	Exit Time	Time Elapsed	Buy/Call Sell/Put	Entry Price	Exit Price	Quantity	Profit/Loss	Total
1									
2									
3									
4									
5									
6									
7									
8									
9									
10									

Total Trades	Winning Trades	Losing Trades	Win Rate %

Notes

DATE:_____

TRADING POWDER:_____

DAILY GOAL: _____

ACCOUNT BALANCE:_____

MAXIMUM RISK AMOUNT PER TRADE:_____

MARKET ANALYSIS

Check the momentum of the market based on Key Indices, Commodities, and ETFs.

Type of Market Day	Key Indices and Commodities					
	S&P 500	Dow 30	Nasdaq	Russell 2000	Crude Oil	Gold
GREEN						
RED						

INDICATORS OVERVIEW

	Ticker Symbol																	
Indicators	5M	15M	30M	1HR	4HR	1D	5M	15M	30M	1HR	4HR	1D	5M	15M	30M	1HR	4HR	1D
Moving Averages																		
5 day																		
9 day																		
50 day																		
100 day																		
200 day																		
Bollinger Bands																		
Upper Band																		
Lower Band																		
DMI																		
Bullish																		
Bearish																		
MACD																		
Bullish																		
Bearish																		
RSI																		
Overbought																		
Oversold																		
Stochastic																		
Overbought																		
Oversold																		

Company Ticker	Chart Momentum																
	5 MIN			15 MIN			30 MIN			1 HR			4 HR			1 DAY		

Instrument(s) Traded	Hard Shares		Options		Forex		Crypto		
Trade #	Entry Time	Exit Time	Time Elapsed	Buy/Call Sell/Put	Entry Price	Exit Price	Quantity	Profit/Loss	Total
1									
2									
3									
4									
5									
6									
7									
8									
9									
10									

Total Trades	Winning Trades	Losing Trades	Win Rate %
Notes			

DATE:_____   ACCOUNT BALANCE:_____

TRADING POWDER:_____   MAXIMUM RISK AMOUNT PER TRADE:_____

DAILY GOAL: _____

MARKET ANALYSIS

Check the momentum of the market based on Key Indices, Commodities, and ETFs.

Type of Market Day	Key Indices and Commodities					
	S&P 500	Dow 30	Nasdaq	Russell 2000	Crude Oil	Gold
GREEN						
RED						

INDICATORS OVERVIEW

	Ticker Symbol																	
Indicators	5M	15M	30M	1HR	4HR	1D	5M	15M	30M	1HR	4HR	1D	5M	15M	30M	1HR	4HR	1D
Moving Averages																		
5 day																		
9 day																		
50 day																		
100 day																		
200 day																		
Bollinger Bands																		
Upper Band																		
Lower Band																		
DMI																		
Bullish																		
Bearish																		
MACD																		
Bullish																		
Bearish																		
RSI																		
Overbought																		
Oversold																		
Stochastic																		
Overbought																		
Oversold																		

Company Ticker	Chart Momentum											
	5 MIN		15 MIN		30 MIN		1 HR		4 HR		1 DAY	

Instrument(s) Traded	Hard Shares		Options		Forex		Crypto			
Trade #	Entry Time	Exit Time	Time Elapsed	Buy/Call Sell/Put	Entry Price	Exit Price	Quantity	Profit/Loss	Total
1									
2									
3									
4									
5									
6									
7									
8									
9									
10									

Total Trades	Winning Trades	Losing Trades	Win Rate %
Notes			

DATE:_____   ACCOUNT BALANCE:_____

TRADING POWDER:_____   MAXIMUM RISK AMOUNT PER TRADE:_____

DAILY GOAL: _____

MARKET ANALYSIS

Check the momentum of the market based on Key Indices, Commodities, and ETFs.

Type of Market Day	Key Indices and Commodities					
	S&P 500	Dow 30	Nasdaq	Russell 2000	Crude Oil	Gold
GREEN						
RED						

INDICATORS OVERVIEW

	Ticker Symbol																	
Indicators	5M	15M	30M	1HR	4HR	1D	5M	15M	30M	1HR	4HR	1D	5M	15M	30M	1HR	4HR	1D
Moving Averages																		
5 day																		
9 day																		
50 day																		
100 day																		
200 day																		
Bollinger Bands																		
Upper Band																		
Lower Band																		
DMI																		
Bullish																		
Bearish																		
MACD																		
Bullish																		
Bearish																		
RSI																		
Overbought																		
Oversold																		
Stochastic																		
Overbought																		
Oversold																		

Company Ticker	Chart Momentum																
	5 MIN			15 MIN			30 MIN			1 HR			4 HR			1 DAY		

Instrument(s) Traded	Hard Shares		Options		Forex		Crypto		
Trade #	Entry Time	Exit Time	Time Elapsed	Buy/Call Sell/Put	Entry Price	Exit Price	Quantity	Profit/Loss	Total
1									
2									
3									
4									
5									
6									
7									
8									
9									
10									

Total Trades	Winning Trades	Losing Trades	Win Rate %

Notes

DATE:_____   ACCOUNT BALANCE:_____

TRADING POWDER:_____   MAXIMUM RISK AMOUNT PER TRADE:_____

DAILY GOAL: _____

MARKET ANALYSIS

Check the momentum of the market based on Key Indices, Commodities, and ETFs.

Type of Market Day	Key Indices and Commodities					
	S&P 500	Dow 30	Nasdaq	Russell 2000	Crude Oil	Gold
GREEN						
RED						

INDICATORS OVERVIEW

	Ticker Symbol																	
Indicators	5M	15M	30M	1HR	4HR	1D	5M	15M	30M	1HR	4HR	1D	5M	15M	30M	1HR	4HR	1D
Moving Averages																		
5 day																		
9 day																		
50 day																		
100 day																		
200 day																		
Bollinger Bands																		
Upper Band																		
Lower Band																		
DMI																		
Bullish																		
Bearish																		
MACD																		
Bullish																		
Bearish																		
RSI																		
Overbought																		
Oversold																		
Stochastic																		
Overbought																		
Oversold																		

Company Ticker	Chart Momentum												
	5 MIN		15 MIN		30 MIN		1 HR		4 HR		1 DAY		

Instrument(s) Traded	Hard Shares		Options		Forex		Crypto		
Trade #	Entry Time	Exit Time	Time Elapsed	Buy/Call Sell/Put	Entry Price	Exit Price	Quantity	Profit/Loss	Total
1									
2									
3									
4									
5									
6									
7									
8									
9									
10									

Total Trades	Winning Trades	Losing Trades	Win Rate %

Notes

DATE:_____   ACCOUNT BALANCE:_____

TRADING POWDER:_____   MAXIMUM RISK AMOUNT PER TRADE:_____

DAILY GOAL: _____

MARKET ANALYSIS

Check the momentum of the market based on Key Indices, Commodities, and ETFs.

Type of Market Day	Key Indices and Commodities					
	S&P 500	Dow 30	Nasdaq	Russell 2000	Crude Oil	Gold
GREEN						
RED						

INDICATORS OVERVIEW

	Ticker Symbol																	
Indicators	5M	15M	30M	1HR	4HR	1D	5M	15M	30M	1HR	4HR	1D	5M	15M	30M	1HR	4HR	1D
Moving Averages																		
5 day																		
9 day																		
50 day																		
100 day																		
200 day																		
Bollinger Bands																		
Upper Band																		
Lower Band																		
DMI																		
Bullish																		
Bearish																		
MACD																		
Bullish																		
Bearish																		
RSI																		
Overbought																		
Oversold																		
Stochastic																		
Overbought																		
Oversold																		

Company Ticker	Chart Momentum											
	5 MIN		15 MIN		30 MIN		1 HR		4 HR		1 DAY	

Instrument(s) Traded	Hard Shares		Options		Forex		Crypto		
Trade #	Entry Time	Exit Time	Time Elapsed	Buy/Call Sell/Put	Entry Price	Exit Price	Quantity	Profit/Loss	Total
1									
2									
3									
4									
5									
6									
7									
8									
9									
10									

Total Trades	Winning Trades	Losing Trades	Win Rate %

Notes

DATE:_____   ACCOUNT BALANCE:_____

TRADING POWDER:_____   MAXIMUM RISK AMOUNT PER TRADE:_____

DAILY GOAL: _____

MARKET ANALYSIS

Check the momentum of the market based on Key Indices, Commodities, and ETFs.

Type of Market Day	Key Indices and Commodities					
	S&P 500	Dow 30	Nasdaq	Russell 2000	Crude Oil	Gold
GREEN						
RED						

INDICATORS OVERVIEW

	Ticker Symbol																	
Indicators	5M	15M	30M	1HR	4HR	1D	5M	15M	30M	1HR	4HR	1D	5M	15M	30M	1HR	4HR	1D
Moving Averages																		
5 day																		
9 day																		
50 day																		
100 day																		
200 day																		
Bollinger Bands																		
Upper Band																		
Lower Band																		
DMI																		
Bullish																		
Bearish																		
MACD																		
Bullish																		
Bearish																		
RSI																		
Overbought																		
Oversold																		
Stochastic																		
Overbought																		
Oversold																		

Company Ticker	Chart Momentum												
	5 MIN			15 MIN			30 MIN			1 HR			4 HR			1 DAY		

Company Ticker	5 MIN			15 MIN			30 MIN			1 HR			4 HR			1 DAY		

Instrument(s) Traded	Hard Shares		Options		Forex		Crypto		
Trade #	Entry Time	Exit Time	Time Elapsed	Buy/Call Sell/Put	Entry Price	Exit Price	Quantity	Profit/Loss	Total
1									
2									
3									
4									
5									
6									
7									
8									
9									
10									

Total Trades	Winning Trades	Losing Trades	Win Rate %

Notes

DATE:_____ ACCOUNT BALANCE:_____

TRADING POWDER:_____ MAXIMUM RISK AMOUNT PER TRADE:_____

DAILY GOAL: _____

MARKET ANALYSIS

Check the momentum of the market based on Key Indices, Commodities, and ETFs.

Type of Market Day	Key Indices and Commodities					
	S&P 500	Dow 30	Nasdaq	Russell 2000	Crude Oil	Gold
GREEN						
RED						

INDICATORS OVERVIEW

Indicators	Ticker Symbol																	
	5M	15M	30M	1HR	4HR	1D	5M	15M	30M	1HR	4HR	1D	5M	15M	30M	1HR	4HR	1D
Moving Averages																		
5 day																		
9 day																		
50 day																		
100 day																		
200 day																		
Bollinger Bands																		
Upper Band																		
Lower Band																		
DMI																		
Bullish																		
Bearish																		
MACD																		
Bullish																		
Bearish																		
RSI																		
Overbought																		
Oversold																		
Stochastic																		
Overbought																		
Oversold																		

Company Ticker	Chart Momentum																
	5 MIN			15 MIN			30 MIN			1 HR			4 HR			1 DAY		

Instrument(s) Traded	Hard Shares		Options		Forex		Crypto		
Trade #	Entry Time	Exit Time	Time Elapsed	Buy/Call Sell/Put	Entry Price	Exit Price	Quantity	Profit/Loss	Total
1									
2									
3									
4									
5									
6									
7									
8									
9									
10									

Total Trades	Winning Trades	Losing Trades	Win Rate %

Notes

DATE:_____   ACCOUNT BALANCE:_____

TRADING POWDER:_____   MAXIMUM RISK AMOUNT PER TRADE:_____

DAILY GOAL: _____

MARKET ANALYSIS

Check the momentum of the market based on Key Indices, Commodities, and ETFs.

Type of Market Day	Key Indices and Commodities					
	S&P 500	Dow 30	Nasdaq	Russell 2000	Crude Oil	Gold
GREEN						
RED						

INDICATORS OVERVIEW

	Ticker Symbol																	
Indicators	5M	15M	30M	1HR	4HR	1D	5M	15M	30M	1HR	4HR	1D	5M	15M	30M	1HR	4HR	1D
Moving Averages																		
5 day																		
9 day																		
50 day																		
100 day																		
200 day																		
Bollinger Bands																		
Upper Band																		
Lower Band																		
DMI																		
Bullish																		
Bearish																		
MACD																		
Bullish																		
Bearish																		
RSI																		
Overbought																		
Oversold																		
Stochastic																		
Overbought																		
Oversold																		

Company Ticker	Chart Momentum												
	5 MIN			15 MIN			30 MIN			1 HR		4 HR	1 DAY

Instrument(s) Traded	Hard Shares		Options		Forex		Crypto		
Trade #	Entry Time	Exit Time	Time Elapsed	Buy/Call Sell/Put	Entry Price	Exit Price	Quantity	Profit/Loss	Total
1									
2									
3									
4									
5									
6									
7									
8									
9									
10									

Total Trades	Winning Trades	Losing Trades	Win Rate %

Notes

DATE:_____   ACCOUNT BALANCE:_____

TRADING POWDER:_____   MAXIMUM RISK AMOUNT PER TRADE:_____

DAILY GOAL: _____

MARKET ANALYSIS

Check the momentum of the market based on Key Indices, Commodities, and ETFs.

Type of Market Day	Key Indices and Commodities					
	S&P 500	Dow 30	Nasdaq	Russell 2000	Crude Oil	Gold
GREEN						
RED						

INDICATORS OVERVIEW

	Ticker Symbol																	
Indicators	5M	15M	30M	1HR	4HR	1D	5M	15M	30M	1HR	4HR	1D	5M	15M	30M	1HR	4HR	1D
Moving Averages																		
5 day																		
9 day																		
50 day																		
100 day																		
200 day																		
Bollinger Bands																		
Upper Band																		
Lower Band																		
DMI																		
Bullish																		
Bearish																		
MACD																		
Bullish																		
Bearish																		
RSI																		
Overbought																		
Oversold																		
Stochastic																		
Overbought																		
Oversold																		

Company Ticker	Chart Momentum											
	5 MIN		15 MIN		30 MIN		1 HR		4 HR		1 DAY	

Instrument(s) Traded	Hard Shares		Options		Forex		Crypto		
Trade #	Entry Time	Exit Time	Time Elapsed	Buy/Call Sell/Put	Entry Price	Exit Price	Quantity	Profit/Loss	Total
1									
2									
3									
4									
5									
6									
7									
8									
9									
10									

Total Trades	Winning Trades	Losing Trades	Win Rate %

Notes

DATE:_____   ACCOUNT BALANCE:_____

TRADING POWDER:_____   MAXIMUM RISK AMOUNT PER TRADE:_____

DAILY GOAL: _____

MARKET ANALYSIS

Check the momentum of the market based on Key Indices, Commodities, and ETFs.

Type of Market Day	Key Indices and Commodities					
	S&P 500	Dow 30	Nasdaq	Russell 2000	Crude Oil	Gold
GREEN						
RED						

INDICATORS OVERVIEW

	Ticker Symbol																	
Indicators	5M	15M	30M	1HR	4HR	1D	5M	15M	30M	1HR	4HR	1D	5M	15M	30M	1HR	4HR	1D
Moving Averages																		
5 day																		
9 day																		
50 day																		
100 day																		
200 day																		
Bollinger Bands																		
Upper Band																		
Lower Band																		
DMI																		
Bullish																		
Bearish																		
MACD																		
Bullish																		
Bearish																		
RSI																		
Overbought																		
Oversold																		
Stochastic																		
Overbought																		
Oversold																		

Company Ticker	Chart Momentum											
	5 MIN		15 MIN		30 MIN		1 HR		4 HR		1 DAY	

Instrument(s) Traded	Hard Shares		Options		Forex		Crypto		
Trade #	Entry Time	Exit Time	Time Elapsed	Buy/Call Sell/Put	Entry Price	Exit Price	Quantity	Profit/Loss	Total
1									
2									
3									
4									
5									
6									
7									
8									
9									
10									

Total Trades	Winning Trades	Losing Trades	Win Rate %

Notes

DATE:_____   ACCOUNT BALANCE:_____

TRADING POWDER:_____   MAXIMUM RISK AMOUNT PER TRADE:_____

DAILY GOAL: _____

MARKET ANALYSIS

Check the momentum of the market based on Key Indices, Commodities, and ETFs.

Type of Market Day	Key Indices and Commodities					
	S&P 500	Dow 30	Nasdaq	Russell 2000	Crude Oil	Gold
GREEN						
RED						

INDICATORS OVERVIEW

| | Ticker Symbol | | | | | | | | | | | | | | | | | |
| | | | | | | | | | | | | | | | | | |
Indicators	5M	15M	30M	1HR	4HR	1D	5M	15M	30M	1HR	4HR	1D	5M	15M	30M	1HR	4HR	1D
Moving Averages																		
5 day																		
9 day																		
50 day																		
100 day																		
200 day																		
Bollinger Bands																		
Upper Band																		
Lower Band																		
DMI																		
Bullish																		
Bearish																		
MACD																		
Bullish																		
Bearish																		
RSI																		
Overbought																		
Oversold																		
Stochastic																		
Overbought																		
Oversold																		

Company Ticker	Chart Momentum																	
	5 MIN			15 MIN			30 MIN			1 HR			4 HR			1 DAY		

Instrument(s) Traded	Hard Shares		Options		Forex		Crypto		
Trade #	Entry Time	Exit Time	Time Elapsed	Buy/Call Sell/Put	Entry Price	Exit Price	Quantity	Profit/Loss	Total
1									
2									
3									
4									
5									
6									
7									
8									
9									
10									

Total Trades	Winning Trades	Losing Trades	Win Rate %

Notes

DATE:_____   ACCOUNT BALANCE:_____

TRADING POWDER:_____   MAXIMUM RISK AMOUNT PER TRADE:_____

DAILY GOAL: _____

MARKET ANALYSIS

Check the momentum of the market based on Key Indices, Commodities, and ETFs.

Type of Market Day	Key Indices and Commodities					
	S&P 500	Dow 30	Nasdaq	Russell 2000	Crude Oil	Gold
GREEN						
RED						

INDICATORS OVERVIEW

	Ticker Symbol																	
Indicators	5M	15M	30M	1HR	4HR	1D	5M	15M	30M	1HR	4HR	1D	5M	15M	30M	1HR	4HR	1D
Moving Averages																		
5 day																		
9 day																		
50 day																		
100 day																		
200 day																		
Bollinger Bands																		
Upper Band																		
Lower Band																		
DMI																		
Bullish																		
Bearish																		
MACD																		
Bullish																		
Bearish																		
RSI																		
Overbought																		
Oversold																		
Stochastic																		
Overbought																		
Oversold																		

Company Ticker	Chart Momentum												
	5 MIN		15 MIN		30 MIN		1 HR		4 HR		1 DAY		

Instrument(s) Traded	Hard Shares		Options		Forex		Crypto		
Trade #	Entry Time	Exit Time	Time Elapsed	Buy/Call Sell/Put	Entry Price	Exit Price	Quantity	Profit/Loss	Total
1									
2									
3									
4									
5									
6									
7									
8									
9									
10									

Total Trades	Winning Trades	Losing Trades	Win Rate %

Notes

DATE:_____   ACCOUNT BALANCE:_____

TRADING POWDER:_____   MAXIMUM RISK AMOUNT PER TRADE:_____

DAILY GOAL: _____

MARKET ANALYSIS

Check the momentum of the market based on Key Indices, Commodities, and ETFs.

Type of Market Day	Key Indices and Commodities					
	S&P 500	Dow 30	Nasdaq	Russell 2000	Crude Oil	Gold
GREEN						
RED						

INDICATORS OVERVIEW

	Ticker Symbol																	
Indicators	5M	15M	30M	1HR	4HR	1D	5M	15M	30M	1HR	4HR	1D	5M	15M	30M	1HR	4HR	1D
Moving Averages																		
5 day																		
9 day																		
50 day																		
100 day																		
200 day																		
Bollinger Bands																		
Upper Band																		
Lower Band																		
DMI																		
Bullish																		
Bearish																		
MACD																		
Bullish																		
Bearish																		
RSI																		
Overbought																		
Oversold																		
Stochastic																		
Overbought																		
Oversold																		

Company Ticker	Chart Momentum																
	5 MIN			15 MIN			30 MIN			1 HR			4 HR			1 DAY		

Instrument(s) Traded	Hard Shares		Options		Forex		Crypto		
Trade #	Entry Time	Exit Time	Time Elapsed	Buy/Call Sell/Put	Entry Price	Exit Price	Quantity	Profit/Loss	Total
1									
2									
3									
4									
5									
6									
7									
8									
9									
10									

Total Trades	Winning Trades	Losing Trades	Win Rate %

Notes

DATE:_____   ACCOUNT BALANCE:_____

TRADING POWDER:_____   MAXIMUM RISK AMOUNT PER TRADE:_____

DAILY GOAL: _____

MARKET ANALYSIS

Check the momentum of the market based on Key Indices, Commodities, and ETFs.

Type of Market Day	Key Indices and Commodities					
	S&P 500	Dow 30	Nasdaq	Russell 2000	Crude Oil	Gold
GREEN						
RED						

INDICATORS OVERVIEW

	Ticker Symbol																	
Indicators	5M	15M	30M	1HR	4HR	1D	5M	15M	30M	1HR	4HR	1D	5M	15M	30M	1HR	4HR	1D
Moving Averages																		
5 day																		
9 day																		
50 day																		
100 day																		
200 day																		
Bollinger Bands																		
Upper Band																		
Lower Band																		
DMI																		
Bullish																		
Bearish																		
MACD																		
Bullish																		
Bearish																		
RSI																		
Overbought																		
Oversold																		
Stochastic																		
Overbought																		
Oversold																		

Company Ticker	Chart Momentum											
	5 MIN		15 MIN		30 MIN		1 HR		4 HR		1 DAY	

Instrument(s) Traded	Hard Shares		Options		Forex		Crypto			
Trade #	Entry Time	Exit Time	Time Elapsed	Buy/Call Sell/Put	Entry Price	Exit Price	Quantity	Profit/Loss	Total
1									
2									
3									
4									
5									
6									
7									
8									
9									
10									

Total Trades	Winning Trades	Losing Trades	Win Rate %

Notes

DATE:_____   ACCOUNT BALANCE:_____

TRADING POWDER:_____   MAXIMUM RISK AMOUNT PER TRADE:_____

DAILY GOAL: _____

MARKET ANALYSIS

Check the momentum of the market based on Key Indices, Commodities, and ETFs.

Type of Market Day	Key Indices and Commodities					
	S&P 500	Dow 30	Nasdaq	Russell 2000	Crude Oil	Gold
GREEN						
RED						

INDICATORS OVERVIEW

	Ticker Symbol																	
Indicators	5M	15M	30M	1HR	4HR	1D	5M	15M	30M	1HR	4HR	1D	5M	15M	30M	1HR	4HR	1D
Moving Averages																		
5 day																		
9 day																		
50 day																		
100 day																		
200 day																		
Bollinger Bands																		
Upper Band																		
Lower Band																		
DMI																		
Bullish																		
Bearish																		
MACD																		
Bullish																		
Bearish																		
RSI																		
Overbought																		
Oversold																		
Stochastic																		
Overbought																		
Oversold																		

Company Ticker	Chart Momentum																
	5 MIN			15 MIN			30 MIN			1 HR			4 HR			1 DAY		

Instrument(s) Traded	Hard Shares		Options		Forex		Crypto		
Trade #	Entry Time	Exit Time	Time Elapsed	Buy/Call Sell/Put	Entry Price	Exit Price	Quantity	Profit/Loss	Total
1									
2									
3									
4									
5									
6									
7									
8									
9									
10									

Total Trades	Winning Trades	Losing Trades	Win Rate %

Notes

DATE:_____   ACCOUNT BALANCE:_____

TRADING POWDER:_____   MAXIMUM RISK AMOUNT PER TRADE:_____

DAILY GOAL: _____

MARKET ANALYSIS

Check the momentum of the market based on Key Indices, Commodities, and ETFs.

Type of Market Day	Key Indices and Commodities					
	S&P 500	Dow 30	Nasdaq	Russell 2000	Crude Oil	Gold
GREEN						
RED						

INDICATORS OVERVIEW

	Ticker Symbol																	
Indicators	5M	15M	30M	1HR	4HR	1D	5M	15M	30M	1HR	4HR	1D	5M	15M	30M	1HR	4HR	1D
Moving Averages																		
5 day																		
9 day																		
50 day																		
100 day																		
200 day																		
Bollinger Bands																		
Upper Band																		
Lower Band																		
DMI																		
Bullish																		
Bearish																		
MACD																		
Bullish																		
Bearish																		
RSI																		
Overbought																		
Oversold																		
Stochastic																		
Overbought																		
Oversold																		

Company Ticker	Chart Momentum																
	5 MIN			15 MIN			30 MIN			1 HR			4 HR			1 DAY		

Instrument(s) Traded	Hard Shares		Options		Forex		Crypto		
Trade #	Entry Time	Exit Time	Time Elapsed	Buy/Call Sell/Put	Entry Price	Exit Price	Quantity	Profit/Loss	Total
1									
2									
3									
4									
5									
6									
7									
8									
9									
10									

Total Trades	Winning Trades	Losing Trades	Win Rate %

Notes

DATE:_____

ACCOUNT BALANCE:_____

TRADING POWDER:_____

MAXIMUM RISK AMOUNT PER TRADE:_____

DAILY GOAL: _____

MARKET ANALYSIS

Check the momentum of the market based on Key Indices, Commodities, and ETFs.

Type of Market Day	Key Indices and Commodities					
	S&P 500	Dow 30	Nasdaq	Russell 2000	Crude Oil	Gold
GREEN						
RED						

INDICATORS OVERVIEW

	Ticker Symbol																	
Indicators	5M	15M	30M	1HR	4HR	1D	5M	15M	30M	1HR	4HR	1D	5M	15M	30M	1HR	4HR	1D
Moving Averages																		
5 day																		
9 day																		
50 day																		
100 day																		
200 day																		
Bollinger Bands																		
Upper Band																		
Lower Band																		
DMI																		
Bullish																		
Bearish																		
MACD																		
Bullish																		
Bearish																		
RSI																		
Overbought																		
Oversold																		
Stochastic																		
Overbought																		
Oversold																		

Company Ticker	Chart Momentum																	
	5 MIN			15 MIN			30 MIN			1 HR			4 HR			1 DAY		

Instrument(s) Traded	Hard Shares		Options		Forex		Crypto		
Trade #	Entry Time	Exit Time	Time Elapsed	Buy/Call Sell/Put	Entry Price	Exit Price	Quantity	Profit/Loss	Total
1									
2									
3									
4									
5									
6									
7									
8									
9									
10									

Total Trades	Winning Trades	Losing Trades	Win Rate %

Notes

DATE:_____   ACCOUNT BALANCE:_____

TRADING POWDER:_____   MAXIMUM RISK AMOUNT PER TRADE:_____

DAILY GOAL: _____

MARKET ANALYSIS

Check the momentum of the market based on Key Indices, Commodities, and ETFs.

Type of Market Day	Key Indices and Commodities					
	S&P 500	Dow 30	Nasdaq	Russell 2000	Crude Oil	Gold
GREEN						
RED						

INDICATORS OVERVIEW

| | Ticker Symbol | | | | | | | | | | | | | | | | | |
| | | | | | | | | | | | | | | | | | | |
Indicators	5M	15M	30M	1HR	4HR	1D	5M	15M	30M	1HR	4HR	1D	5M	15M	30M	1HR	4HR	1D
Moving Averages																		
5 day																		
9 day																		
50 day																		
100 day																		
200 day																		
Bollinger Bands																		
Upper Band																		
Lower Band																		
DMI																		
Bullish																		
Bearish																		
MACD																		
Bullish																		
Bearish																		
RSI																		
Overbought																		
Oversold																		
Stochastic																		
Overbought																		
Oversold																		

Company Ticker	Chart Momentum																
	5 MIN			15 MIN			30 MIN			1 HR			4 HR			1 DAY		

Instrument(s) Traded	Hard Shares		Options		Forex		Crypto		
Trade #	Entry Time	Exit Time	Time Elapsed	Buy/Call Sell/Put	Entry Price	Exit Price	Quantity	Profit/Loss	Total
1									
2									
3									
4									
5									
6									
7									
8									
9									
10									

Total Trades	Winning Trades	Losing Trades	Win Rate %

Notes

DATE:_____   ACCOUNT BALANCE:_____

TRADING POWDER:_____   MAXIMUM RISK AMOUNT PER TRADE:_____

DAILY GOAL: _____

MARKET ANALYSIS

Check the momentum of the market based on Key Indices, Commodities, and ETFs.

Type of Market Day	Key Indices and Commodities					
	S&P 500	Dow 30	Nasdaq	Russell 2000	Crude Oil	Gold
GREEN						
RED						

INDICATORS OVERVIEW

	Ticker Symbol																	
Indicators	5M	15M	30M	1HR	4HR	1D	5M	15M	30M	1HR	4HR	1D	5M	15M	30M	1HR	4HR	1D
Moving Averages																		
5 day																		
9 day																		
50 day																		
100 day																		
200 day																		
Bollinger Bands																		
Upper Band																		
Lower Band																		
DMI																		
Bullish																		
Bearish																		
MACD																		
Bullish																		
Bearish																		
RSI																		
Overbought																		
Oversold																		
Stochastic																		
Overbought																		
Oversold																		

Company Ticker	Chart Momentum																
	5 MIN			15 MIN			30 MIN			1 HR			4 HR			1 DAY		

Instrument(s) Traded	Hard Shares		Options		Forex		Crypto		
Trade #	Entry Time	Exit Time	Time Elapsed	Buy/Call Sell/Put	Entry Price	Exit Price	Quantity	Profit/Loss	Total
1									
2									
3									
4									
5									
6									
7									
8									
9									
10									

Total Trades	Winning Trades	Losing Trades	Win Rate %

Notes

DATE:_____   ACCOUNT BALANCE:_____

TRADING POWDER:_____   MAXIMUM RISK AMOUNT PER TRADE:_____

DAILY GOAL: _____

MARKET ANALYSIS

Check the momentum of the market based on Key Indices, Commodities, and ETFs.

Type of Market Day	Key Indices and Commodities					
	S&P 500	Dow 30	Nasdaq	Russell 2000	Crude Oil	Gold
GREEN						
RED						

INDICATORS OVERVIEW

	Ticker Symbol																	
Indicators	5M	15M	30M	1HR	4HR	1D	5M	15M	30M	1HR	4HR	1D	5M	15M	30M	1HR	4HR	1D
Moving Averages																		
5 day																		
9 day																		
50 day																		
100 day																		
200 day																		
Bollinger Bands																		
Upper Band																		
Lower Band																		
DMI																		
Bullish																		
Bearish																		
MACD																		
Bullish																		
Bearish																		
RSI																		
Overbought																		
Oversold																		
Stochastic																		
Overbought																		
Oversold																		

Company Ticker	Chart Momentum																
	5 MIN			15 MIN			30 MIN			1 HR			4 HR			1 DAY		

Instrument(s) Traded	Hard Shares		Options		Forex		Crypto		
Trade #	Entry Time	Exit Time	Time Elapsed	Buy/Call Sell/Put	Entry Price	Exit Price	Quantity	Profit/Loss	Total
1									
2									
3									
4									
5									
6									
7									
8									
9									
10									

Total Trades	Winning Trades	Losing Trades	Win Rate %

Notes

DATE:_____ ACCOUNT BALANCE:_____

TRADING POWDER:_____ MAXIMUM RISK AMOUNT PER TRADE:_____

DAILY GOAL: _____

MARKET ANALYSIS

Check the momentum of the market based on Key Indices, Commodities, and ETFs.

Type of Market Day	Key Indices and Commodities					
	S&P 500	Dow 30	Nasdaq	Russell 2000	Crude Oil	Gold
GREEN						
RED						

INDICATORS OVERVIEW

	Ticker Symbol																	
Indicators	5M	15M	30M	1HR	4HR	1D	5M	15M	30M	1HR	4HR	1D	5M	15M	30M	1HR	4HR	1D
Moving Averages																		
5 day																		
9 day																		
50 day																		
100 day																		
200 day																		
Bollinger Bands																		
Upper Band																		
Lower Band																		
DMI																		
Bullish																		
Bearish																		
MACD																		
Bullish																		
Bearish																		
RSI																		
Overbought																		
Oversold																		
Stochastic																		
Overbought																		
Oversold																		

Company Ticker	Chart Momentum												
	5 MIN		15 MIN		30 MIN		1 HR		4 HR		1 DAY		

Instrument(s) Traded	Hard Shares		Options		Forex		Crypto		
Trade #	Entry Time	Exit Time	Time Elapsed	Buy/Call Sell/Put	Entry Price	Exit Price	Quantity	Profit/Loss	Total
1									
2									
3									
4									
5									
6									
7									
8									
9									
10									

Total Trades	Winning Trades	Losing Trades	Win Rate %

Notes

DATE:_____   ACCOUNT BALANCE:_____

TRADING POWDER:_____   MAXIMUM RISK AMOUNT PER TRADE:_____

DAILY GOAL: _____

MARKET ANALYSIS

Check the momentum of the market based on Key Indices, Commodities, and ETFs.

Type of Market Day	Key Indices and Commodities					
	S&P 500	Dow 30	Nasdaq	Russell 2000	Crude Oil	Gold
GREEN						
RED						

INDICATORS OVERVIEW

	Ticker Symbol																	
Indicators	5M	15M	30M	1HR	4HR	1D	5M	15M	30M	1HR	4HR	1D	5M	15M	30M	1HR	4HR	1D
Moving Averages																		
5 day																		
9 day																		
50 day																		
100 day																		
200 day																		
Bollinger Bands																		
Upper Band																		
Lower Band																		
DMI																		
Bullish																		
Bearish																		
MACD																		
Bullish																		
Bearish																		
RSI																		
Overbought																		
Oversold																		
Stochastic																		
Overbought																		
Oversold																		

Company Ticker	Chart Momentum																
	5 MIN			15 MIN			30 MIN			1 HR			4 HR			1 DAY		

Instrument(s) Traded	Hard Shares		Options		Forex		Crypto		
Trade #	Entry Time	Exit Time	Time Elapsed	Buy/Call Sell/Put	Entry Price	Exit Price	Quantity	Profit/Loss	Total
1									
2									
3									
4									
5									
6									
7									
8									
9									
10									

Total Trades	Winning Trades	Losing Trades	Win Rate %

Notes

DATE:_____   ACCOUNT BALANCE:_____

TRADING POWDER:_____   MAXIMUM RISK AMOUNT PER TRADE:_____

DAILY GOAL: _____

MARKET ANALYSIS

Check the momentum of the market based on Key Indices, Commodities, and ETFs.

Type of Market Day	Key Indices and Commodities					
	S&P 500	Dow 30	Nasdaq	Russell 2000	Crude Oil	Gold
GREEN						
RED						

INDICATORS OVERVIEW

	Ticker Symbol																	
Indicators	5M	15M	30M	1HR	4HR	1D	5M	15M	30M	1HR	4HR	1D	5M	15M	30M	1HR	4HR	1D
Moving Averages																		
5 day																		
9 day																		
50 day																		
100 day																		
200 day																		
Bollinger Bands																		
Upper Band																		
Lower Band																		
DMI																		
Bullish																		
Bearish																		
MACD																		
Bullish																		
Bearish																		
RSI																		
Overbought																		
Oversold																		
Stochastic																		
Overbought																		
Oversold																		

Company Ticker	Chart Momentum																
	5 MIN			15 MIN			30 MIN			1 HR			4 HR			1 DAY		

Instrument(s) Traded	Hard Shares		Options		Forex		Crypto		
Trade #	Entry Time	Exit Time	Time Elapsed	Buy/Call Sell/Put	Entry Price	Exit Price	Quantity	Profit/Loss	Total
1									
2									
3									
4									
5									
6									
7									
8									
9									
10									

Total Trades	Winning Trades	Losing Trades	Win Rate %

Notes

DATE:_____   ACCOUNT BALANCE:_____

TRADING POWDER:_____   MAXIMUM RISK AMOUNT PER TRADE:_____

DAILY GOAL: _____

MARKET ANALYSIS

Check the momentum of the market based on Key Indices, Commodities, and ETFs.

Type of Market Day	Key Indices and Commodities					
	S&P 500	Dow 30	Nasdaq	Russell 2000	Crude Oil	Gold
GREEN						
RED						

INDICATORS OVERVIEW

	Ticker Symbol																	
Indicators	5M	15M	30M	1HR	4HR	1D	5M	15M	30M	1HR	4HR	1D	5M	15M	30M	1HR	4HR	1D
Moving Averages																		
5 day																		
9 day																		
50 day																		
100 day																		
200 day																		
Bollinger Bands																		
Upper Band																		
Lower Band																		
DMI																		
Bullish																		
Bearish																		
MACD																		
Bullish																		
Bearish																		
RSI																		
Overbought																		
Oversold																		
Stochastic																		
Overbought																		
Oversold																		

Company Ticker	Chart Momentum																	
	5 MIN			15 MIN			30 MIN			1 HR			4 HR			1 DAY		

Instrument(s) Traded	Hard Shares		Options		Forex		Crypto		
Trade #	Entry Time	Exit Time	Time Elapsed	Buy/Call Sell/Put	Entry Price	Exit Price	Quantity	Profit/Loss	Total
1									
2									
3									
4									
5									
6									
7									
8									
9									
10									

Total Trades	Winning Trades	Losing Trades	Win Rate %

Notes

DATE:_____   ACCOUNT BALANCE:_____

TRADING POWDER:_____   MAXIMUM RISK AMOUNT PER TRADE:_____

DAILY GOAL: _____

MARKET ANALYSIS

Check the momentum of the market based on Key Indices, Commodities, and ETFs.

Type of Market Day	Key Indices and Commodities					
	S&P 500	Dow 30	Nasdaq	Russell 2000	Crude Oil	Gold
GREEN						
RED						

INDICATORS OVERVIEW

	Ticker Symbol																	
Indicators	5M	15M	30M	1HR	4HR	1D	5M	15M	30M	1HR	4HR	1D	5M	15M	30M	1HR	4HR	1D
Moving Averages																		
5 day																		
9 day																		
50 day																		
100 day																		
200 day																		
Bollinger Bands																		
Upper Band																		
Lower Band																		
DMI																		
Bullish																		
Bearish																		
MACD																		
Bullish																		
Bearish																		
RSI																		
Overbought																		
Oversold																		
Stochastic																		
Overbought																		
Oversold																		

Company Ticker	Chart Momentum																
	5 MIN			15 MIN			30 MIN			1 HR			4 HR			1 DAY		

Instrument(s) Traded	Hard Shares		Options		Forex		Crypto		
Trade #	Entry Time	Exit Time	Time Elapsed	Buy/Call Sell/Put	Entry Price	Exit Price	Quantity	Profit/Loss	Total
1									
2									
3									
4									
5									
6									
7									
8									
9									
10									

Total Trades	Winning Trades	Losing Trades	Win Rate %

Notes

DATE:_____   ACCOUNT BALANCE:_____

TRADING POWDER:_____   MAXIMUM RISK AMOUNT PER TRADE:_____

DAILY GOAL: _____

MARKET ANALYSIS

Check the momentum of the market based on Key Indices, Commodities, and ETFs.

Type of Market Day	Key Indices and Commodities					
	S&P 500	Dow 30	Nasdaq	Russell 2000	Crude Oil	Gold
GREEN						
RED						

INDICATORS OVERVIEW

	Ticker Symbol																	
Indicators	5M	15M	30M	1HR	4HR	1D	5M	15M	30M	1HR	4HR	1D	5M	15M	30M	1HR	4HR	1D
Moving Averages																		
5 day																		
9 day																		
50 day																		
100 day																		
200 day																		
Bollinger Bands																		
Upper Band																		
Lower Band																		
DMI																		
Bullish																		
Bearish																		
MACD																		
Bullish																		
Bearish																		
RSI																		
Overbought																		
Oversold																		
Stochastic																		
Overbought																		
Oversold																		

Company Ticker	Chart Momentum																
	5 MIN			15 MIN			30 MIN			1 HR			4 HR			1 DAY		

Instrument(s) Traded	Hard Shares		Options		Forex		Crypto		
Trade #	Entry Time	Exit Time	Time Elapsed	Buy/Call Sell/Put	Entry Price	Exit Price	Quantity	Profit/Loss	Total
1									
2									
3									
4									
5									
6									
7									
8									
9									
10									

Total Trades	Winning Trades	Losing Trades	Win Rate %

Notes

DATE:_____   ACCOUNT BALANCE:_____

TRADING POWDER:_____   MAXIMUM RISK AMOUNT PER TRADE:_____

DAILY GOAL: _____

MARKET ANALYSIS

Check the momentum of the market based on Key Indices, Commodities, and ETFs.

Type of Market Day	Key Indices and Commodities					
	S&P 500	Dow 30	Nasdaq	Russell 2000	Crude Oil	Gold
GREEN						
RED						

INDICATORS OVERVIEW

	Ticker Symbol																	
Indicators	5M	15M	30M	1HR	4HR	1D	5M	15M	30M	1HR	4HR	1D	5M	15M	30M	1HR	4HR	1D
Moving Averages																		
5 day																		
9 day																		
50 day																		
100 day																		
200 day																		
Bollinger Bands																		
Upper Band																		
Lower Band																		
DMI																		
Bullish																		
Bearish																		
MACD																		
Bullish																		
Bearish																		
RSI																		
Overbought																		
Oversold																		
Stochastic																		
Overbought																		
Oversold																		

Company Ticker	Chart Momentum											
	5 MIN		15 MIN		30 MIN		1 HR		4 HR		1 DAY	

Instrument(s) Traded	Hard Shares		Options		Forex		Crypto		
Trade #	Entry Time	Exit Time	Time Elapsed	Buy/Call Sell/Put	Entry Price	Exit Price	Quantity	Profit/Loss	Total
1									
2									
3									
4									
5									
6									
7									
8									
9									
10									

Total Trades	Winning Trades	Losing Trades	Win Rate %

Notes

DATE:_____ ACCOUNT BALANCE:_____

TRADING POWDER:_____ MAXIMUM RISK AMOUNT PER TRADE:_____

DAILY GOAL: _____

MARKET ANALYSIS

Check the momentum of the market based on Key Indices, Commodities, and ETFs.

Type of Market Day	Key Indices and Commodities					
	S&P 500	Dow 30	Nasdaq	Russell 2000	Crude Oil	Gold
GREEN						
RED						

INDICATORS OVERVIEW

	Ticker Symbol																	
Indicators	5M	15M	30M	1HR	4HR	1D	5M	15M	30M	1HR	4HR	1D	5M	15M	30M	1HR	4HR	1D
Moving Averages																		
5 day																		
9 day																		
50 day																		
100 day																		
200 day																		
Bollinger Bands																		
Upper Band																		
Lower Band																		
DMI																		
Bullish																		
Bearish																		
MACD																		
Bullish																		
Bearish																		
RSI																		
Overbought																		
Oversold																		
Stochastic																		
Overbought																		
Oversold																		

Company Ticker	Chart Momentum																	
	5 MIN			15 MIN			30 MIN			1 HR			4 HR			1 DAY		

Instrument(s) Traded	Hard Shares		Options		Forex		Crypto		
Trade #	Entry Time	Exit Time	Time Elapsed	Buy/Call Sell/Put	Entry Price	Exit Price	Quantity	Profit/Loss	Total
1									
2									
3									
4									
5									
6									
7									
8									
9									
10									

Total Trades	Winning Trades	Losing Trades	Win Rate %

Notes

DATE:_____ **ACCOUNT BALANCE:**_____

TRADING POWDER:_____ **MAXIMUM RISK AMOUNT PER TRADE:**_____

DAILY GOAL: _____

MARKET ANALYSIS

Check the momentum of the market based on Key Indices, Commodities, and ETFs.

Type of Market Day	Key Indices and Commodities					
	S&P 500	Dow 30	Nasdaq	Russell 2000	Crude Oil	Gold
GREEN						
RED						

INDICATORS OVERVIEW

	Ticker Symbol																	
Indicators	5M	15M	30M	1HR	4HR	1D	5M	15M	30M	1HR	4HR	1D	5M	15M	30M	1HR	4HR	1D
Moving Averages																		
5 day																		
9 day																		
50 day																		
100 day																		
200 day																		
Bollinger Bands																		
Upper Band																		
Lower Band																		
DMI																		
Bullish																		
Bearish																		
MACD																		
Bullish																		
Bearish																		
RSI																		
Overbought																		
Oversold																		
Stochastic																		
Overbought																		
Oversold																		

Company Ticker	Chart Momentum																
	5 MIN			15 MIN			30 MIN			1 HR			4 HR			1 DAY		

Instrument(s) Traded	Hard Shares		Options		Forex		Crypto		
Trade #	Entry Time	Exit Time	Time Elapsed	Buy/Call Sell/Put	Entry Price	Exit Price	Quantity	Profit/Loss	Total
1									
2									
3									
4									
5									
6									
7									
8									
9									
10									

Total Trades	Winning Trades	Losing Trades	Win Rate %

Notes

DATE:_____   ACCOUNT BALANCE:_____

TRADING POWDER:_____   MAXIMUM RISK AMOUNT PER TRADE:_____

DAILY GOAL: _____

MARKET ANALYSIS

Check the momentum of the market based on Key Indices, Commodities, and ETFs.

Type of Market Day	Key Indices and Commodities					
	S&P 500	Dow 30	Nasdaq	Russell 2000	Crude Oil	Gold
GREEN						
RED						

INDICATORS OVERVIEW

	Ticker Symbol																	
Indicators	5M	15M	30M	1HR	4HR	1D	5M	15M	30M	1HR	4HR	1D	5M	15M	30M	1HR	4HR	1D
Moving Averages																		
5 day																		
9 day																		
50 day																		
100 day																		
200 day																		
Bollinger Bands																		
Upper Band																		
Lower Band																		
DMI																		
Bullish																		
Bearish																		
MACD																		
Bullish																		
Bearish																		
RSI																		
Overbought																		
Oversold																		
Stochastic																		
Overbought																		
Oversold																		

Company Ticker	Chart Momentum											
	5 MIN		15 MIN		30 MIN		1 HR		4 HR		1 DAY	

Instrument(s) Traded	Hard Shares		Options		Forex		Crypto			
Trade #	Entry Time	Exit Time	Time Elapsed	Buy/Call Sell/Put	Entry Price	Exit Price	Quantity	Profit/Loss	Total	
1										
2										
3										
4										
5										
6										
7										
8										
9										
10										

Total Trades	Winning Trades	Losing Trades	Win Rate %

Notes

DATE:_____   ACCOUNT BALANCE:_____

TRADING POWDER:_____   MAXIMUM RISK AMOUNT PER TRADE:_____

DAILY GOAL: _____

MARKET ANALYSIS

Check the momentum of the market based on Key Indices, Commodities, and ETFs.

Type of Market Day	Key Indices and Commodities					
	S&P 500	Dow 30	Nasdaq	Russell 2000	Crude Oil	Gold
GREEN						
RED						

INDICATORS OVERVIEW

	Ticker Symbol																	
Indicators	5M	15M	30M	1HR	4HR	1D	5M	15M	30M	1HR	4HR	1D	5M	15M	30M	1HR	4HR	1D
Moving Averages																		
5 day																		
9 day																		
50 day																		
100 day																		
200 day																		
Bollinger Bands																		
Upper Band																		
Lower Band																		
DMI																		
Bullish																		
Bearish																		
MACD																		
Bullish																		
Bearish																		
RSI																		
Overbought																		
Oversold																		
Stochastic																		
Overbought																		
Oversold																		

Company Ticker	Chart Momentum																
	5 MIN			15 MIN			30 MIN			1 HR			4 HR			1 DAY		

Instrument(s) Traded	Hard Shares		Options		Forex		Crypto		
Trade #	Entry Time	Exit Time	Time Elapsed	Buy/Call Sell/Put	Entry Price	Exit Price	Quantity	Profit/Loss	Total
1									
2									
3									
4									
5									
6									
7									
8									
9									
10									

Total Trades	Winning Trades	Losing Trades	Win Rate %

Notes

DATE:_____   ACCOUNT BALANCE:_____

TRADING POWDER:_____   MAXIMUM RISK AMOUNT PER TRADE:_____

DAILY GOAL: _____

MARKET ANALYSIS

Check the momentum of the market based on Key Indices, Commodities, and ETFs.

Type of Market Day	Key Indices and Commodities					
	S&P 500	Dow 30	Nasdaq	Russell 2000	Crude Oil	Gold
GREEN						
RED						

INDICATORS OVERVIEW

	Ticker Symbol																	
Indicators	5M	15M	30M	1HR	4HR	1D	5M	15M	30M	1HR	4HR	1D	5M	15M	30M	1HR	4HR	1D
Moving Averages																		
5 day																		
9 day																		
50 day																		
100 day																		
200 day																		
Bollinger Bands																		
Upper Band																		
Lower Band																		
DMI																		
Bullish																		
Bearish																		
MACD																		
Bullish																		
Bearish																		
RSI																		
Overbought																		
Oversold																		
Stochastic																		
Overbought																		
Oversold																		

Company Ticker	Chart Momentum											
	5 MIN		15 MIN		30 MIN		1 HR		4 HR		1 DAY	

Instrument(s) Traded	Hard Shares		Options		Forex		Crypto		
Trade #	Entry Time	Exit Time	Time Elapsed	Buy/Call Sell/Put	Entry Price	Exit Price	Quantity	Profit/Loss	Total
1									
2									
3									
4									
5									
6									
7									
8									
9									
10									

Total Trades	Winning Trades	Losing Trades	Win Rate %

Notes

DATE:_____   ACCOUNT BALANCE:_____

TRADING POWDER:_____   MAXIMUM RISK AMOUNT PER TRADE:_____

DAILY GOAL: _____

MARKET ANALYSIS

Check the momentum of the market based on Key Indices, Commodities, and ETFs.

Type of Market Day	Key Indices and Commodities					
	S&P 500	Dow 30	Nasdaq	Russell 2000	Crude Oil	Gold
GREEN						
RED						

INDICATORS OVERVIEW

	Ticker Symbol																	
	---	---	---	---	---	---	---	---	---	---	---	---	---	---	---	---	---	---
Indicators	5M	15M	30M	1HR	4HR	1D	5M	15M	30M	1HR	4HR	1D	5M	15M	30M	1HR	4HR	1D
Moving Averages																		
5 day																		
9 day																		
50 day																		
100 day																		
200 day																		
Bollinger Bands																		
Upper Band																		
Lower Band																		
DMI																		
Bullish																		
Bearish																		
MACD																		
Bullish																		
Bearish																		
RSI																		
Overbought																		
Oversold																		
Stochastic																		
Overbought																		
Oversold																		

Company Ticker	Chart Momentum																
	5 MIN			15 MIN			30 MIN			1 HR			4 HR			1 DAY	

Instrument(s) Traded	Hard Shares		Options		Forex		Crypto		
Trade #	Entry Time	Exit Time	Time Elapsed	Buy/Call Sell/Put	Entry Price	Exit Price	Quantity	Profit/Loss	Total
1									
2									
3									
4									
5									
6									
7									
8									
9									
10									

Total Trades	Winning Trades	Losing Trades	Win Rate %

Notes

DATE:_____   ACCOUNT BALANCE:_____

TRADING POWDER:_____   MAXIMUM RISK AMOUNT PER TRADE:_____

DAILY GOAL: _____

MARKET ANALYSIS

Check the momentum of the market based on Key Indices, Commodities, and ETFs.

Type of Market Day	Key Indices and Commodities					
	S&P 500	Dow 30	Nasdaq	Russell 2000	Crude Oil	Gold
GREEN						
RED						

INDICATORS OVERVIEW

	Ticker Symbol																	
Indicators	5M	15M	30M	1HR	4HR	1D	5M	15M	30M	1HR	4HR	1D	5M	15M	30M	1HR	4HR	1D
Moving Averages																		
5 day																		
9 day																		
50 day																		
100 day																		
200 day																		
Bollinger Bands																		
Upper Band																		
Lower Band																		
DMI																		
Bullish																		
Bearish																		
MACD																		
Bullish																		
Bearish																		
RSI																		
Overbought																		
Oversold																		
Stochastic																		
Overbought																		
Oversold																		

Company Ticker	Chart Momentum																
	5 MIN			15 MIN			30 MIN			1 HR			4 HR			1 DAY		

Instrument(s) Traded	Hard Shares		Options		Forex		Crypto		
Trade #	Entry Time	Exit Time	Time Elapsed	Buy/Call Sell/Put	Entry Price	Exit Price	Quantity	Profit/Loss	Total
1									
2									
3									
4									
5									
6									
7									
8									
9									
10									

Total Trades	Winning Trades	Losing Trades	Win Rate %

Notes

DATE:_____   **ACCOUNT BALANCE:**_____

TRADING POWDER:_____   **MAXIMUM RISK AMOUNT PER TRADE:**_____

DAILY GOAL: _____

MARKET ANALYSIS

Check the momentum of the market based on Key Indices, Commodities, and ETFs.

Type of Market Day	Key Indices and Commodities					
	S&P 500	Dow 30	Nasdaq	Russell 2000	Crude Oil	Gold
GREEN						
RED						

INDICATORS OVERVIEW

	Ticker Symbol																	
Indicators	5M	15M	30M	1HR	4HR	1D	5M	15M	30M	1HR	4HR	1D	5M	15M	30M	1HR	4HR	1D
Moving Averages																		
5 day																		
9 day																		
50 day																		
100 day																		
200 day																		
Bollinger Bands																		
Upper Band																		
Lower Band																		
DMI																		
Bullish																		
Bearish																		
MACD																		
Bullish																		
Bearish																		
RSI																		
Overbought																		
Oversold																		
Stochastic																		
Overbought																		
Oversold																		

Company Ticker	Chart Momentum																	
	5 MIN			15 MIN			30 MIN			1 HR			4 HR			1 DAY		

Instrument(s) Traded	Hard Shares		Options		Forex		Crypto		
Trade #	Entry Time	Exit Time	Time Elapsed	Buy/Call Sell/Put	Entry Price	Exit Price	Quantity	Profit/Loss	Total
1									
2									
3									
4									
5									
6									
7									
8									
9									
10									

Total Trades	Winning Trades	Losing Trades	Win Rate %

Notes

DATE:_____   ACCOUNT BALANCE:_____

TRADING POWDER:_____   MAXIMUM RISK AMOUNT PER TRADE:_____

DAILY GOAL: _____

MARKET ANALYSIS

Check the momentum of the market based on Key Indices, Commodities, and ETFs.

Type of Market Day	Key Indices and Commodities					
	S&P 500	Dow 30	Nasdaq	Russell 2000	Crude Oil	Gold
GREEN						
RED						

INDICATORS OVERVIEW

	Ticker Symbol																	
Indicators	5M	15M	30M	1HR	4HR	1D	5M	15M	30M	1HR	4HR	1D	5M	15M	30M	1HR	4HR	1D
Moving Averages																		
5 day																		
9 day																		
50 day																		
100 day																		
200 day																		
Bollinger Bands																		
Upper Band																		
Lower Band																		
DMI																		
Bullish																		
Bearish																		
MACD																		
Bullish																		
Bearish																		
RSI																		
Overbought																		
Oversold																		
Stochastic																		
Overbought																		
Oversold																		

Company Ticker	Chart Momentum																
	5 MIN			15 MIN			30 MIN			1 HR			4 HR			1 DAY		

Instrument(s) Traded	Hard Shares		Options		Forex		Crypto		
Trade #	Entry Time	Exit Time	Time Elapsed	Buy/Call Sell/Put	Entry Price	Exit Price	Quantity	Profit/Loss	Total
1									
2									
3									
4									
5									
6									
7									
8									
9									
10									

Total Trades	Winning Trades	Losing Trades	Win Rate %

Notes

DATE:_____   ACCOUNT BALANCE:_____

TRADING POWDER:_____   MAXIMUM RISK AMOUNT PER TRADE:_____

DAILY GOAL: _____

MARKET ANALYSIS

Check the momentum of the market based on Key Indices, Commodities, and ETFs.

Type of Market Day	Key Indices and Commodities					
	S&P 500	Dow 30	Nasdaq	Russell 2000	Crude Oil	Gold
GREEN						
RED						

INDICATORS OVERVIEW

| | Ticker Symbol | | | | | | | | | | | | | | | | | |
| | | | | | | | | | | | | | | | | | |
Indicators	5M	15M	30M	1HR	4HR	1D	5M	15M	30M	1HR	4HR	1D	5M	15M	30M	1HR	4HR	1D
Moving Averages																		
5 day																		
9 day																		
50 day																		
100 day																		
200 day																		
Bollinger Bands																		
Upper Band																		
Lower Band																		
DMI																		
Bullish																		
Bearish																		
MACD																		
Bullish																		
Bearish																		
RSI																		
Overbought																		
Oversold																		
Stochastic																		
Overbought																		
Oversold																		

Company Ticker	Chart Momentum																
	5 MIN			15 MIN			30 MIN			1 HR			4 HR			1 DAY		

Instrument(s) Traded	Hard Shares		Options		Forex		Crypto		
Trade #	Entry Time	Exit Time	Time Elapsed	Buy/Call Sell/Put	Entry Price	Exit Price	Quantity	Profit/Loss	Total
1									
2									
3									
4									
5									
6									
7									
8									
9									
10									

Total Trades	Winning Trades	Losing Trades	Win Rate %

Notes

DATE:_____   **ACCOUNT BALANCE:**_____

TRADING POWDER:_____   **MAXIMUM RISK AMOUNT PER TRADE:**_____

DAILY GOAL: _____

MARKET ANALYSIS

Check the momentum of the market based on Key Indices, Commodities, and ETFs.

Type of Market Day	Key Indices and Commodities					
	S&P 500	Dow 30	Nasdaq	Russell 2000	Crude Oil	Gold
GREEN						
RED						

INDICATORS OVERVIEW

	Ticker Symbol																	
Indicators	5M	15M	30M	1HR	4HR	1D	5M	15M	30M	1HR	4HR	1D	5M	15M	30M	1HR	4HR	1D
Moving Averages																		
5 day																		
9 day																		
50 day																		
100 day																		
200 day																		
Bollinger Bands																		
Upper Band																		
Lower Band																		
DMI																		
Bullish																		
Bearish																		
MACD																		
Bullish																		
Bearish																		
RSI																		
Overbought																		
Oversold																		
Stochastic																		
Overbought																		
Oversold																		

Company Ticker	Chart Momentum																
	5 MIN			15 MIN			30 MIN			1 HR			4 HR			1 DAY		

Instrument(s) Traded	Hard Shares		Options		Forex		Crypto		
Trade #	Entry Time	Exit Time	Time Elapsed	Buy/Call Sell/Put	Entry Price	Exit Price	Quantity	Profit/Loss	Total
1									
2									
3									
4									
5									
6									
7									
8									
9									
10									

Total Trades	Winning Trades	Losing Trades	Win Rate %

Notes

DATE:_____   ACCOUNT BALANCE:_____

TRADING POWDER:_____   MAXIMUM RISK AMOUNT PER TRADE:_____

DAILY GOAL: _____

MARKET ANALYSIS

Check the momentum of the market based on Key Indices, Commodities, and ETFs.

Type of Market Day	Key Indices and Commodities					
	S&P 500	Dow 30	Nasdaq	Russell 2000	Crude Oil	Gold
GREEN						
RED						

INDICATORS OVERVIEW

	Ticker Symbol																	
Indicators	5M	15M	30M	1HR	4HR	1D	5M	15M	30M	1HR	4HR	1D	5M	15M	30M	1HR	4HR	1D
Moving Averages																		
5 day																		
9 day																		
50 day																		
100 day																		
200 day																		
Bollinger Bands																		
Upper Band																		
Lower Band																		
DMI																		
Bullish																		
Bearish																		
MACD																		
Bullish																		
Bearish																		
RSI																		
Overbought																		
Oversold																		
Stochastic																		
Overbought																		
Oversold																		

Company Ticker	Chart Momentum																
	5 MIN			15 MIN			30 MIN			1 HR			4 HR			1 DAY		

Instrument(s) Traded	Hard Shares		Options		Forex		Crypto		
Trade #	Entry Time	Exit Time	Time Elapsed	Buy/Call Sell/Put	Entry Price	Exit Price	Quantity	Profit/Loss	Total
1									
2									
3									
4									
5									
6									
7									
8									
9									
10									

Total Trades	Winning Trades	Losing Trades	Win Rate %
Notes			

DATE:_____   ACCOUNT BALANCE:_____

TRADING POWDER:_____   MAXIMUM RISK AMOUNT PER TRADE:_____

DAILY GOAL: _____

MARKET ANALYSIS

Check the momentum of the market based on Key Indices, Commodities, and ETFs.

Type of Market Day	Key Indices and Commodities					
	S&P 500	Dow 30	Nasdaq	Russell 2000	Crude Oil	Gold
GREEN						
RED						

INDICATORS OVERVIEW

	Ticker Symbol																	
Indicators	5M	15M	30M	1HR	4HR	1D	5M	15M	30M	1HR	4HR	1D	5M	15M	30M	1HR	4HR	1D
Moving Averages																		
5 day																		
9 day																		
50 day																		
100 day																		
200 day																		
Bollinger Bands																		
Upper Band																		
Lower Band																		
DMI																		
Bullish																		
Bearish																		
MACD																		
Bullish																		
Bearish																		
RSI																		
Overbought																		
Oversold																		
Stochastic																		
Overbought																		
Oversold																		

Company Ticker	Chart Momentum																
	5 MIN			15 MIN			30 MIN			1 HR			4 HR			1 DAY		

Instrument(s) Traded	Hard Shares		Options		Forex		Crypto		
Trade #	Entry Time	Exit Time	Time Elapsed	Buy/Call Sell/Put	Entry Price	Exit Price	Quantity	Profit/Loss	Total
1									
2									
3									
4									
5									
6									
7									
8									
9									
10									

Total Trades	Winning Trades	Losing Trades	Win Rate %

Notes

DATE:_____   **ACCOUNT BALANCE:**_____

TRADING POWDER:_____   **MAXIMUM RISK AMOUNT PER TRADE:**_____

DAILY GOAL: _____

MARKET ANALYSIS

Check the momentum of the market based on Key Indices, Commodities, and ETFs.

Type of Market Day	Key Indices and Commodities					
	S&P 500	Dow 30	Nasdaq	Russell 2000	Crude Oil	Gold
GREEN						
RED						

INDICATORS OVERVIEW

	Ticker Symbol																	
Indicators	5M	15M	30M	1HR	4HR	1D	5M	15M	30M	1HR	4HR	1D	5M	15M	30M	1HR	4HR	1D
Moving Averages																		
5 day																		
9 day																		
50 day																		
100 day																		
200 day																		
Bollinger Bands																		
Upper Band																		
Lower Band																		
DMI																		
Bullish																		
Bearish																		
MACD																		
Bullish																		
Bearish																		
RSI																		
Overbought																		
Oversold																		
Stochastic																		
Overbought																		
Oversold																		

Company Ticker	Chart Momentum												
	5 MIN			15 MIN			30 MIN			1 HR		4 HR		1 DAY

Instrument(s) Traded	Hard Shares			Options		Forex		Crypto		
Trade #	Entry Time	Exit Time	Time Elapsed	Buy/Call Sell/Put	Entry Price	Exit Price	Quantity	Profit/Loss	Total
1									
2									
3									
4									
5									
6									
7									
8									
9									
10									

Total Trades	Winning Trades	Losing Trades	Win Rate %

Notes

DATE:_____   ACCOUNT BALANCE:_____

TRADING POWDER:_____   MAXIMUM RISK AMOUNT PER TRADE:_____

DAILY GOAL: _____

MARKET ANALYSIS

Check the momentum of the market based on Key Indices, Commodities, and ETFs.

Type of Market Day	Key Indices and Commodities					
	S&P 500	Dow 30	Nasdaq	Russell 2000	Crude Oil	Gold
GREEN						
RED						

INDICATORS OVERVIEW

	Ticker Symbol																	
Indicators	5M	15M	30M	1HR	4HR	1D	5M	15M	30M	1HR	4HR	1D	5M	15M	30M	1HR	4HR	1D
Moving Averages																		
5 day																		
9 day																		
50 day																		
100 day																		
200 day																		
Bollinger Bands																		
Upper Band																		
Lower Band																		
DMI																		
Bullish																		
Bearish																		
MACD																		
Bullish																		
Bearish																		
RSI																		
Overbought																		
Oversold																		
Stochastic																		
Overbought																		
Oversold																		

Company Ticker	Chart Momentum											
	5 MIN		15 MIN		30 MIN		1 HR		4 HR		1 DAY	

Instrument(s) Traded	Hard Shares		Options		Forex		Crypto		
Trade #	Entry Time	Exit Time	Time Elapsed	Buy/Call Sell/Put	Entry Price	Exit Price	Quantity	Profit/Loss	Total
1									
2									
3									
4									
5									
6									
7									
8									
9									
10									

Total Trades	Winning Trades	Losing Trades	Win Rate %

Notes

DATE:_____   ACCOUNT BALANCE:_____

TRADING POWDER:_____   MAXIMUM RISK AMOUNT PER TRADE:_____

DAILY GOAL: _____

MARKET ANALYSIS

Check the momentum of the market based on Key Indices, Commodities, and ETFs.

Type of Market Day	Key Indices and Commodities					
	S&P 500	Dow 30	Nasdaq	Russell 2000	Crude Oil	Gold
GREEN						
RED						

INDICATORS OVERVIEW

| | Ticker Symbol | | | | | | | | | | | | | | | | | |
| | | | | | | | | | | | | | | | | | |
Indicators	5M	15M	30M	1HR	4HR	1D	5M	15M	30M	1HR	4HR	1D	5M	15M	30M	1HR	4HR	1D
Moving Averages																		
5 day																		
9 day																		
50 day																		
100 day																		
200 day																		
Bollinger Bands																		
Upper Band																		
Lower Band																		
DMI																		
Bullish																		
Bearish																		
MACD																		
Bullish																		
Bearish																		
RSI																		
Overbought																		
Oversold																		
Stochastic																		
Overbought																		
Oversold																		

Company Ticker	Chart Momentum																
	5 MIN			15 MIN			30 MIN			1 HR			4 HR			1 DAY		

Instrument(s) Traded	Hard Shares		Options		Forex		Crypto			
Trade #	Entry Time	Exit Time	Time Elapsed	Buy/Call Sell/Put	Entry Price	Exit Price	Quantity	Profit/Loss	Total	
1										
2										
3										
4										
5										
6										
7										
8										
9										
10										

Total Trades	Winning Trades	Losing Trades	Win Rate %

Notes

DATE:_____   ACCOUNT BALANCE:_____

TRADING POWDER:_____   MAXIMUM RISK AMOUNT PER TRADE:_____

DAILY GOAL: _____

MARKET ANALYSIS

Check the momentum of the market based on Key Indices, Commodities, and ETFs.

Type of Market Day	Key Indices and Commodities					
	S&P 500	Dow 30	Nasdaq	Russell 2000	Crude Oil	Gold
GREEN						
RED						

INDICATORS OVERVIEW

	Ticker Symbol																	
Indicators	5M	15M	30M	1HR	4HR	1D	5M	15M	30M	1HR	4HR	1D	5M	15M	30M	1HR	4HR	1D
Moving Averages																		
5 day																		
9 day																		
50 day																		
100 day																		
200 day																		
Bollinger Bands																		
Upper Band																		
Lower Band																		
DMI																		
Bullish																		
Bearish																		
MACD																		
Bullish																		
Bearish																		
RSI																		
Overbought																		
Oversold																		
Stochastic																		
Overbought																		
Oversold																		

Company Ticker	Chart Momentum																
	5 MIN			15 MIN			30 MIN			1 HR			4 HR			1 DAY		

Instrument(s) Traded	Hard Shares		Options		Forex		Crypto		
Trade #	Entry Time	Exit Time	Time Elapsed	Buy/Call Sell/Put	Entry Price	Exit Price	Quantity	Profit/Loss	Total
1									
2									
3									
4									
5									
6									
7									
8									
9									
10									

Total Trades	Winning Trades	Losing Trades	Win Rate %

Notes

DATE:_____ **ACCOUNT BALANCE:**_____

TRADING POWDER:_____ **MAXIMUM RISK AMOUNT PER TRADE:**_____

DAILY GOAL:_____

MARKET ANALYSIS

Check the momentum of the market based on Key Indices, Commodities, and ETFs.

Type of Market Day	Key Indices and Commodities					
	S&P 500	Dow 30	Nasdaq	Russell 2000	Crude Oil	Gold
GREEN						
RED						

INDICATORS OVERVIEW

	Ticker Symbol																	
Indicators	5M	15M	30M	1HR	4HR	1D	5M	15M	30M	1HR	4HR	1D	5M	15M	30M	1HR	4HR	1D
Moving Averages																		
5 day																		
9 day																		
50 day																		
100 day																		
200 day																		
Bollinger Bands																		
Upper Band																		
Lower Band																		
DMI																		
Bullish																		
Bearish																		
MACD																		
Bullish																		
Bearish																		
RSI																		
Overbought																		
Oversold																		
Stochastic																		
Overbought																		
Oversold																		

Company Ticker	Chart Momentum																
	5 MIN			15 MIN			30 MIN			1 HR			4 HR			1 DAY		

Instrument(s) Traded	Hard Shares		Options		Forex		Crypto		
Trade #	Entry Time	Exit Time	Time Elapsed	Buy/Call Sell/Put	Entry Price	Exit Price	Quantity	Profit/Loss	Total
1									
2									
3									
4									
5									
6									
7									
8									
9									
10									

Total Trades	Winning Trades	Losing Trades	Win Rate %

Notes

DATE:_____   ACCOUNT BALANCE:_____

TRADING POWDER:_____   MAXIMUM RISK AMOUNT PER TRADE:_____

DAILY GOAL: _____

MARKET ANALYSIS

Check the momentum of the market based on Key Indices, Commodities, and ETFs.

Type of Market Day	Key Indices and Commodities					
	S&P 500	Dow 30	Nasdaq	Russell 2000	Crude Oil	Gold
GREEN						
RED						

INDICATORS OVERVIEW

	Ticker Symbol																	
Indicators	5M	15M	30M	1HR	4HR	1D	5M	15M	30M	1HR	4HR	1D	5M	15M	30M	1HR	4HR	1D
Moving Averages																		
5 day																		
9 day																		
50 day																		
100 day																		
200 day																		
Bollinger Bands																		
Upper Band																		
Lower Band																		
DMI																		
Bullish																		
Bearish																		
MACD																		
Bullish																		
Bearish																		
RSI																		
Overbought																		
Oversold																		
Stochastic																		
Overbought																		
Oversold																		

Company Ticker	Chart Momentum											
	5 MIN		15 MIN		30 MIN		1 HR		4 HR		1 DAY	

Instrument(s) Traded	Hard Shares		Options		Forex		Crypto		
Trade #	Entry Time	Exit Time	Time Elapsed	Buy/Call Sell/Put	Entry Price	Exit Price	Quantity	Profit/Loss	Total
1									
2									
3									
4									
5									
6									
7									
8									
9									
10									

Total Trades	Winning Trades	Losing Trades	Win Rate %

Notes

DATE:_____

TRADING POWDER:_____

DAILY GOAL: _____

ACCOUNT BALANCE:_____

MAXIMUM RISK AMOUNT PER TRADE:_____

MARKET ANALYSIS

Check the momentum of the market based on Key Indices, Commodities, and ETFs.

Type of Market Day	Key Indices and Commodities					
	S&P 500	Dow 30	Nasdaq	Russell 2000	Crude Oil	Gold
GREEN						
RED						

INDICATORS OVERVIEW

| | Ticker Symbol | | | | | | | | | | | | | | | | | |
| | | | | | | | | | | | | | | | | | | |
Indicators	5M	15M	30M	1HR	4HR	1D	5M	15M	30M	1HR	4HR	1D	5M	15M	30M	1HR	4HR	1D
Moving Averages																		
5 day																		
9 day																		
50 day																		
100 day																		
200 day																		
Bollinger Bands																		
Upper Band																		
Lower Band																		
DMI																		
Bullish																		
Bearish																		
MACD																		
Bullish																		
Bearish																		
RSI																		
Overbought																		
Oversold																		
Stochastic																		
Overbought																		
Oversold																		

Company Ticker	Chart Momentum																
	5 MIN			15 MIN			30 MIN			1 HR			4 HR			1 DAY		

Instrument(s) Traded	Hard Shares		Options		Forex		Crypto		
Trade #	Entry Time	Exit Time	Time Elapsed	Buy/Call Sell/Put	Entry Price	Exit Price	Quantity	Profit/Loss	Total
1									
2									
3									
4									
5									
6									
7									
8									
9									
10									

Total Trades	Winning Trades	Losing Trades	Win Rate %

Notes

DATE:_____   ACCOUNT BALANCE:_____

TRADING POWDER:_____   MAXIMUM RISK AMOUNT PER TRADE:_____

DAILY GOAL: _____

MARKET ANALYSIS

Check the momentum of the market based on Key Indices, Commodities, and ETFs.

Type of Market Day	Key Indices and Commodities					
	S&P 500	Dow 30	Nasdaq	Russell 2000	Crude Oil	Gold
GREEN						
RED						

INDICATORS OVERVIEW

	Ticker Symbol																	
Indicators	5M	15M	30M	1HR	4HR	1D	5M	15M	30M	1HR	4HR	1D	5M	15M	30M	1HR	4HR	1D
Moving Averages																		
5 day																		
9 day																		
50 day																		
100 day																		
200 day																		
Bollinger Bands																		
Upper Band																		
Lower Band																		
DMI																		
Bullish																		
Bearish																		
MACD																		
Bullish																		
Bearish																		
RSI																		
Overbought																		
Oversold																		
Stochastic																		
Overbought																		
Oversold																		

Company Ticker	Chart Momentum																
	5 MIN			15 MIN			30 MIN			1 HR			4 HR			1 DAY		

Instrument(s) Traded	Hard Shares		Options		Forex		Crypto		
Trade #	Entry Time	Exit Time	Time Elapsed	Buy/Call Sell/Put	Entry Price	Exit Price	Quantity	Profit/Loss	Total
1									
2									
3									
4									
5									
6									
7									
8									
9									
10									

Total Trades	Winning Trades	Losing Trades	Win Rate %

Notes

DATE:_____   ACCOUNT BALANCE:_____

TRADING POWDER:_____   MAXIMUM RISK AMOUNT PER TRADE:_____

DAILY GOAL: _____

MARKET ANALYSIS

Check the momentum of the market based on Key Indices, Commodities, and ETFs.

Type of Market Day	Key Indices and Commodities					
	S&P 500	Dow 30	Nasdaq	Russell 2000	Crude Oil	Gold
GREEN						
RED						

INDICATORS OVERVIEW

| | Ticker Symbol | | | | | | | | | | | | | | | | | |
| | | | | | | | | | | | | | | | | | |
Indicators	5M	15M	30M	1HR	4HR	1D	5M	15M	30M	1HR	4HR	1D	5M	15M	30M	1HR	4HR	1D
Moving Averages																		
5 day																		
9 day																		
50 day																		
100 day																		
200 day																		
Bollinger Bands																		
Upper Band																		
Lower Band																		
DMI																		
Bullish																		
Bearish																		
MACD																		
Bullish																		
Bearish																		
RSI																		
Overbought																		
Oversold																		
Stochastic																		
Overbought																		
Oversold																		

Company Ticker	Chart Momentum																
	5 MIN			15 MIN			30 MIN			1 HR			4 HR			1 DAY		

Instrument(s) Traded	Hard Shares		Options		Forex		Crypto		
Trade #	Entry Time	Exit Time	Time Elapsed	Buy/Call Sell/Put	Entry Price	Exit Price	Quantity	Profit/Loss	Total
1									
2									
3									
4									
5									
6									
7									
8									
9									
10									

Total Trades	Winning Trades	Losing Trades	Win Rate %

Notes

DATE:_____   ACCOUNT BALANCE:_____

TRADING POWDER:_____   MAXIMUM RISK AMOUNT PER TRADE:_____

DAILY GOAL: _____

MARKET ANALYSIS

Check the momentum of the market based on Key Indices, Commodities, and ETFs.

Type of Market Day	Key Indices and Commodities					
	S&P 500	Dow 30	Nasdaq	Russell 2000	Crude Oil	Gold
GREEN						
RED						

INDICATORS OVERVIEW

	Ticker Symbol																	
Indicators	5M	15M	30M	1HR	4HR	1D	5M	15M	30M	1HR	4HR	1D	5M	15M	30M	1HR	4HR	1D
Moving Averages																		
5 day																		
9 day																		
50 day																		
100 day																		
200 day																		
Bollinger Bands																		
Upper Band																		
Lower Band																		
DMI																		
Bullish																		
Bearish																		
MACD																		
Bullish																		
Bearish																		
RSI																		
Overbought																		
Oversold																		
Stochastic																		
Overbought																		
Oversold																		

Company Ticker	Chart Momentum																
	5 MIN			15 MIN			30 MIN			1 HR			4 HR			1 DAY		

Instrument(s) Traded	Hard Shares		Options		Forex		Crypto		
Trade #	Entry Time	Exit Time	Time Elapsed	Buy/Call Sell/Put	Entry Price	Exit Price	Quantity	Profit/Loss	Total
1									
2									
3									
4									
5									
6									
7									
8									
9									
10									

Total Trades	Winning Trades	Losing Trades	Win Rate %

Notes

DATE:_____   ACCOUNT BALANCE:_____

TRADING POWDER:_____   MAXIMUM RISK AMOUNT PER TRADE:_____

DAILY GOAL: _____

MARKET ANALYSIS

Check the momentum of the market based on Key Indices, Commodities, and ETFs.

Type of Market Day	Key Indices and Commodities					
	S&P 500	Dow 30	Nasdaq	Russell 2000	Crude Oil	Gold
GREEN						
RED						

INDICATORS OVERVIEW

	Ticker Symbol																	
Indicators	5M	15M	30M	1HR	4HR	1D	5M	15M	30M	1HR	4HR	1D	5M	15M	30M	1HR	4HR	1D
Moving Averages																		
5 day																		
9 day																		
50 day																		
100 day																		
200 day																		
Bollinger Bands																		
Upper Band																		
Lower Band																		
DMI																		
Bullish																		
Bearish																		
MACD																		
Bullish																		
Bearish																		
RSI																		
Overbought																		
Oversold																		
Stochastic																		
Overbought																		
Oversold																		

Company Ticker	Chart Momentum																
	5 MIN			15 MIN			30 MIN			1 HR			4 HR			1 DAY		

Instrument(s) Traded	Hard Shares		Options		Forex		Crypto		
Trade #	Entry Time	Exit Time	Time Elapsed	Buy/Call Sell/Put	Entry Price	Exit Price	Quantity	Profit/Loss	Total
1									
2									
3									
4									
5									
6									
7									
8									
9									
10									

Total Trades	Winning Trades	Losing Trades	Win Rate %

Notes

DATE:_____   ACCOUNT BALANCE:_____

TRADING POWDER:_____   MAXIMUM RISK AMOUNT PER TRADE:_____

DAILY GOAL: _____

MARKET ANALYSIS

Check the momentum of the market based on Key Indices, Commodities, and ETFs.

Type of Market Day	Key Indices and Commodities					
	S&P 500	Dow 30	Nasdaq	Russell 2000	Crude Oil	Gold
GREEN						
RED						

INDICATORS OVERVIEW

	Ticker Symbol																	
Indicators	5M	15M	30M	1HR	4HR	1D	5M	15M	30M	1HR	4HR	1D	5M	15M	30M	1HR	4HR	1D
Moving Averages																		
5 day																		
9 day																		
50 day																		
100 day																		
200 day																		
Bollinger Bands																		
Upper Band																		
Lower Band																		
DMI																		
Bullish																		
Bearish																		
MACD																		
Bullish																		
Bearish																		
RSI																		
Overbought																		
Oversold																		
Stochastic																		
Overbought																		
Oversold																		

Company Ticker	Chart Momentum																
	5 MIN			15 MIN			30 MIN			1 HR			4 HR			1 DAY		

Instrument(s) Traded	Hard Shares		Options		Forex		Crypto		
Trade #	Entry Time	Exit Time	Time Elapsed	Buy/Call Sell/Put	Entry Price	Exit Price	Quantity	Profit/Loss	Total
1									
2									
3									
4									
5									
6									
7									
8									
9									
10									

Total Trades	Winning Trades	Losing Trades	Win Rate %

Notes

DATE:_____   ACCOUNT BALANCE:_____

TRADING POWDER:_____   MAXIMUM RISK AMOUNT PER TRADE:_____

DAILY GOAL: _____

MARKET ANALYSIS

Check the momentum of the market based on Key Indices, Commodities, and ETFs.

Type of Market Day	Key Indices and Commodities					
	S&P 500	Dow 30	Nasdaq	Russell 2000	Crude Oil	Gold
GREEN						
RED						

INDICATORS OVERVIEW

	Ticker Symbol																	
Indicators	5M	15M	30M	1HR	4HR	1D	5M	15M	30M	1HR	4HR	1D	5M	15M	30M	1HR	4HR	1D
Moving Averages																		
5 day																		
9 day																		
50 day																		
100 day																		
200 day																		
Bollinger Bands																		
Upper Band																		
Lower Band																		
DMI																		
Bullish																		
Bearish																		
MACD																		
Bullish																		
Bearish																		
RSI																		
Overbought																		
Oversold																		
Stochastic																		
Overbought																		
Oversold																		

Company Ticker	Chart Momentum																
	5 MIN			15 MIN			30 MIN			1 HR			4 HR			1 DAY		

Instrument(s) Traded	Hard Shares		Options		Forex		Crypto		
Trade #	Entry Time	Exit Time	Time Elapsed	Buy/Call Sell/Put	Entry Price	Exit Price	Quantity	Profit/Loss	Total
1									
2									
3									
4									
5									
6									
7									
8									
9									
10									

Total Trades	Winning Trades	Losing Trades	Win Rate %

Notes

DATE:_____ ACCOUNT BALANCE:_____

TRADING POWDER:_____ MAXIMUM RISK AMOUNT PER TRADE:_____

DAILY GOAL: _____

MARKET ANALYSIS

Check the momentum of the market based on Key Indices, Commodities, and ETFs.

Type of Market Day	Key Indices and Commodities					
	S&P 500	Dow 30	Nasdaq	Russell 2000	Crude Oil	Gold
GREEN						
RED						

INDICATORS OVERVIEW

	Ticker Symbol																	
Indicators	5M	15M	30M	1HR	4HR	1D	5M	15M	30M	1HR	4HR	1D	5M	15M	30M	1HR	4HR	1D
Moving Averages																		
5 day																		
9 day																		
50 day																		
100 day																		
200 day																		
Bollinger Bands																		
Upper Band																		
Lower Band																		
DMI																		
Bullish																		
Bearish																		
MACD																		
Bullish																		
Bearish																		
RSI																		
Overbought																		
Oversold																		
Stochastic																		
Overbought																		
Oversold																		

Company Ticker	Chart Momentum																
	5 MIN			15 MIN			30 MIN			1 HR			4 HR			1 DAY		

Instrument(s) Traded	Hard Shares		Options		Forex		Crypto		
Trade #	Entry Time	Exit Time	Time Elapsed	Buy/Call Sell/Put	Entry Price	Exit Price	Quantity	Profit/Loss	Total
1									
2									
3									
4									
5									
6									
7									
8									
9									
10									

Total Trades	Winning Trades	Losing Trades	Win Rate %

Notes

DATE:_____   ACCOUNT BALANCE:_____

TRADING POWDER:_____   MAXIMUM RISK AMOUNT PER TRADE:_____

DAILY GOAL:_____

MARKET ANALYSIS

Check the momentum of the market based on Key Indices, Commodities, and ETFs.

Type of Market Day	Key Indices and Commodities					
	S&P 500	Dow 30	Nasdaq	Russell 2000	Crude Oil	Gold
GREEN						
RED						

INDICATORS OVERVIEW

	Ticker Symbol																	
Indicators	5M	15M	30M	1HR	4HR	1D	5M	15M	30M	1HR	4HR	1D	5M	15M	30M	1HR	4HR	1D
Moving Averages																		
5 day																		
9 day																		
50 day																		
100 day																		
200 day																		
Bollinger Bands																		
Upper Band																		
Lower Band																		
DMI																		
Bullish																		
Bearish																		
MACD																		
Bullish																		
Bearish																		
RSI																		
Overbought																		
Oversold																		
Stochastic																		
Overbought																		
Oversold																		

Company Ticker	Chart Momentum																
	5 MIN			15 MIN			30 MIN			1 HR			4 HR			1 DAY		

Instrument(s) Traded	Hard Shares		Options		Forex		Crypto		
Trade #	Entry Time	Exit Time	Time Elapsed	Buy/Call Sell/Put	Entry Price	Exit Price	Quantity	Profit/Loss	Total
1									
2									
3									
4									
5									
6									
7									
8									
9									
10									

Total Trades	Winning Trades	Losing Trades	Win Rate %

Notes

DATE:_____   ACCOUNT BALANCE:_____

TRADING POWDER:_____   MAXIMUM RISK AMOUNT PER TRADE:_____

DAILY GOAL: _____

MARKET ANALYSIS

Check the momentum of the market based on Key Indices, Commodities, and ETFs.

Type of Market Day	Key Indices and Commodities					
	S&P 500	Dow 30	Nasdaq	Russell 2000	Crude Oil	Gold
GREEN						
RED						

INDICATORS OVERVIEW

	Ticker Symbol																	
Indicators	5M	15M	30M	1HR	4HR	1D	5M	15M	30M	1HR	4HR	1D	5M	15M	30M	1HR	4HR	1D
Moving Averages																		
5 day																		
9 day																		
50 day																		
100 day																		
200 day																		
Bollinger Bands																		
Upper Band																		
Lower Band																		
DMI																		
Bullish																		
Bearish																		
MACD																		
Bullish																		
Bearish																		
RSI																		
Overbought																		
Oversold																		
Stochastic																		
Overbought																		
Oversold																		

Company Ticker	Chart Momentum																
	5 MIN			15 MIN			30 MIN			1 HR			4 HR			1 DAY		

Instrument(s) Traded	Hard Shares		Options		Forex		Crypto		
Trade #	Entry Time	Exit Time	Time Elapsed	Buy/Call Sell/Put	Entry Price	Exit Price	Quantity	Profit/Loss	Total
1									
2									
3									
4									
5									
6									
7									
8									
9									
10									

Total Trades	Winning Trades	Losing Trades	Win Rate %

Notes

DATE:_____

ACCOUNT BALANCE:_____

TRADING POWDER:_____

MAXIMUM RISK AMOUNT PER TRADE:_____

DAILY GOAL:_____

MARKET ANALYSIS

Check the momentum of the market based on Key Indices, Commodities, and ETFs.

Type of Market Day	Key Indices and Commodities					
	S&P 500	Dow 30	Nasdaq	Russell 2000	Crude Oil	Gold
GREEN						
RED						

INDICATORS OVERVIEW

	Ticker Symbol																	
Indicators	5M	15M	30M	1HR	4HR	1D	5M	15M	30M	1HR	4HR	1D	5M	15M	30M	1HR	4HR	1D
Moving Averages																		
5 day																		
9 day																		
50 day																		
100 day																		
200 day																		
Bollinger Bands																		
Upper Band																		
Lower Band																		
DMI																		
Bullish																		
Bearish																		
MACD																		
Bullish																		
Bearish																		
RSI																		
Overbought																		
Oversold																		
Stochastic																		
Overbought																		
Oversold																		

Company Ticker	Chart Momentum												
	5 MIN		15 MIN		30 MIN		1 HR		4 HR		1 DAY		

Instrument(s) Traded	Hard Shares		Options		Forex		Crypto		
Trade #	Entry Time	Exit Time	Time Elapsed	Buy/Call Sell/Put	Entry Price	Exit Price	Quantity	Profit/Loss	Total
1									
2									
3									
4									
5									
6									
7									
8									
9									
10									

Total Trades	Winning Trades	Losing Trades	Win Rate %

Notes

DATE:_____   ACCOUNT BALANCE:_____

TRADING POWDER:_____   MAXIMUM RISK AMOUNT PER TRADE:_____

DAILY GOAL: _____

MARKET ANALYSIS

Check the momentum of the market based on Key Indices, Commodities, and ETFs.

Type of Market Day	Key Indices and Commodities					
	S&P 500	Dow 30	Nasdaq	Russell 2000	Crude Oil	Gold
GREEN						
RED						

INDICATORS OVERVIEW

	Ticker Symbol																	
Indicators	5M	15M	30M	1HR	4HR	1D	5M	15M	30M	1HR	4HR	1D	5M	15M	30M	1HR	4HR	1D
Moving Averages																		
5 day																		
9 day																		
50 day																		
100 day																		
200 day																		
Bollinger Bands																		
Upper Band																		
Lower Band																		
DMI																		
Bullish																		
Bearish																		
MACD																		
Bullish																		
Bearish																		
RSI																		
Overbought																		
Oversold																		
Stochastic																		
Overbought																		
Oversold																		

Company Ticker	Chart Momentum											
	5 MIN		15 MIN		30 MIN		1 HR		4 HR		1 DAY	

Instrument(s) Traded	Hard Shares		Options		Forex		Crypto		
Trade #	Entry Time	Exit Time	Time Elapsed	Buy/Call Sell/Put	Entry Price	Exit Price	Quantity	Profit/Loss	Total
1									
2									
3									
4									
5									
6									
7									
8									
9									
10									

Total Trades	Winning Trades	Losing Trades	Win Rate %

Notes

DATE:_____   ACCOUNT BALANCE:_____

TRADING POWDER:_____   MAXIMUM RISK AMOUNT PER TRADE:_____

DAILY GOAL: _____

MARKET ANALYSIS

Check the momentum of the market based on Key Indices, Commodities, and ETFs.

Type of Market Day	Key Indices and Commodities					
	S&P 500	Dow 30	Nasdaq	Russell 2000	Crude Oil	Gold
GREEN						
RED						

INDICATORS OVERVIEW

	Ticker Symbol																	
Indicators	5M	15M	30M	1HR	4HR	1D	5M	15M	30M	1HR	4HR	1D	5M	15M	30M	1HR	4HR	1D
Moving Averages																		
5 day																		
9 day																		
50 day																		
100 day																		
200 day																		
Bollinger Bands																		
Upper Band																		
Lower Band																		
DMI																		
Bullish																		
Bearish																		
MACD																		
Bullish																		
Bearish																		
RSI																		
Overbought																		
Oversold																		
Stochastic																		
Overbought																		
Oversold																		

Company Ticker	Chart Momentum																
	5 MIN			15 MIN			30 MIN			1 HR			4 HR			1 DAY		

Instrument(s) Traded	Hard Shares		Options		Forex		Crypto		
Trade #	Entry Time	Exit Time	Time Elapsed	Buy/Call Sell/Put	Entry Price	Exit Price	Quantity	Profit/Loss	Total
1									
2									
3									
4									
5									
6									
7									
8									
9									
10									

Total Trades	Winning Trades	Losing Trades	Win Rate %

Notes

DATE:_____   ACCOUNT BALANCE:_____

TRADING POWDER:_____   MAXIMUM RISK AMOUNT PER TRADE:_____

DAILY GOAL: _____

MARKET ANALYSIS

Check the momentum of the market based on Key Indices, Commodities, and ETFs.

Type of Market Day	Key Indices and Commodities					
	S&P 500	Dow 30	Nasdaq	Russell 2000	Crude Oil	Gold
GREEN						
RED						

INDICATORS OVERVIEW

	Ticker Symbol																	
Indicators	5M	15M	30M	1HR	4HR	1D	5M	15M	30M	1HR	4HR	1D	5M	15M	30M	1HR	4HR	1D
Moving Averages																		
5 day																		
9 day																		
50 day																		
100 day																		
200 day																		
Bollinger Bands																		
Upper Band																		
Lower Band																		
DMI																		
Bullish																		
Bearish																		
MACD																		
Bullish																		
Bearish																		
RSI																		
Overbought																		
Oversold																		
Stochastic																		
Overbought																		
Oversold																		

Company Ticker	Chart Momentum																
	5 MIN			15 MIN			30 MIN			1 HR			4 HR			1 DAY		

Instrument(s) Traded	Hard Shares		Options		Forex		Crypto		
Trade #	Entry Time	Exit Time	Time Elapsed	Buy/Call Sell/Put	Entry Price	Exit Price	Quantity	Profit/Loss	Total
1									
2									
3									
4									
5									
6									
7									
8									
9									
10									

Total Trades	Winning Trades	Losing Trades	Win Rate %

Notes

DATE:_____   ACCOUNT BALANCE:_____

TRADING POWDER:_____   MAXIMUM RISK AMOUNT PER TRADE:_____

DAILY GOAL: _____

MARKET ANALYSIS

Check the momentum of the market based on Key Indices, Commodities, and ETFs.

Type of Market Day	Key Indices and Commodities					
	S&P 500	Dow 30	Nasdaq	Russell 2000	Crude Oil	Gold
GREEN						
RED						

INDICATORS OVERVIEW

	Ticker Symbol																	
Indicators	5M	15M	30M	1HR	4HR	1D	5M	15M	30M	1HR	4HR	1D	5M	15M	30M	1HR	4HR	1D
Moving Averages																		
5 day																		
9 day																		
50 day																		
100 day																		
200 day																		
Bollinger Bands																		
Upper Band																		
Lower Band																		
DMI																		
Bullish																		
Bearish																		
MACD																		
Bullish																		
Bearish																		
RSI																		
Overbought																		
Oversold																		
Stochastic																		
Overbought																		
Oversold																		

Company Ticker	Chart Momentum																	
	5 MIN			15 MIN			30 MIN			1 HR			4 HR			1 DAY		

Instrument(s) Traded	Hard Shares		Options		Forex		Crypto		
Trade #	Entry Time	Exit Time	Time Elapsed	Buy/Call Sell/Put	Entry Price	Exit Price	Quantity	Profit/Loss	Total
1									
2									
3									
4									
5									
6									
7									
8									
9									
10									

Total Trades	Winning Trades	Losing Trades	Win Rate %

Notes

DATE:_____

ACCOUNT BALANCE:_____

TRADING POWDER:_____

MAXIMUM RISK AMOUNT PER TRADE:_____

DAILY GOAL: _____

MARKET ANALYSIS

Check the momentum of the market based on Key Indices, Commodities, and ETFs.

Type of Market Day	Key Indices and Commodities					
	S&P 500	Dow 30	Nasdaq	Russell 2000	Crude Oil	Gold
GREEN						
RED						

INDICATORS OVERVIEW

	Ticker Symbol																	
Indicators	5M	15M	30M	1HR	4HR	1D	5M	15M	30M	1HR	4HR	1D	5M	15M	30M	1HR	4HR	1D
Moving Averages																		
5 day																		
9 day																		
50 day																		
100 day																		
200 day																		
Bollinger Bands																		
Upper Band																		
Lower Band																		
DMI																		
Bullish																		
Bearish																		
MACD																		
Bullish																		
Bearish																		
RSI																		
Overbought																		
Oversold																		
Stochastic																		
Overbought																		
Oversold																		

Company Ticker	Chart Momentum																
	5 MIN		15 MIN		30 MIN		1 HR		4 HR		1 DAY						

Instrument(s) Traded	Hard Shares		Options		Forex		Crypto			
Trade #	Entry Time	Exit Time	Time Elapsed	Buy/Call Sell/Put	Entry Price	Exit Price	Quantity	Profit/Loss	Total
1									
2									
3									
4									
5									
6									
7									
8									
9									
10									

Total Trades	Winning Trades	Losing Trades	Win Rate %

Notes

DATE:_____   ACCOUNT BALANCE:_____

TRADING POWDER:_____   MAXIMUM RISK AMOUNT PER TRADE:_____

DAILY GOAL: _____

MARKET ANALYSIS

Check the momentum of the market based on Key Indices, Commodities, and ETFs.

Type of Market Day	Key Indices and Commodities					
	S&P 500	Dow 30	Nasdaq	Russell 2000	Crude Oil	Gold
GREEN						
RED						

INDICATORS OVERVIEW

	Ticker Symbol																	
Indicators	5M	15M	30M	1HR	4HR	1D	5M	15M	30M	1HR	4HR	1D	5M	15M	30M	1HR	4HR	1D
Moving Averages																		
5 day																		
9 day																		
50 day																		
100 day																		
200 day																		
Bollinger Bands																		
Upper Band																		
Lower Band																		
DMI																		
Bullish																		
Bearish																		
MACD																		
Bullish																		
Bearish																		
RSI																		
Overbought																		
Oversold																		
Stochastic																		
Overbought																		
Oversold																		

Company Ticker	Chart Momentum																	
	5 MIN			15 MIN			30 MIN			1 HR			4 HR			1 DAY		

Instrument(s) Traded	Hard Shares		Options		Forex		Crypto		
Trade #	Entry Time	Exit Time	Time Elapsed	Buy/Call Sell/Put	Entry Price	Exit Price	Quantity	Profit/Loss	Total
1									
2									
3									
4									
5									
6									
7									
8									
9									
10									

Total Trades	Winning Trades	Losing Trades	Win Rate %

Notes

DATE:_____

ACCOUNT BALANCE:_____

TRADING POWDER:_____

MAXIMUM RISK AMOUNT PER TRADE:_____

DAILY GOAL: _____

MARKET ANALYSIS

Check the momentum of the market based on Key Indices, Commodities, and ETFs.

Type of Market Day	Key Indices and Commodities					
	S&P 500	Dow 30	Nasdaq	Russell 2000	Crude Oil	Gold
GREEN						
RED						

INDICATORS OVERVIEW

	Ticker Symbol																	
Indicators	5M	15M	30M	1HR	4HR	1D	5M	15M	30M	1HR	4HR	1D	5M	15M	30M	1HR	4HR	1D
Moving Averages																		
5 day																		
9 day																		
50 day																		
100 day																		
200 day																		
Bollinger Bands																		
Upper Band																		
Lower Band																		
DMI																		
Bullish																		
Bearish																		
MACD																		
Bullish																		
Bearish																		
RSI																		
Overbought																		
Oversold																		
Stochastic																		
Overbought																		
Oversold																		

Company Ticker	Chart Momentum												
	5 MIN			15 MIN			30 MIN			1 HR		4 HR	1 DAY

Instrument(s) Traded	Hard Shares		Options		Forex		Crypto		
Trade #	Entry Time	Exit Time	Time Elapsed	Buy/Call Sell/Put	Entry Price	Exit Price	Quantity	Profit/Loss	Total
1									
2									
3									
4									
5									
6									
7									
8									
9									
10									

Total Trades	Winning Trades	Losing Trades	Win Rate %

Notes

DATE:_____

ACCOUNT BALANCE:_____

TRADING POWDER:_____

MAXIMUM RISK AMOUNT PER TRADE:_____

DAILY GOAL:_____

MARKET ANALYSIS

Check the momentum of the market based on Key Indices, Commodities, and ETFs.

Type of Market Day	Key Indices and Commodities					
	S&P 500	Dow 30	Nasdaq	Russell 2000	Crude Oil	Gold
GREEN						
RED						

INDICATORS OVERVIEW

	Ticker Symbol																	
Indicators	5M	15M	30M	1HR	4HR	1D	5M	15M	30M	1HR	4HR	1D	5M	15M	30M	1HR	4HR	1D
Moving Averages																		
5 day																		
9 day																		
50 day																		
100 day																		
200 day																		
Bollinger Bands																		
Upper Band																		
Lower Band																		
DMI																		
Bullish																		
Bearish																		
MACD																		
Bullish																		
Bearish																		
RSI																		
Overbought																		
Oversold																		
Stochastic																		
Overbought																		
Oversold																		

Company Ticker	Chart Momentum																
	5 MIN			15 MIN			30 MIN			1 HR			4 HR			1 DAY		

Instrument(s) Traded	Hard Shares		Options		Forex		Crypto	
Trade #	Entry Time	Exit Time	Time Elapsed	Buy/Call Sell/Put	Entry Price	Exit Price	Quantity	Profit/Loss	Total
1									
2									
3									
4									
5									
6									
7									
8									
9									
10									

Total Trades	Winning Trades	Losing Trades	Win Rate %

Notes

DATE:_____   ACCOUNT BALANCE:_____

TRADING POWDER:_____   MAXIMUM RISK AMOUNT PER TRADE:_____

DAILY GOAL: _____

MARKET ANALYSIS

Check the momentum of the market based on Key Indices, Commodities, and ETFs.

Type of Market Day	Key Indices and Commodities					
	S&P 500	Dow 30	Nasdaq	Russell 2000	Crude Oil	Gold
GREEN						
RED						

INDICATORS OVERVIEW

	Ticker Symbol																	
Indicators	5M	15M	30M	1HR	4HR	1D	5M	15M	30M	1HR	4HR	1D	5M	15M	30M	1HR	4HR	1D
Moving Averages																		
5 day																		
9 day																		
50 day																		
100 day																		
200 day																		
Bollinger Bands																		
Upper Band																		
Lower Band																		
DMI																		
Bullish																		
Bearish																		
MACD																		
Bullish																		
Bearish																		
RSI																		
Overbought																		
Oversold																		
Stochastic																		
Overbought																		
Oversold																		

Company Ticker	Chart Momentum																
	5 MIN			15 MIN			30 MIN			1 HR			4 HR			1 DAY		

Instrument(s) Traded	Hard Shares		Options		Forex		Crypto		
Trade #	Entry Time	Exit Time	Time Elapsed	Buy/Call Sell/Put	Entry Price	Exit Price	Quantity	Profit/Loss	Total
1									
2									
3									
4									
5									
6									
7									
8									
9									
10									

Total Trades	Winning Trades	Losing Trades	Win Rate %

Notes

DATE:_____   **ACCOUNT BALANCE:**_____

TRADING POWDER:_____   **MAXIMUM RISK AMOUNT PER TRADE:**_____

DAILY GOAL: _____

MARKET ANALYSIS

Check the momentum of the market based on Key Indices, Commodities, and ETFs.

Type of Market Day	Key Indices and Commodities					
	S&P 500	Dow 30	Nasdaq	Russell 2000	Crude Oil	Gold
GREEN						
RED						

INDICATORS OVERVIEW

| | Ticker Symbol | | | | | | | | | | | | | | | | | |
Indicators	5M	15M	30M	1HR	4HR	1D	5M	15M	30M	1HR	4HR	1D	5M	15M	30M	1HR	4HR	1D
Moving Averages																		
5 day																		
9 day																		
50 day																		
100 day																		
200 day																		
Bollinger Bands																		
Upper Band																		
Lower Band																		
DMI																		
Bullish																		
Bearish																		
MACD																		
Bullish																		
Bearish																		
RSI																		
Overbought																		
Oversold																		
Stochastic																		
Overbought																		
Oversold																		

Company Ticker	Chart Momentum																
	5 MIN			15 MIN			30 MIN			1 HR			4 HR			1 DAY		

Instrument(s) Traded	Hard Shares		Options		Forex		Crypto		
Trade #	Entry Time	Exit Time	Time Elapsed	Buy/Call Sell/Put	Entry Price	Exit Price	Quantity	Profit/Loss	Total
1									
2									
3									
4									
5									
6									
7									
8									
9									
10									

Total Trades	Winning Trades	Losing Trades	Win Rate %

Notes

DATE:_____   ACCOUNT BALANCE:_____

TRADING POWDER:_____   MAXIMUM RISK AMOUNT PER TRADE:_____

DAILY GOAL: _____

MARKET ANALYSIS

Check the momentum of the market based on Key Indices, Commodities, and ETFs.

Type of Market Day	Key Indices and Commodities					
	S&P 500	Dow 30	Nasdaq	Russell 2000	Crude Oil	Gold
GREEN						
RED						

INDICATORS OVERVIEW

	Ticker Symbol																	
Indicators	5M	15M	30M	1HR	4HR	1D	5M	15M	30M	1HR	4HR	1D	5M	15M	30M	1HR	4HR	1D
Moving Averages																		
5 day																		
9 day																		
50 day																		
100 day																		
200 day																		
Bollinger Bands																		
Upper Band																		
Lower Band																		
DMI																		
Bullish																		
Bearish																		
MACD																		
Bullish																		
Bearish																		
RSI																		
Overbought																		
Oversold																		
Stochastic																		
Overbought																		
Oversold																		

Company Ticker	Chart Momentum											
	5 MIN		15 MIN		30 MIN		1 HR		4 HR		1 DAY	

Instrument(s) Traded	Hard Shares		Options		Forex		Crypto		
Trade #	Entry Time	Exit Time	Time Elapsed	Buy/Call Sell/Put	Entry Price	Exit Price	Quantity	Profit/Loss	Total
1									
2									
3									
4									
5									
6									
7									
8									
9									
10									

Total Trades	Winning Trades	Losing Trades	Win Rate %

Notes

DATE:_____   ACCOUNT BALANCE:_____

TRADING POWDER:_____   MAXIMUM RISK AMOUNT PER TRADE:_____

DAILY GOAL: _____

MARKET ANALYSIS

Check the momentum of the market based on Key Indices, Commodities, and ETFs.

Type of Market Day	Key Indices and Commodities					
	S&P 500	Dow 30	Nasdaq	Russell 2000	Crude Oil	Gold
GREEN						
RED						

INDICATORS OVERVIEW

	Ticker Symbol																	
Indicators	5M	15M	30M	1HR	4HR	1D	5M	15M	30M	1HR	4HR	1D	5M	15M	30M	1HR	4HR	1D
Moving Averages																		
5 day																		
9 day																		
50 day																		
100 day																		
200 day																		
Bollinger Bands																		
Upper Band																		
Lower Band																		
DMI																		
Bullish																		
Bearish																		
MACD																		
Bullish																		
Bearish																		
RSI																		
Overbought																		
Oversold																		
Stochastic																		
Overbought																		
Oversold																		

Company Ticker	Chart Momentum																
	5 MIN			15 MIN			30 MIN			1 HR			4 HR			1 DAY		

Instrument(s) Traded	Hard Shares		Options		Forex		Crypto		
Trade #	Entry Time	Exit TIme	Time Elapsed	Buy/Call Sell/Put	Entry Price	Exit Price	Quantity	Profit/Loss	Total
1									
2									
3									
4									
5									
6									
7									
8									
9									
10									

Total Trades	Winning Trades	Losing Trades	Win Rate %

Notes

DATE:_____   ACCOUNT BALANCE:_____

TRADING POWDER:_____   MAXIMUM RISK AMOUNT PER TRADE:_____

DAILY GOAL: _____

MARKET ANALYSIS

Check the momentum of the market based on Key Indices, Commodities, and ETFs.

Type of Market Day	Key Indices and Commodities					
	S&P 500	Dow 30	Nasdaq	Russell 2000	Crude Oil	Gold
GREEN						
RED						

INDICATORS OVERVIEW

	Ticker Symbol																	
Indicators	5M	15M	30M	1HR	4HR	1D	5M	15M	30M	1HR	4HR	1D	5M	15M	30M	1HR	4HR	1D
Moving Averages																		
5 day																		
9 day																		
50 day																		
100 day																		
200 day																		
Bollinger Bands																		
Upper Band																		
Lower Band																		
DMI																		
Bullish																		
Bearish																		
MACD																		
Bullish																		
Bearish																		
RSI																		
Overbought																		
Oversold																		
Stochastic																		
Overbought																		
Oversold																		

Company Ticker	Chart Momentum											
	5 MIN		15 MIN		30 MIN		1 HR		4 HR		1 DAY	

Instrument(s) Traded	Hard Shares		Options		Forex		Crypto		
Trade #	Entry Time	Exit Time	Time Elapsed	Buy/Call Sell/Put	Entry Price	Exit Price	Quantity	Profit/Loss	Total
1									
2									
3									
4									
5									
6									
7									
8									
9									
10									

Total Trades	Winning Trades	Losing Trades	Win Rate %

Notes

DATE:_____   ACCOUNT BALANCE:_____

TRADING POWDER:_____   MAXIMUM RISK AMOUNT PER TRADE:_____

DAILY GOAL: _____

MARKET ANALYSIS

Check the momentum of the market based on Key Indices, Commodities, and ETFs.

Type of Market Day	Key Indices and Commodities					
	S&P 500	Dow 30	Nasdaq	Russell 2000	Crude Oil	Gold
GREEN						
RED						

INDICATORS OVERVIEW

	Ticker Symbol																	
Indicators	5M	15M	30M	1HR	4HR	1D	5M	15M	30M	1HR	4HR	1D	5M	15M	30M	1HR	4HR	1D
Moving Averages																		
5 day																		
9 day																		
50 day																		
100 day																		
200 day																		
Bollinger Bands																		
Upper Band																		
Lower Band																		
DMI																		
Bullish																		
Bearish																		
MACD																		
Bullish																		
Bearish																		
RSI																		
Overbought																		
Oversold																		
Stochastic																		
Overbought																		
Oversold																		

Company Ticker	Chart Momentum																	
	5 MIN			15 MIN			30 MIN			1 HR			4 HR			1 DAY		

Instrument(s) Traded	Hard Shares		Options		Forex		Crypto		
Trade #	Entry Time	Exit Time	Time Elapsed	Buy/Call Sell/Put	Entry Price	Exit Price	Quantity	Profit/Loss	Total
1									
2									
3									
4									
5									
6									
7									
8									
9									
10									

Total Trades	Winning Trades	Losing Trades	Win Rate %

Notes

DATE:_____   ACCOUNT BALANCE:_____

TRADING POWDER:_____   MAXIMUM RISK AMOUNT PER TRADE:_____

DAILY GOAL: _____

MARKET ANALYSIS

Check the momentum of the market based on Key Indices, Commodities, and ETFs.

Type of Market Day	Key Indices and Commodities					
	S&P 500	Dow 30	Nasdaq	Russell 2000	Crude Oil	Gold
GREEN						
RED						

INDICATORS OVERVIEW

	Ticker Symbol																	
Indicators	5M	15M	30M	1HR	4HR	1D	5M	15M	30M	1HR	4HR	1D	5M	15M	30M	1HR	4HR	1D
Moving Averages																		
5 day																		
9 day																		
50 day																		
100 day																		
200 day																		
Bollinger Bands																		
Upper Band																		
Lower Band																		
DMI																		
Bullish																		
Bearish																		
MACD																		
Bullish																		
Bearish																		
RSI																		
Overbought																		
Oversold																		
Stochastic																		
Overbought																		
Oversold																		

Company Ticker	Chart Momentum																	
	5 MIN			15 MIN			30 MIN			1 HR			4 HR			1 DAY		

Instrument(s) Traded	Hard Shares		Options		Forex		Crypto		
Trade #	Entry Time	Exit Time	Time Elapsed	Buy/Call Sell/Put	Entry Price	Exit Price	Quantity	Profit/Loss	Total
1									
2									
3									
4									
5									
6									
7									
8									
9									
10									

Total Trades	Winning Trades	Losing Trades	Win Rate %
Notes			

DATE:_____   ACCOUNT BALANCE:_____

TRADING POWDER:_____   MAXIMUM RISK AMOUNT PER TRADE:_____

DAILY GOAL: _____

MARKET ANALYSIS

Check the momentum of the market based on Key Indices, Commodities, and ETFs.

Type of Market Day	Key Indices and Commodities					
	S&P 500	Dow 30	Nasdaq	Russell 2000	Crude Oil	Gold
GREEN						
RED						

INDICATORS OVERVIEW

	Ticker Symbol																	
Indicators	5M	15M	30M	1HR	4HR	1D	5M	15M	30M	1HR	4HR	1D	5M	15M	30M	1HR	4HR	1D
Moving Averages																		
5 day																		
9 day																		
50 day																		
100 day																		
200 day																		
Bollinger Bands																		
Upper Band																		
Lower Band																		
DMI																		
Bullish																		
Bearish																		
MACD																		
Bullish																		
Bearish																		
RSI																		
Overbought																		
Oversold																		
Stochastic																		
Overbought																		
Oversold																		

Company Ticker	Chart Momentum																	
	5 MIN			15 MIN			30 MIN			1 HR			4 HR			1 DAY		

Instrument(s) Traded	Hard Shares		Options		Forex		Crypto		
Trade #	Entry Time	Exit Time	Time Elapsed	Buy/Call Sell/Put	Entry Price	Exit Price	Quantity	Profit/Loss	Total
1									
2									
3									
4									
5									
6									
7									
8									
9									
10									

Total Trades	Winning Trades	Losing Trades	Win Rate %

Notes

DATE:_____   ACCOUNT BALANCE:_____

TRADING POWDER:_____   MAXIMUM RISK AMOUNT PER TRADE:_____

DAILY GOAL: _____

MARKET ANALYSIS

Check the momentum of the market based on Key Indices, Commodities, and ETFs.

Type of Market Day	Key Indices and Commodities					
	S&P 500	Dow 30	Nasdaq	Russell 2000	Crude Oil	Gold
GREEN						
RED						

INDICATORS OVERVIEW

	Ticker Symbol																	
Indicators	5M	15M	30M	1HR	4HR	1D	5M	15M	30M	1HR	4HR	1D	5M	15M	30M	1HR	4HR	1D
Moving Averages																		
5 day																		
9 day																		
50 day																		
100 day																		
200 day																		
Bollinger Bands																		
Upper Band																		
Lower Band																		
DMI																		
Bullish																		
Bearish																		
MACD																		
Bullish																		
Bearish																		
RSI																		
Overbought																		
Oversold																		
Stochastic																		
Overbought																		
Oversold																		

Company Ticker	Chart Momentum											
	5 MIN		15 MIN		30 MIN		1 HR		4 HR		1 DAY	

Instrument(s) Traded	Hard Shares		Options		Forex		Crypto			
Trade #	Entry Time	Exit Time	Time Elapsed	Buy/Call Sell/Put	Entry Price	Exit Price	Quantity	Profit/Loss	Total
1									
2									
3									
4									
5									
6									
7									
8									
9									
10									

Total Trades	Winning Trades	Losing Trades	Win Rate %

Notes

DATE:_____   ACCOUNT BALANCE:_____

TRADING POWDER:_____   MAXIMUM RISK AMOUNT PER TRADE:_____

DAILY GOAL: _____

MARKET ANALYSIS

Check the momentum of the market based on Key Indices, Commodities, and ETFs.

Type of Market Day	Key Indices and Commodities					
	S&P 500	Dow 30	Nasdaq	Russell 2000	Crude Oil	Gold
GREEN						
RED						

INDICATORS OVERVIEW

| | Ticker Symbol | | | | | | | | | | | | | | | | | |
| | | | | | | | | | | | | | | | | | | |
Indicators	5M	15M	30M	1HR	4HR	1D	5M	15M	30M	1HR	4HR	1D	5M	15M	30M	1HR	4HR	1D
Moving Averages																		
5 day																		
9 day																		
50 day																		
100 day																		
200 day																		
Bollinger Bands																		
Upper Band																		
Lower Band																		
DMI																		
Bullish																		
Bearish																		
MACD																		
Bullish																		
Bearish																		
RSI																		
Overbought																		
Oversold																		
Stochastic																		
Overbought																		
Oversold																		

Company Ticker	Chart Momentum																
	5 MIN			15 MIN			30 MIN			1 HR			4 HR			1 DAY		

Instrument(s) Traded	Hard Shares		Options		Forex		Crypto		
Trade #	Entry Time	Exit Time	Time Elapsed	Buy/Call Sell/Put	Entry Price	Exit Price	Quantity	Profit/Loss	Total
1									
2									
3									
4									
5									
6									
7									
8									
9									
10									

Total Trades	Winning Trades	Losing Trades	Win Rate %

Notes

DATE:_____   ACCOUNT BALANCE:_____

TRADING POWDER:_____   MAXIMUM RISK AMOUNT PER TRADE:_____

DAILY GOAL: _____

MARKET ANALYSIS

Check the momentum of the market based on Key Indices, Commodities, and ETFs.

Type of Market Day	Key Indices and Commodities					
	S&P 500	Dow 30	Nasdaq	Russell 2000	Crude Oil	Gold
GREEN						
RED						

INDICATORS OVERVIEW

	Ticker Symbol																
Indicators	5M	15M	30M	1HR	4HR	1D	5M	15M	30M	1HR	4HR	1D	5M	15M	30M	1HR	4HR	1D
Moving Averages																	
5 day																	
9 day																	
50 day																	
100 day																	
200 day																	
Bollinger Bands																	
Upper Band																	
Lower Band																	
DMI																	
Bullish																	
Bearish																	
MACD																	
Bullish																	
Bearish																	
RSI																	
Overbought																	
Oversold																	
Stochastic																	
Overbought																	
Oversold																	

Company Ticker	Chart Momentum											
	5 MIN		15 MIN		30 MIN		1 HR		4 HR		1 DAY	

Instrument(s) Traded	Hard Shares		Options		Forex		Crypto			
Trade #	Entry Time	Exit Time	Time Elapsed	Buy/Call Sell/Put	Entry Price	Exit Price	Quantity	Profit/Loss	Total	
1										
2										
3										
4										
5										
6										
7										
8										
9										
10										

Total Trades	Winning Trades	Losing Trades	Win Rate %

Notes

DATE:_____   ACCOUNT BALANCE:_____

TRADING POWDER:_____   MAXIMUM RISK AMOUNT PER TRADE:_____

DAILY GOAL: _____

MARKET ANALYSIS

Check the momentum of the market based on Key Indices, Commodities, and ETFs.

Type of Market Day	Key Indices and Commodities					
	S&P 500	Dow 30	Nasdaq	Russell 2000	Crude Oil	Gold
GREEN						
RED						

INDICATORS OVERVIEW

	Ticker Symbol																	
Indicators	5M	15M	30M	1HR	4HR	1D	5M	15M	30M	1HR	4HR	1D	5M	15M	30M	1HR	4HR	1D
Moving Averages																		
5 day																		
9 day																		
50 day																		
100 day																		
200 day																		
Bollinger Bands																		
Upper Band																		
Lower Band																		
DMI																		
Bullish																		
Bearish																		
MACD																		
Bullish																		
Bearish																		
RSI																		
Overbought																		
Oversold																		
Stochastic																		
Overbought																		
Oversold																		

Company Ticker	Chart Momentum																
	5 MIN			15 MIN			30 MIN			1 HR			4 HR			1 DAY		

Instrument(s) Traded	Hard Shares		Options		Forex		Crypto		
Trade #	Entry Time	Exit Time	Time Elapsed	Buy/Call Sell/Put	Entry Price	Exit Price	Quantity	Profit/Loss	Total
1									
2									
3									
4									
5									
6									
7									
8									
9									
10									

Total Trades	Winning Trades	Losing Trades	Win Rate %

Notes

DATE:_____   **ACCOUNT BALANCE:**_____

TRADING POWDER:_____   **MAXIMUM RISK AMOUNT PER TRADE:**_____

DAILY GOAL: _____

MARKET ANALYSIS

Check the momentum of the market based on Key Indices, Commodities, and ETFs.

Type of Market Day	Key Indices and Commodities					
	S&P 500	Dow 30	Nasdaq	Russell 2000	Crude Oil	Gold
GREEN						
RED						

INDICATORS OVERVIEW

	Ticker Symbol																	
Indicators	5M	15M	30M	1HR	4HR	1D	5M	15M	30M	1HR	4HR	1D	5M	15M	30M	1HR	4HR	1D
Moving Averages																		
5 day																		
9 day																		
50 day																		
100 day																		
200 day																		
Bollinger Bands																		
Upper Band																		
Lower Band																		
DMI																		
Bullish																		
Bearish																		
MACD																		
Bullish																		
Bearish																		
RSI																		
Overbought																		
Oversold																		
Stochastic																		
Overbought																		
Oversold																		

Company Ticker	Chart Momentum																
	5 MIN			15 MIN			30 MIN			1 HR			4 HR			1 DAY	

Instrument(s) Traded	Hard Shares		Options		Forex		Crypto		
Trade #	Entry Time	Exit TIme	Time Elapsed	Buy/Call Sell/Put	Entry Price	Exit Price	Quantity	Profit/Loss	Total
1									
2									
3									
4									
5									
6									
7									
8									
9									
10									

Total Trades	Winning Trades	Losing Trades	Win Rate %

Notes

DATE:_____   ACCOUNT BALANCE:_____

TRADING POWDER:_____   MAXIMUM RISK AMOUNT PER TRADE:_____

DAILY GOAL: _____

MARKET ANALYSIS

Check the momentum of the market based on Key Indices, Commodities, and ETFs.

Type of Market Day	Key Indices and Commodities					
	S&P 500	Dow 30	Nasdaq	Russell 2000	Crude Oil	Gold
GREEN						
RED						

INDICATORS OVERVIEW

	Ticker Symbol																	
Indicators	5M	15M	30M	1HR	4HR	1D	5M	15M	30M	1HR	4HR	1D	5M	15M	30M	1HR	4HR	1D
Moving Averages																		
5 day																		
9 day																		
50 day																		
100 day																		
200 day																		
Bollinger Bands																		
Upper Band																		
Lower Band																		
DMI																		
Bullish																		
Bearish																		
MACD																		
Bullish																		
Bearish																		
RSI																		
Overbought																		
Oversold																		
Stochastic																		
Overbought																		
Oversold																		

Company Ticker	Chart Momentum																
	5 MIN			15 MIN			30 MIN			1 HR			4 HR			1 DAY		

Instrument(s) Traded	Hard Shares		Options		Forex		Crypto		
Trade #	Entry Time	Exit Time	Time Elapsed	Buy/Call Sell/Put	Entry Price	Exit Price	Quantity	Profit/Loss	Total
1									
2									
3									
4									
5									
6									
7									
8									
9									
10									

Total Trades	Winning Trades	Losing Trades	Win Rate %

Notes

DATE:_____   ACCOUNT BALANCE:_____

TRADING POWDER:_____   MAXIMUM RISK AMOUNT PER TRADE:_____

DAILY GOAL: _____

MARKET ANALYSIS

Check the momentum of the market based on Key Indices, Commodities, and ETFs.

Type of Market Day	Key Indices and Commodities					
	S&P 500	Dow 30	Nasdaq	Russell 2000	Crude Oil	Gold
GREEN						
YELLOW						
RED						

INDICATORS OVERVIEW

	Ticker Symbol																	
Indicators	5M	15M	30M	1HR	4HR	1D	5M	15M	30M	1HR	4HR	1D	5M	15M	30M	1HR	4HR	1D
Moving Averages																		
5 day																		
9 day																		
50 day																		
100 day																		
200 day																		
Bollinger Bands																		
Upper Band																		
Lower Band																		
DMI																		
Bullish																		
Bearish																		
MACD																		
Bullish																		
Bearish																		
RSI																		
Overbought																		
Oversold																		
Stochastic																		
Overbought																		
Oversold																		

Company Ticker	Chart Momentum																	
	5 MIN			15 MIN			30 MIN			1 HR			4 HR			1 DAY		

Instrument(s) Traded	Hard Shares		Options		Forex		Crypto		
Trade #	Entry Time	Exit Time	Time Elapsed	Buy/Call Sell/Put	Entry Price	Exit Price	Quantity	Profit/Loss	Total
1									
2									
3									
4									
5									
6									
7									
8									
9									
10									

Total Trades	Winning Trades	Losing Trades	Win Rate %

Notes

DATE:_____   ACCOUNT BALANCE:_____

TRADING POWDER:_____   MAXIMUM RISK AMOUNT PER TRADE:_____

DAILY GOAL: _____

MARKET ANALYSIS

Check the momentum of the market based on Key Indices, Commodities, and ETFs.

Type of Market Day	Key Indices and Commodities					
	S&P 500	Dow 30	Nasdaq	Russell 2000	Crude Oil	Gold
GREEN						
RED						

INDICATORS OVERVIEW

	Ticker Symbol																	
Indicators	5M	15M	30M	1HR	4HR	1D	5M	15M	30M	1HR	4HR	1D	5M	15M	30M	1HR	4HR	1D
Moving Averages																		
5 day																		
9 day																		
50 day																		
100 day																		
200 day																		
Bollinger Bands																		
Upper Band																		
Lower Band																		
DMI																		
Bullish																		
Bearish																		
MACD																		
Bullish																		
Bearish																		
RSI																		
Overbought																		
Oversold																		
Stochastic																		
Overbought																		
Oversold																		

Company Ticker	Chart Momentum																
	5 MIN			15 MIN			30 MIN			1 HR			4 HR			1 DAY		

Instrument(s) Traded	Hard Shares		Options		Forex		Crypto		
Trade #	Entry Time	Exit Time	Time Elapsed	Buy/Call Sell/Put	Entry Price	Exit Price	Quantity	Profit/Loss	Total
1									
2									
3									
4									
5									
6									
7									
8									
9									
10									

Total Trades	Winning Trades	Losing Trades	Win Rate %
Notes			

DATE:_____   ACCOUNT BALANCE:_____

TRADING POWDER:_____   MAXIMUM RISK AMOUNT PER TRADE:_____

DAILY GOAL: _____

MARKET ANALYSIS

Check the momentum of the market based on Key Indices, Commodities, and ETFs.

Type of Market Day	Key Indices and Commodities					
	S&P 500	Dow 30	Nasdaq	Russell 2000	Crude Oil	Gold
GREEN						
RED						

INDICATORS OVERVIEW

	Ticker Symbol																	
Indicators	5M	15M	30M	1HR	4HR	1D	5M	15M	30M	1HR	4HR	1D	5M	15M	30M	1HR	4HR	1D
Moving Averages																		
5 day																		
9 day																		
50 day																		
100 day																		
200 day																		
Bollinger Bands																		
Upper Band																		
Lower Band																		
DMI																		
Bullish																		
Bearish																		
MACD																		
Bullish																		
Bearish																		
RSI																		
Overbought																		
Oversold																		
Stochastic																		
Overbought																		
Oversold																		

Company Ticker	Chart Momentum												
	5 MIN		15 MIN		30 MIN		1 HR		4 HR		1 DAY		

Instrument(s) Traded	Hard Shares		Options		Forex		Crypto		
Trade #	Entry Time	Exit Time	Time Elapsed	Buy/Call Sell/Put	Entry Price	Exit Price	Quantity	Profit/Loss	Total
1									
2									
3									
4									
5									
6									
7									
8									
9									
10									

Total Trades	Winning Trades	Losing Trades	Win Rate %

Notes

DATE:_____   ACCOUNT BALANCE:_____

TRADING POWDER:_____   MAXIMUM RISK AMOUNT PER TRADE:_____

DAILY GOAL: _____

MARKET ANALYSIS

Check the momentum of the market based on Key Indices, Commodities, and ETFs.

Type of Market Day	Key Indices and Commodities					
	S&P 500	Dow 30	Nasdaq	Russell 2000	Crude Oil	Gold
GREEN						
RED						

INDICATORS OVERVIEW

| | Ticker Symbol | | | | | | | | | | | | | | | | | |
| | | | | | | | | | | | | | | | | | |
Indicators	5M	15M	30M	1HR	4HR	1D	5M	15M	30M	1HR	4HR	1D	5M	15M	30M	1HR	4HR	1D
Moving Averages																		
5 day																		
9 day																		
50 day																		
100 day																		
200 day																		
Bollinger Bands																		
Upper Band																		
Lower Band																		
DMI																		
Bullish																		
Bearish																		
MACD																		
Bullish																		
Bearish																		
RSI																		
Overbought																		
Oversold																		
Stochastic																		
Overbought																		
Oversold																		

Company Ticker	Chart Momentum																	
	5 MIN			15 MIN			30 MIN			1 HR			4 HR			1 DAY		

Instrument(s) Traded	Hard Shares		Options		Forex		Crypto		
Trade #	Entry Time	Exit Time	Time Elapsed	Buy/Call Sell/Put	Entry Price	Exit Price	Quantity	Profit/Loss	Total
1									
2									
3									
4									
5									
6									
7									
8									
9									
10									

Total Trades	Winning Trades	Losing Trades	Win Rate %

Notes

DATE:_____   ACCOUNT BALANCE:_____

TRADING POWDER:_____   MAXIMUM RISK AMOUNT PER TRADE:_____

DAILY GOAL: _____

MARKET ANALYSIS

Check the momentum of the market based on Key Indices, Commodities, and ETFs.

Type of Market Day	Key Indices and Commodities					
	S&P 500	Dow 30	Nasdaq	Russell 2000	Crude Oil	Gold
GREEN						
RED						

INDICATORS OVERVIEW

	Ticker Symbol																	
Indicators	5M	15M	30M	1HR	4HR	1D	5M	15M	30M	1HR	4HR	1D	5M	15M	30M	1HR	4HR	1D
Moving Averages																		
5 day																		
9 day																		
50 day																		
100 day																		
200 day																		
Bollinger Bands																		
Upper Band																		
Lower Band																		
DMI																		
Bullish																		
Bearish																		
MACD																		
Bullish																		
Bearish																		
RSI																		
Overbought																		
Oversold																		
Stochastic																		
Overbought																		
Oversold																		

Company Ticker	Chart Momentum											
	5 MIN		15 MIN		30 MIN		1 HR		4 HR		1 DAY	

Instrument(s) Traded	Hard Shares		Options		Forex		Crypto		
Trade #	Entry Time	Exit Time	Time Elapsed	Buy/Call Sell/Put	Entry Price	Exit Price	Quantity	Profit/Loss	Total
1									
2									
3									
4									
5									
6									
7									
8									
9									
10									

Total Trades	Winning Trades	Losing Trades	Win Rate %

Notes

DATE:_____   ACCOUNT BALANCE:_____

TRADING POWDER:_____   MAXIMUM RISK AMOUNT PER TRADE:_____

DAILY GOAL: _____

MARKET ANALYSIS

Check the momentum of the market based on Key Indices, Commodities, and ETFs.

Type of Market Day	Key Indices and Commodities					
	S&P 500	Dow 30	Nasdaq	Russell 2000	Crude Oil	Gold
GREEN						
RED						

INDICATORS OVERVIEW

	Ticker Symbol																	
Indicators	5M	15M	30M	1HR	4HR	1D	5M	15M	30M	1HR	4HR	1D	5M	15M	30M	1HR	4HR	1D
Moving Averages																		
5 day																		
9 day																		
50 day																		
100 day																		
200 day																		
Bollinger Bands																		
Upper Band																		
Lower Band																		
DMI																		
Bullish																		
Bearish																		
MACD																		
Bullish																		
Bearish																		
RSI																		
Overbought																		
Oversold																		
Stochastic																		
Overbought																		
Oversold																		

Company Ticker	Chart Momentum																
	5 MIN			15 MIN			30 MIN			1 HR			4 HR			1 DAY		

Instrument(s) Traded	Hard Shares		Options		Forex		Crypto		
Trade #	Entry Time	Exit Time	Time Elapsed	Buy/Call Sell/Put	Entry Price	Exit Price	Quantity	Profit/Loss	Total
1									
2									
3									
4									
5									
6									
7									
8									
9									
10									

Total Trades	Winning Trades	Losing Trades	Win Rate %

Notes

DATE:_____   ACCOUNT BALANCE:_____

TRADING POWDER:_____   MAXIMUM RISK AMOUNT PER TRADE:_____

DAILY GOAL: _____

MARKET ANALYSIS

Check the momentum of the market based on Key Indices, Commodities, and ETFs.

Type of Market Day	Key Indices and Commodities					
	S&P 500	Dow 30	Nasdaq	Russell 2000	Crude Oil	Gold
GREEN						
RED						

INDICATORS OVERVIEW

	Ticker Symbol																	
Indicators	5M	15M	30M	1HR	4HR	1D	5M	15M	30M	1HR	4HR	1D	5M	15M	30M	1HR	4HR	1D
Moving Averages																		
5 day																		
9 day																		
50 day																		
100 day																		
200 day																		
Bollinger Bands																		
Upper Band																		
Lower Band																		
DMI																		
Bullish																		
Bearish																		
MACD																		
Bullish																		
Bearish																		
RSI																		
Overbought																		
Oversold																		
Stochastic																		
Overbought																		
Oversold																		

Company Ticker	Chart Momentum																
	5 MIN			15 MIN			30 MIN			1 HR			4 HR			1 DAY		

Instrument(s) Traded	Hard Shares		Options		Forex		Crypto		
Trade #	Entry Time	Exit Time	Time Elapsed	Buy/Call Sell/Put	Entry Price	Exit Price	Quantity	Profit/Loss	Total
1									
2									
3									
4									
5									
6									
7									
8									
9									
10									

Total Trades	Winning Trades	Losing Trades	Win Rate %

Notes

DATE:_____ ACCOUNT BALANCE:_____

TRADING POWDER:_____ MAXIMUM RISK AMOUNT PER TRADE:_____

DAILY GOAL: _____

MARKET ANALYSIS

Check the momentum of the market based on Key Indices, Commodities, and ETFs.

Type of Market Day	Key Indices and Commodities					
	S&P 500	Dow 30	Nasdaq	Russell 2000	Crude Oil	Gold
GREEN						
RED						

INDICATORS OVERVIEW

	Ticker Symbol																	
Indicators	5M	15M	30M	1HR	4HR	1D	5M	15M	30M	1HR	4HR	1D	5M	15M	30M	1HR	4HR	1D
Moving Averages																		
5 day																		
9 day																		
50 day																		
100 day																		
200 day																		
Bollinger Bands																		
Upper Band																		
Lower Band																		
DMI																		
Bullish																		
Bearish																		
MACD																		
Bullish																		
Bearish																		
RSI																		
Overbought																		
Oversold																		
Stochastic																		
Overbought																		
Oversold																		

Company Ticker	Chart Momentum																
	5 MIN			15 MIN			30 MIN			1 HR			4 HR			1 DAY		

Instrument(s) Traded	Hard Shares		Options		Forex		Crypto		
Trade #	Entry Time	Exit Time	Time Elapsed	Buy/Call Sell/Put	Entry Price	Exit Price	Quantity	Profit/Loss	Total
1									
2									
3									
4									
5									
6									
7									
8									
9									
10									

Total Trades	Winning Trades	Losing Trades	Win Rate %

Notes

DATE:_____   **ACCOUNT BALANCE:**_____

TRADING POWDER:_____   **MAXIMUM RISK AMOUNT PER TRADE:**_____

DAILY GOAL: _____

MARKET ANALYSIS

Check the momentum of the market based on Key Indices, Commodities, and ETFs.

Type of Market Day	Key Indices and Commodities					
	S&P 500	Dow 30	Nasdaq	Russell 2000	Crude Oil	Gold
GREEN						
RED						

INDICATORS OVERVIEW

	Ticker Symbol																	
Indicators	5M	15M	30M	1HR	4HR	1D	5M	15M	30M	1HR	4HR	1D	5M	15M	30M	1HR	4HR	1D
Moving Averages																		
5 day																		
9 day																		
50 day																		
100 day																		
200 day																		
Bollinger Bands																		
Upper Band																		
Lower Band																		
DMI																		
Bullish																		
Bearish																		
MACD																		
Bullish																		
Bearish																		
RSI																		
Overbought																		
Oversold																		
Stochastic																		
Overbought																		
Oversold																		

Company Ticker	Chart Momentum											
	5 MIN		15 MIN		30 MIN		1 HR		4 HR		1 DAY	

Instrument(s) Traded	Hard Shares		Options		Forex		Crypto		
Trade #	Entry Time	Exit Time	Time Elapsed	Buy/Call Sell/Put	Entry Price	Exit Price	Quantity	Profit/Loss	Total
1									
2									
3									
4									
5									
6									
7									
8									
9									
10									

Total Trades	Winning Trades	Losing Trades	Win Rate %

Notes

DATE:_____   ACCOUNT BALANCE:_____

TRADING POWDER:_____   MAXIMUM RISK AMOUNT PER TRADE:_____

DAILY GOAL: _____

MARKET ANALYSIS

Check the momentum of the market based on Key Indices, Commodities, and ETFs.

Type of Market Day	Key Indices and Commodities					
	S&P 500	Dow 30	Nasdaq	Russell 2000	Crude Oil	Gold
GREEN						
RED						

INDICATORS OVERVIEW

	Ticker Symbol																	
Indicators	5M	15M	30M	1HR	4HR	1D	5M	15M	30M	1HR	4HR	1D	5M	15M	30M	1HR	4HR	1D
Moving Averages																		
5 day																		
9 day																		
50 day																		
100 day																		
200 day																		
Bollinger Bands																		
Upper Band																		
Lower Band																		
DMI																		
Bullish																		
Bearish																		
MACD																		
Bullish																		
Bearish																		
RSI																		
Overbought																		
Oversold																		
Stochastic																		
Overbought																		
Oversold																		

Company Ticker	Chart Momentum																
	5 MIN			15 MIN			30 MIN			1 HR			4 HR			1 DAY		

Instrument(s) Traded	Hard Shares		Options		Forex		Crypto		
Trade #	Entry Time	Exit Time	Time Elapsed	Buy/Call Sell/Put	Entry Price	Exit Price	Quantity	Profit/Loss	Total
1									
2									
3									
4									
5									
6									
7									
8									
9									
10									

Total Trades	Winning Trades	Losing Trades	Win Rate %

Notes

DATE:_____ ACCOUNT BALANCE:_____

TRADING POWDER:_____ MAXIMUM RISK AMOUNT PER TRADE:_____

DAILY GOAL:_____

MARKET ANALYSIS

Check the momentum of the market based on Key Indices, Commodities, and ETFs.

Type of Market Day	Key Indices and Commodities					
	S&P 500	Dow 30	Nasdaq	Russell 2000	Crude Oil	Gold
GREEN						
RED						

INDICATORS OVERVIEW

	Ticker Symbol																	
Indicators	5M	15M	30M	1HR	4HR	1D	5M	15M	30M	1HR	4HR	1D	5M	15M	30M	1HR	4HR	1D
Moving Averages																		
5 day																		
9 day																		
50 day																		
100 day																		
200 day																		
Bollinger Bands																		
Upper Band																		
Lower Band																		
DMI																		
Bullish																		
Bearish																		
MACD																		
Bullish																		
Bearish																		
RSI																		
Overbought																		
Oversold																		
Stochastic																		
Overbought																		
Oversold																		

Company Ticker	Chart Momentum											
	5 MIN		15 MIN		30 MIN		1 HR		4 HR		1 DAY	

Instrument(s) Traded	Hard Shares		Options		Forex		Crypto		
Trade #	Entry Time	Exit Time	Time Elapsed	Buy/Call Sell/Put	Entry Price	Exit Price	Quantity	Profit/Loss	Total
1									
2									
3									
4									
5									
6									
7									
8									
9									
10									

Total Trades	Winning Trades	Losing Trades	Win Rate %

Notes

DATE:_____   ACCOUNT BALANCE:_____

TRADING POWDER:_____   MAXIMUM RISK AMOUNT PER TRADE:_____

DAILY GOAL: _____

MARKET ANALYSIS

Check the momentum of the market based on Key Indices, Commodities, and ETFs.

Type of Market Day	Key Indices and Commodities					
	S&P 500	Dow 30	Nasdaq	Russell 2000	Crude Oil	Gold
GREEN						
RED						

INDICATORS OVERVIEW

	Ticker Symbol																	
Indicators	5M	15M	30M	1HR	4HR	1D	5M	15M	30M	1HR	4HR	1D	5M	15M	30M	1HR	4HR	1D
Moving Averages																		
5 day																		
9 day																		
50 day																		
100 day																		
200 day																		
Bollinger Bands																		
Upper Band																		
Lower Band																		
DMI																		
Bullish																		
Bearish																		
MACD																		
Bullish																		
Bearish																		
RSI																		
Overbought																		
Oversold																		
Stochastic																		
Overbought																		
Oversold																		

Company Ticker	Chart Momentum																
	5 MIN			15 MIN			30 MIN			1 HR			4 HR			1 DAY		

Instrument(s) Traded	Hard Shares		Options		Forex		Crypto		
Trade #	Entry Time	Exit Time	Time Elapsed	Buy/Call Sell/Put	Entry Price	Exit Price	Quantity	Profit/Loss	Total
1									
2									
3									
4									
5									
6									
7									
8									
9									
10									

Total Trades	Winning Trades	Losing Trades	Win Rate %

Notes

DATE:_____ ACCOUNT BALANCE:_____

TRADING POWDER:_____ MAXIMUM RISK AMOUNT PER TRADE:_____

DAILY GOAL: _____

MARKET ANALYSIS

Check the momentum of the market based on Key Indices, Commodities, and ETFs.

Type of Market Day	Key Indices and Commodities					
	S&P 500	Dow 30	Nasdaq	Russell 2000	Crude Oil	Gold
GREEN						
RED						

INDICATORS OVERVIEW

	Ticker Symbol																	
Indicators	5M	15M	30M	1HR	4HR	1D	5M	15M	30M	1HR	4HR	1D	5M	15M	30M	1HR	4HR	1D
Moving Averages																		
5 day																		
9 day																		
50 day																		
100 day																		
200 day																		
Bollinger Bands																		
Upper Band																		
Lower Band																		
DMI																		
Bullish																		
Bearish																		
MACD																		
Bullish																		
Bearish																		
RSI																		
Overbought																		
Oversold																		
Stochastic																		
Overbought																		
Oversold																		

Company Ticker	Chart Momentum																
	5 MIN			15 MIN			30 MIN			1 HR			4 HR			1 DAY		

Instrument(s) Traded	Hard Shares		Options		Forex		Crypto		
Trade #	Entry Time	Exit Time	Time Elapsed	Buy/Call Sell/Put	Entry Price	Exit Price	Quantity	Profit/Loss	Total
1									
2									
3									
4									
5									
6									
7									
8									
9									
10									

Total Trades	Winning Trades	Losing Trades	Win Rate %

Notes

DATE:_____ ACCOUNT BALANCE:_____

TRADING POWDER:_____ MAXIMUM RISK AMOUNT PER TRADE:_____

DAILY GOAL: _____

MARKET ANALYSIS

Check the momentum of the market based on Key Indices, Commodities, and ETFs.

Type of Market Day	Key Indices and Commodities					
	S&P 500	Dow 30	Nasdaq	Russell 2000	Crude Oil	Gold
GREEN						
RED						

INDICATORS OVERVIEW

	Ticker Symbol																	
Indicators	5M	15M	30M	1HR	4HR	1D	5M	15M	30M	1HR	4HR	1D	5M	15M	30M	1HR	4HR	1D
Moving Averages																		
5 day																		
9 day																		
50 day																		
100 day																		
200 day																		
Bollinger Bands																		
Upper Band																		
Lower Band																		
DMI																		
Bullish																		
Bearish																		
MACD																		
Bullish																		
Bearish																		
RSI																		
Overbought																		
Oversold																		
Stochastic																		
Overbought																		
Oversold																		

Company Ticker	Chart Momentum																
	5 MIN			15 MIN			30 MIN			1 HR			4 HR			1 DAY		

Instrument(s) Traded	Hard Shares		Options		Forex		Crypto		
Trade #	Entry Time	Exit Time	Time Elapsed	Buy/Call Sell/Put	Entry Price	Exit Price	Quantity	Profit/Loss	Total
1									
2									
3									
4									
5									
6									
7									
8									
9									
10									

Total Trades	Winning Trades	Losing Trades	Win Rate %

Notes

DATE:_____   ACCOUNT BALANCE:_____

TRADING POWDER:_____   MAXIMUM RISK AMOUNT PER TRADE:_____

DAILY GOAL: _____

MARKET ANALYSIS

Check the momentum of the market based on Key Indices, Commodities, and ETFs.

Type of Market Day	Key Indices and Commodities					
	S&P 500	Dow 30	Nasdaq	Russell 2000	Crude Oil	Gold
GREEN						
RED						

INDICATORS OVERVIEW

	Ticker Symbol																	
Indicators	5M	15M	30M	1HR	4HR	1D	5M	15M	30M	1HR	4HR	1D	5M	15M	30M	1HR	4HR	1D
Moving Averages																		
5 day																		
9 day																		
50 day																		
100 day																		
200 day																		
Bollinger Bands																		
Upper Band																		
Lower Band																		
DMI																		
Bullish																		
Bearish																		
MACD																		
Bullish																		
Bearish																		
RSI																		
Overbought																		
Oversold																		
Stochastic																		
Overbought																		
Oversold																		

Company Ticker	Chart Momentum												
	5 MIN			15 MIN			30 MIN		1 HR		4 HR		1 DAY

Instrument(s) Traded	Hard Shares		Options		Forex		Crypto		
Trade #	Entry Time	Exit Time	Time Elapsed	Buy/Call Sell/Put	Entry Price	Exit Price	Quantity	Profit/Loss	Total
1									
2									
3									
4									
5									
6									
7									
8									
9									
10									

Total Trades	Winning Trades	Losing Trades	Win Rate %

Notes

DATE:_____   ACCOUNT BALANCE:_____

TRADING POWDER:_____   MAXIMUM RISK AMOUNT PER TRADE:_____

DAILY GOAL: _____

MARKET ANALYSIS

Check the momentum of the market based on Key Indices, Commodities, and ETFs.

Type of Market Day	Key Indices and Commodities					
	S&P 500	Dow 30	Nasdaq	Russell 2000	Crude Oil	Gold
GREEN						
RED						

INDICATORS OVERVIEW

	Ticker Symbol																	
Indicators	5M	15M	30M	1HR	4HR	1D	5M	15M	30M	1HR	4HR	1D	5M	15M	30M	1HR	4HR	1D
Moving Averages																		
5 day																		
9 day																		
50 day																		
100 day																		
200 day																		
Bollinger Bands																		
Upper Band																		
Lower Band																		
DMI																		
Bullish																		
Bearish																		
MACD																		
Bullish																		
Bearish																		
RSI																		
Overbought																		
Oversold																		
Stochastic																		
Overbought																		
Oversold																		

Company Ticker	Chart Momentum																
	5 MIN			15 MIN			30 MIN			1 HR			4 HR			1 DAY		

Instrument(s) Traded	Hard Shares		Options		Forex		Crypto		
Trade #	Entry Time	Exit Time	Time Elapsed	Buy/Call Sell/Put	Entry Price	Exit Price	Quantity	Profit/Loss	Total
1									
2									
3									
4									
5									
6									
7									
8									
9									
10									

Total Trades	Winning Trades	Losing Trades	Win Rate %

Notes

DATE:_____   ACCOUNT BALANCE:_____

TRADING POWDER:_____   MAXIMUM RISK AMOUNT PER TRADE:_____

DAILY GOAL: _____

MARKET ANALYSIS

Check the momentum of the market based on Key Indices, Commodities, and ETFs.

Type of Market Day	Key Indices and Commodities					
	S&P 500	Dow 30	Nasdaq	Russell 2000	Crude Oil	Gold
GREEN						
RED						

INDICATORS OVERVIEW

	Ticker Symbol																	
Indicators	5M	15M	30M	1HR	4HR	1D	5M	15M	30M	1HR	4HR	1D	5M	15M	30M	1HR	4HR	1D
Moving Averages																		
5 day																		
9 day																		
50 day																		
100 day																		
200 day																		
Bollinger Bands																		
Upper Band																		
Lower Band																		
DMI																		
Bullish																		
Bearish																		
MACD																		
Bullish																		
Bearish																		
RSI																		
Overbought																		
Oversold																		
Stochastic																		
Overbought																		
Oversold																		

Company Ticker	Chart Momentum																
	5 MIN			15 MIN			30 MIN			1 HR			4 HR			1 DAY		

Instrument(s) Traded	Hard Shares		Options		Forex		Crypto		
Trade #	Entry Time	Exit Time	Time Elapsed	Buy/Call Sell/Put	Entry Price	Exit Price	Quantity	Profit/Loss	Total
1									
2									
3									
4									
5									
6									
7									
8									
9									
10									

Total Trades	Winning Trades	Losing Trades	Win Rate %

Notes

DATE:_____   ACCOUNT BALANCE:_____

TRADING POWDER:_____   MAXIMUM RISK AMOUNT PER TRADE:_____

DAILY GOAL: _____

MARKET ANALYSIS

Check the momentum of the market based on Key Indices, Commodities, and ETFs.

Type of Market Day	Key Indices and Commodities					
	S&P 500	Dow 30	Nasdaq	Russell 2000	Crude Oil	Gold
GREEN						
RED						

INDICATORS OVERVIEW

	Ticker Symbol																	
Indicators	5M	15M	30M	1HR	4HR	1D	5M	15M	30M	1HR	4HR	1D	5M	15M	30M	1HR	4HR	1D
Moving Averages																		
5 day																		
9 day																		
50 day																		
100 day																		
200 day																		
Bollinger Bands																		
Upper Band																		
Lower Band																		
DMI																		
Bullish																		
Bearish																		
MACD																		
Bullish																		
Bearish																		
RSI																		
Overbought																		
Oversold																		
Stochastic																		
Overbought																		
Oversold																		

Company Ticker	Chart Momentum																
	5 MIN			15 MIN			30 MIN			1 HR			4 HR			1 DAY		

Instrument(s) Traded	Hard Shares		Options		Forex		Crypto			
Trade #	Entry Time	Exit Time	Time Elapsed	Buy/Call Sell/Put	Entry Price	Exit Price	Quantity	Profit/Loss	Total
1									
2									
3									
4									
5									
6									
7									
8									
9									
10									

Total Trades	Winning Trades	Losing Trades	Win Rate %

Notes

DATE:_____   ACCOUNT BALANCE:_____

TRADING POWDER:_____   MAXIMUM RISK AMOUNT PER TRADE:_____

DAILY GOAL: _____

MARKET ANALYSIS

Check the momentum of the market based on Key Indices, Commodities, and ETFs.

Type of Market Day	Key Indices and Commodities					
	S&P 500	Dow 30	Nasdaq	Russell 2000	Crude Oil	Gold
GREEN						
RED						

INDICATORS OVERVIEW

	Ticker Symbol																	
Indicators	5M	15M	30M	1HR	4HR	1D	5M	15M	30M	1HR	4HR	1D	5M	15M	30M	1HR	4HR	1D
Moving Averages																		
5 day																		
9 day																		
50 day																		
100 day																		
200 day																		
Bollinger Bands																		
Upper Band																		
Lower Band																		
DMI																		
Bullish																		
Bearish																		
MACD																		
Bullish																		
Bearish																		
RSI																		
Overbought																		
Oversold																		
Stochastic																		
Overbought																		
Oversold																		

Company Ticker	Chart Momentum																
	5 MIN			15 MIN			30 MIN			1 HR			4 HR			1 DAY		

Instrument(s) Traded	Hard Shares		Options		Forex		Crypto		
Trade #	Entry Time	Exit Time	Time Elapsed	Buy/Call Sell/Put	Entry Price	Exit Price	Quantity	Profit/Loss	Total
1									
2									
3									
4									
5									
6									
7									
8									
9									
10									

Total Trades	Winning Trades	Losing Trades	Win Rate %

Notes

DATE:_____   ACCOUNT BALANCE:_____

TRADING POWDER:_____   MAXIMUM RISK AMOUNT PER TRADE:_____

DAILY GOAL: _____

MARKET ANALYSIS

Check the momentum of the market based on Key Indices, Commodities, and ETFs.

Type of Market Day	Key Indices and Commodities					
	S&P 500	Dow 30	Nasdaq	Russell 2000	Crude Oil	Gold
GREEN						
RED						

INDICATORS OVERVIEW

	Ticker Symbol																	
Indicators	5M	15M	30M	1HR	4HR	1D	5M	15M	30M	1HR	4HR	1D	5M	15M	30M	1HR	4HR	1D
Moving Averages																		
5 day																		
9 day																		
50 day																		
100 day																		
200 day																		
Bollinger Bands																		
Upper Band																		
Lower Band																		
DMI																		
Bullish																		
Bearish																		
MACD																		
Bullish																		
Bearish																		
RSI																		
Overbought																		
Oversold																		
Stochastic																		
Overbought																		
Oversold																		

Company Ticker	Chart Momentum																
	5 MIN			15 MIN			30 MIN			1 HR			4 HR			1 DAY		

Instrument(s) Traded	Hard Shares		Options		Forex		Crypto		
Trade #	Entry Time	Exit Time	Time Elapsed	Buy/Call Sell/Put	Entry Price	Exit Price	Quantity	Profit/Loss	Total
1									
2									
3									
4									
5									
6									
7									
8									
9									
10									

Total Trades	Winning Trades	Losing Trades	Win Rate %

Notes

DATE:_____   ACCOUNT BALANCE:_____

TRADING POWDER:_____   MAXIMUM RISK AMOUNT PER TRADE:_____

DAILY GOAL: _____

MARKET ANALYSIS

Check the momentum of the market based on Key Indices, Commodities, and ETFs.

Type of Market Day	Key Indices and Commodities					
	S&P 500	Dow 30	Nasdaq	Russell 2000	Crude Oil	Gold
GREEN						
RED						

INDICATORS OVERVIEW

	Ticker Symbol																	
Indicators	5M	15M	30M	1HR	4HR	1D	5M	15M	30M	1HR	4HR	1D	5M	15M	30M	1HR	4HR	1D
Moving Averages																		
5 day																		
9 day																		
50 day																		
100 day																		
200 day																		
Bollinger Bands																		
Upper Band																		
Lower Band																		
DMI																		
Bullish																		
Bearish																		
MACD																		
Bullish																		
Bearish																		
RSI																		
Overbought																		
Oversold																		
Stochastic																		
Overbought																		
Oversold																		

Company Ticker	Chart Momentum																	
	5 MIN			15 MIN			30 MIN			1 HR			4 HR			1 DAY		

Instrument(s) Traded	Hard Shares		Options		Forex		Crypto		
Trade #	Entry Time	Exit Time	Time Elapsed	Buy/Call Sell/Put	Entry Price	Exit Price	Quantity	Profit/Loss	Total
1									
2									
3									
4									
5									
6									
7									
8									
9									
10									

Total Trades	Winning Trades	Losing Trades	Win Rate %

Notes

DATE:_____ ACCOUNT BALANCE:_____

TRADING POWDER:_____ MAXIMUM RISK AMOUNT PER TRADE:_____

DAILY GOAL: _____

MARKET ANALYSIS

Check the momentum of the market based on Key Indices, Commodities, and ETFs.

Type of Market Day	Key Indices and Commodities					
	S&P 500	Dow 30	Nasdaq	Russell 2000	Crude Oil	Gold
GREEN						
RED						

INDICATORS OVERVIEW

	Ticker Symbol																	
Indicators	5M	15M	30M	1HR	4HR	1D	5M	15M	30M	1HR	4HR	1D	5M	15M	30M	1HR	4HR	1D
Moving Averages																		
5 day																		
9 day																		
50 day																		
100 day																		
200 day																		
Bollinger Bands																		
Upper Band																		
Lower Band																		
DMI																		
Bullish																		
Bearish																		
MACD																		
Bullish																		
Bearish																		
RSI																		
Overbought																		
Oversold																		
Stochastic																		
Overbought																		
Oversold																		

Company Ticker	Chart Momentum																
	5 MIN			15 MIN			30 MIN			1 HR			4 HR			1 DAY		

Instrument(s) Traded	Hard Shares		Options		Forex		Crypto		
Trade #	Entry Time	Exit Time	Time Elapsed	Buy/Call Sell/Put	Entry Price	Exit Price	Quantity	Profit/Loss	Total
1									
2									
3									
4									
5									
6									
7									
8									
9									
10									

Total Trades	Winning Trades	Losing Trades	Win Rate %

Notes

DATE:_____   ACCOUNT BALANCE:_____

TRADING POWDER:_____   MAXIMUM RISK AMOUNT PER TRADE:_____

DAILY GOAL: _____

MARKET ANALYSIS

Check the momentum of the market based on Key Indices, Commodities, and ETFs.

Type of Market Day	Key Indices and Commodities					
	S&P 500	Dow 30	Nasdaq	Russell 2000	Crude Oil	Gold
GREEN						
RED						

INDICATORS OVERVIEW

	Ticker Symbol																	
Indicators	5M	15M	30M	1HR	4HR	1D	5M	15M	30M	1HR	4HR	1D	5M	15M	30M	1HR	4HR	1D
Moving Averages																		
5 day																		
9 day																		
50 day																		
100 day																		
200 day																		
Bollinger Bands																		
Upper Band																		
Lower Band																		
DMI																		
Bullish																		
Bearish																		
MACD																		
Bullish																		
Bearish																		
RSI																		
Overbought																		
Oversold																		
Stochastic																		
Overbought																		
Oversold																		

Company Ticker	Chart Momentum												
	5 MIN		15 MIN		30 MIN		1 HR		4 HR		1 DAY		

Instrument(s) Traded	Hard Shares		Options		Forex		Crypto		
Trade #	Entry Time	Exit Time	Time Elapsed	Buy/Call Sell/Put	Entry Price	Exit Price	Quantity	Profit/Loss	Total
1									
2									
3									
4									
5									
6									
7									
8									
9									
10									

Total Trades	Winning Trades	Losing Trades	Win Rate %

Notes

DATE:_____ ACCOUNT BALANCE:_____

TRADING POWDER:_____ MAXIMUM RISK AMOUNT PER TRADE:_____

DAILY GOAL: _____

MARKET ANALYSIS

Check the momentum of the market based on Key Indices, Commodities, and ETFs.

Type of Market Day	Key Indices and Commodities					
	S&P 500	Dow 30	Nasdaq	Russell 2000	Crude Oil	Gold
GREEN						
RED						

INDICATORS OVERVIEW

	Ticker Symbol																	
Indicators	5M	15M	30M	1HR	4HR	1D	5M	15M	30M	1HR	4HR	1D	5M	15M	30M	1HR	4HR	1D
Moving Averages																		
5 day																		
9 day																		
50 day																		
100 day																		
200 day																		
Bollinger Bands																		
Upper Band																		
Lower Band																		
DMI																		
Bullish																		
Bearish																		
MACD																		
Bullish																		
Bearish																		
RSI																		
Overbought																		
Oversold																		
Stochastic																		
Overbought																		
Oversold																		

Company Ticker	Chart Momentum											
	5 MIN			15 MIN			30 MIN			1 HR	4 HR	1 DAY

Instrument(s) Traded	Hard Shares		Options		Forex		Crypto		
Trade #	Entry Time	Exit Time	Time Elapsed	Buy/Call Sell/Put	Entry Price	Exit Price	Quantity	Profit/Loss	Total
1									
2									
3									
4									
5									
6									
7									
8									
9									
10									

Total Trades	Winning Trades	Losing Trades	Win Rate %

Notes

DATE:_____   ACCOUNT BALANCE:_____

TRADING POWDER:_____   MAXIMUM RISK AMOUNT PER TRADE:_____

DAILY GOAL: _____

MARKET ANALYSIS

Check the momentum of the market based on Key Indices, Commodities, and ETFs.

Type of Market Day	Key Indices and Commodities					
	S&P 500	Dow 30	Nasdaq	Russell 2000	Crude Oil	Gold
GREEN						
RED						

INDICATORS OVERVIEW

	Ticker Symbol																	
Indicators	5M	15M	30M	1HR	4HR	1D	5M	15M	30M	1HR	4HR	1D	5M	15M	30M	1HR	4HR	1D
Moving Averages																		
5 day																		
9 day																		
50 day																		
100 day																		
200 day																		
Bollinger Bands																		
Upper Band																		
Lower Band																		
DMI																		
Bullish																		
Bearish																		
MACD																		
Bullish																		
Bearish																		
RSI																		
Overbought																		
Oversold																		
Stochastic																		
Overbought																		
Oversold																		

Company Ticker	Chart Momentum																
	5 MIN			15 MIN			30 MIN			1 HR			4 HR			1 DAY		

Instrument(s) Traded	Hard Shares		Options		Forex		Crypto		
Trade #	Entry Time	Exit Time	Time Elapsed	Buy/Call Sell/Put	Entry Price	Exit Price	Quantity	Profit/Loss	Total
1									
2									
3									
4									
5									
6									
7									
8									
9									
10									

Total Trades	Winning Trades	Losing Trades	Win Rate %

Notes

DATE:_____   ACCOUNT BALANCE:_____

TRADING POWDER:_____   MAXIMUM RISK AMOUNT PER TRADE:_____

DAILY GOAL: _____

MARKET ANALYSIS

Check the momentum of the market based on Key Indices, Commodities, and ETFs.

Type of Market Day	Key Indices and Commodities					
	S&P 500	Dow 30	Nasdaq	Russell 2000	Crude Oil	Gold
GREEN						
RED						

INDICATORS OVERVIEW

	Ticker Symbol																	
Indicators	5M	15M	30M	1HR	4HR	1D	5M	15M	30M	1HR	4HR	1D	5M	15M	30M	1HR	4HR	1D
Moving Averages																		
5 day																		
9 day																		
50 day																		
100 day																		
200 day																		
Bollinger Bands																		
Upper Band																		
Lower Band																		
DMI																		
Bullish																		
Bearish																		
MACD																		
Bullish																		
Bearish																		
RSI																		
Overbought																		
Oversold																		
Stochastic																		
Overbought																		
Oversold																		

Company Ticker	Chart Momentum																
	5 MIN			15 MIN			30 MIN			1 HR			4 HR			1 DAY		

Instrument(s) Traded	Hard Shares		Options		Forex		Crypto		
Trade #	Entry Time	Exit Time	Time Elapsed	Buy/Call Sell/Put	Entry Price	Exit Price	Quantity	Profit/Loss	Total
1									
2									
3									
4									
5									
6									
7									
8									
9									
10									

Total Trades	Winning Trades	Losing Trades	Win Rate %

Notes

DATE:_____   ACCOUNT BALANCE:_____

TRADING POWDER:_____   MAXIMUM RISK AMOUNT PER TRADE:_____

DAILY GOAL: _____

MARKET ANALYSIS

Check the momentum of the market based on Key Indices, Commodities, and ETFs.

Type of Market Day	Key Indices and Commodities					
	S&P 500	Dow 30	Nasdaq	Russell 2000	Crude Oil	Gold
GREEN						
RED						

INDICATORS OVERVIEW

	Ticker Symbol																	
Indicators	5M	15M	30M	1HR	4HR	1D	5M	15M	30M	1HR	4HR	1D	5M	15M	30M	1HR	4HR	1D
Moving Averages																		
5 day																		
9 day																		
50 day																		
100 day																		
200 day																		
Bollinger Bands																		
Upper Band																		
Lower Band																		
DMI																		
Bullish																		
Bearish																		
MACD																		
Bullish																		
Bearish																		
RSI																		
Overbought																		
Oversold																		
Stochastic																		
Overbought																		
Oversold																		

Company Ticker	Chart Momentum																
	5 MIN			15 MIN			30 MIN			1 HR			4 HR			1 DAY		

Instrument(s) Traded	Hard Shares		Options		Forex		Crypto		
Trade #	Entry Time	Exit Time	Time Elapsed	Buy/Call Sell/Put	Entry Price	Exit Price	Quantity	Profit/Loss	Total
1									
2									
3									
4									
5									
6									
7									
8									
9									
10									

Total Trades	Winning Trades	Losing Trades	Win Rate %

Notes

DATE:_____   ACCOUNT BALANCE:_____

TRADING POWDER:_____   MAXIMUM RISK AMOUNT PER TRADE:_____

DAILY GOAL: _____

MARKET ANALYSIS

Check the momentum of the market based on Key Indices, Commodities, and ETFs.

Type of Market Day	Key Indices and Commodities					
	S&P 500	Dow 30	Nasdaq	Russell 2000	Crude Oil	Gold
GREEN						
RED						

INDICATORS OVERVIEW

| | Ticker Symbol | | | | | | | | | | | | | | | | | |
| | | | | | | | | | | | | | | | | | |
Indicators	5M	15M	30M	1HR	4HR	1D	5M	15M	30M	1HR	4HR	1D	5M	15M	30M	1HR	4HR	1D
Moving Averages																		
5 day																		
9 day																		
50 day																		
100 day																		
200 day																		
Bollinger Bands																		
Upper Band																		
Lower Band																		
DMI																		
Bullish																		
Bearish																		
MACD																		
Bullish																		
Bearish																		
RSI																		
Overbought																		
Oversold																		
Stochastic																		
Overbought																		
Oversold																		

Company Ticker	Chart Momentum																
	5 MIN			15 MIN			30 MIN			1 HR			4 HR			1 DAY		

Instrument(s) Traded	Hard Shares		Options		Forex		Crypto		
Trade #	Entry Time	Exit Time	Time Elapsed	Buy/Call Sell/Put	Entry Price	Exit Price	Quantity	Profit/Loss	Total
1									
2									
3									
4									
5									
6									
7									
8									
9									
10									

Total Trades	Winning Trades	Losing Trades	Win Rate %

Notes

DATE:_____   ACCOUNT BALANCE:_____

TRADING POWDER:_____   MAXIMUM RISK AMOUNT PER TRADE:_____

DAILY GOAL: _____

MARKET ANALYSIS

Check the momentum of the market based on Key Indices, Commodities, and ETFs.

Type of Market Day	Key Indices and Commodities					
	S&P 500	Dow 30	Nasdaq	Russell 2000	Crude Oil	Gold
GREEN						
RED						

INDICATORS OVERVIEW

	Ticker Symbol																	
Indicators	5M	15M	30M	1HR	4HR	1D	5M	15M	30M	1HR	4HR	1D	5M	15M	30M	1HR	4HR	1D
Moving Averages																		
5 day																		
9 day																		
50 day																		
100 day																		
200 day																		
Bollinger Bands																		
Upper Band																		
Lower Band																		
DMI																		
Bullish																		
Bearish																		
MACD																		
Bullish																		
Bearish																		
RSI																		
Overbought																		
Oversold																		
Stochastic																		
Overbought																		
Oversold																		

Company Ticker	Chart Momentum												
	5 MIN		15 MIN		30 MIN		1 HR		4 HR		1 DAY		

Instrument(s) Traded	Hard Shares		Options		Forex		Crypto		
Trade #	Entry Time	Exit Time	Time Elapsed	Buy/Call Sell/Put	Entry Price	Exit Price	Quantity	Profit/Loss	Total
1									
2									
3									
4									
5									
6									
7									
8									
9									
10									

Total Trades	Winning Trades	Losing Trades	Win Rate %

Notes

DATE:_____   ACCOUNT BALANCE:_____

TRADING POWDER:_____   MAXIMUM RISK AMOUNT PER TRADE:_____

DAILY GOAL: _____

MARKET ANALYSIS

Check the momentum of the market based on Key Indices, Commodities, and ETFs.

Type of Market Day	Key Indices and Commodities					
	S&P 500	Dow 30	Nasdaq	Russell 2000	Crude Oil	Gold
GREEN						
RED						

INDICATORS OVERVIEW

	Ticker Symbol																	
Indicators	5M	15M	30M	1HR	4HR	1D	5M	15M	30M	1HR	4HR	1D	5M	15M	30M	1HR	4HR	1D
Moving Averages																		
5 day																		
9 day																		
50 day																		
100 day																		
200 day																		
Bollinger Bands																		
Upper Band																		
Lower Band																		
DMI																		
Bullish																		
Bearish																		
MACD																		
Bullish																		
Bearish																		
RSI																		
Overbought																		
Oversold																		
Stochastic																		
Overbought																		
Oversold																		

Company Ticker	Chart Momentum																
	5 MIN			15 MIN			30 MIN			1 HR			4 HR			1 DAY		

Instrument(s) Traded	Hard Shares		Options		Forex		Crypto		
Trade #	Entry Time	Exit TIme	Time Elapsed	Buy/Call Sell/Put	Entry Price	Exit Price	Quantity	Profit/Loss	Total
1									
2									
3									
4									
5									
6									
7									
8									
9									
10									

Total Trades	Winning Trades	Losing Trades	Win Rate %

Notes

DATE:_____   ACCOUNT BALANCE:_____

TRADING POWDER:_____   MAXIMUM RISK AMOUNT PER TRADE:_____

DAILY GOAL: _____

MARKET ANALYSIS

Check the momentum of the market based on Key Indices, Commodities, and ETFs.

Type of Market Day	Key Indices and Commodities					
	S&P 500	Dow 30	Nasdaq	Russell 2000	Crude Oil	Gold
GREEN						
RED						

INDICATORS OVERVIEW

	Ticker Symbol																	
Indicators	5M	15M	30M	1HR	4HR	1D	5M	15M	30M	1HR	4HR	1D	5M	15M	30M	1HR	4HR	1D
Moving Averages																		
5 day																		
9 day																		
50 day																		
100 day																		
200 day																		
Bollinger Bands																		
Upper Band																		
Lower Band																		
DMI																		
Bullish																		
Bearish																		
MACD																		
Bullish																		
Bearish																		
RSI																		
Overbought																		
Oversold																		
Stochastic																		
Overbought																		
Oversold																		

Company Ticker	Chart Momentum																
	5 MIN			15 MIN			30 MIN			1 HR			4 HR			1 DAY		

Instrument(s) Traded	Hard Shares		Options		Forex		Crypto		
Trade #	Entry Time	Exit Time	Time Elapsed	Buy/Call Sell/Put	Entry Price	Exit Price	Quantity	Profit/Loss	Total
1									
2									
3									
4									
5									
6									
7									
8									
9									
10									

Total Trades	Winning Trades	Losing Trades	Win Rate %
Notes			

DATE:_____   ACCOUNT BALANCE:_____

TRADING POWDER:_____   MAXIMUM RISK AMOUNT PER TRADE:_____

DAILY GOAL: _____

MARKET ANALYSIS

Check the momentum of the market based on Key Indices, Commodities, and ETFs.

Type of Market Day	Key Indices and Commodities					
	S&P 500	Dow 30	Nasdaq	Russell 2000	Crude Oil	Gold
GREEN						
RED						

INDICATORS OVERVIEW

	Ticker Symbol																	
Indicators	5M	15M	30M	1HR	4HR	1D	5M	15M	30M	1HR	4HR	1D	5M	15M	30M	1HR	4HR	1D
Moving Averages																		
5 day																		
9 day																		
50 day																		
100 day																		
200 day																		
Bollinger Bands																		
Upper Band																		
Lower Band																		
DMI																		
Bullish																		
Bearish																		
MACD																		
Bullish																		
Bearish																		
RSI																		
Overbought																		
Oversold																		
Stochastic																		
Overbought																		
Oversold																		

Company Ticker	Chart Momentum																
	5 MIN			15 MIN			30 MIN			1 HR			4 HR			1 DAY		

Instrument(s) Traded	Hard Shares		Options		Forex		Crypto		
Trade #	Entry Time	Exit Time	Time Elapsed	Buy/Call Sell/Put	Entry Price	Exit Price	Quantity	Profit/Loss	Total
1									
2									
3									
4									
5									
6									
7									
8									
9									
10									

Total Trades	Winning Trades	Losing Trades	Win Rate %

Notes

DATE:_____   ACCOUNT BALANCE:_____

TRADING POWDER:_____   MAXIMUM RISK AMOUNT PER TRADE:_____

DAILY GOAL: _____

MARKET ANALYSIS

Check the momentum of the market based on Key Indices, Commodities, and ETFs.

Type of Market Day	Key Indices and Commodities					
	S&P 500	Dow 30	Nasdaq	Russell 2000	Crude Oil	Gold
GREEN						
RED						

INDICATORS OVERVIEW

	Ticker Symbol																	
Indicators	5M	15M	30M	1HR	4HR	1D	5M	15M	30M	1HR	4HR	1D	5M	15M	30M	1HR	4HR	1D
Moving Averages																		
5 day																		
9 day																		
50 day																		
100 day																		
200 day																		
Bollinger Bands																		
Upper Band																		
Lower Band																		
DMI																		
Bullish																		
Bearish																		
MACD																		
Bullish																		
Bearish																		
RSI																		
Overbought																		
Oversold																		
Stochastic																		
Overbought																		
Oversold																		

Company Ticker	Chart Momentum											
	5 MIN		15 MIN		30 MIN		1 HR		4 HR		1 DAY	

Instrument(s) Traded	Hard Shares		Options		Forex		Crypto			
Trade #	Entry Time	Exit Time	Time Elapsed	Buy/Call Sell/Put	Entry Price	Exit Price	Quantity	Profit/Loss	Total
1									
2									
3									
4									
5									
6									
7									
8									
9									
10									

Total Trades	Winning Trades	Losing Trades	Win Rate %

Notes

DATE:_____   ACCOUNT BALANCE:_____

TRADING POWDER:_____   MAXIMUM RISK AMOUNT PER TRADE:_____

DAILY GOAL: _____

MARKET ANALYSIS

Check the momentum of the market based on Key Indices, Commodities, and ETFs.

Type of Market Day	Key Indices and Commodities					
	S&P 500	Dow 30	Nasdaq	Russell 2000	Crude Oil	Gold
GREEN						
RED						

INDICATORS OVERVIEW

| | Ticker Symbol | | | | | | | | | | | | | | | | | |
| | | | | | | | | | | | | | | | | | |
Indicators	5M	15M	30M	1HR	4HR	1D	5M	15M	30M	1HR	4HR	1D	5M	15M	30M	1HR	4HR	1D
Moving Averages																		
5 day																		
9 day																		
50 day																		
100 day																		
200 day																		
Bollinger Bands																		
Upper Band																		
Lower Band																		
DMI																		
Bullish																		
Bearish																		
MACD																		
Bullish																		
Bearish																		
RSI																		
Overbought																		
Oversold																		
Stochastic																		
Overbought																		
Oversold																		

Company Ticker	Chart Momentum																	
	5 MIN			15 MIN			30 MIN			1 HR			4 HR			1 DAY		

Instrument(s) Traded	Hard Shares		Options		Forex		Crypto		
Trade #	Entry Time	Exit Time	Time Elapsed	Buy/Call Sell/Put	Entry Price	Exit Price	Quantity	Profit/Loss	Total
1									
2									
3									
4									
5									
6									
7									
8									
9									
10									

Total Trades	Winning Trades	Losing Trades	Win Rate %

Notes

DATE:_____   ACCOUNT BALANCE:_____

TRADING POWDER:_____   MAXIMUM RISK AMOUNT PER TRADE:_____

DAILY GOAL: _____

MARKET ANALYSIS

Check the momentum of the market based on Key Indices, Commodities, and ETFs.

Type of Market Day	Key Indices and Commodities					
	S&P 500	Dow 30	Nasdaq	Russell 2000	Crude Oil	Gold
GREEN						
RED						

INDICATORS OVERVIEW

	Ticker Symbol																	
Indicators	5M	15M	30M	1HR	4HR	1D	5M	15M	30M	1HR	4HR	1D	5M	15M	30M	1HR	4HR	1D
Moving Averages																		
5 day																		
9 day																		
50 day																		
100 day																		
200 day																		
Bollinger Bands																		
Upper Band																		
Lower Band																		
DMI																		
Bullish																		
Bearish																		
MACD																		
Bullish																		
Bearish																		
RSI																		
Overbought																		
Oversold																		
Stochastic																		
Overbought																		
Oversold																		

Company Ticker	Chart Momentum													
	5 MIN			15 MIN			30 MIN			1 HR		4 HR		1 DAY

Instrument(s) Traded	Hard Shares		Options		Forex		Crypto		
Trade #	Entry Time	Exit Time	Time Elapsed	Buy/Call Sell/Put	Entry Price	Exit Price	Quantity	Profit/Loss	Total
1									
2									
3									
4									
5									
6									
7									
8									
9									
10									

Total Trades	Winning Trades	Losing Trades	Win Rate %

Notes

DATE:_____

ACCOUNT BALANCE:_____

TRADING POWDER:_____

MAXIMUM RISK AMOUNT PER TRADE:_____

DAILY GOAL: _____

MARKET ANALYSIS

Check the momentum of the market based on Key Indices, Commodities, and ETFs.

Type of Market Day	Key Indices and Commodities					
	S&P 500	Dow 30	Nasdaq	Russell 2000	Crude Oil	Gold
GREEN						
RED						

INDICATORS OVERVIEW

	Ticker Symbol																	
Indicators	5M	15M	30M	1HR	4HR	1D	5M	15M	30M	1HR	4HR	1D	5M	15M	30M	1HR	4HR	1D
Moving Averages																		
5 day																		
9 day																		
50 day																		
100 day																		
200 day																		
Bollinger Bands																		
Upper Band																		
Lower Band																		
DMI																		
Bullish																		
Bearish																		
MACD																		
Bullish																		
Bearish																		
RSI																		
Overbought																		
Oversold																		
Stochastic																		
Overbought																		
Oversold																		

Company Ticker	Chart Momentum											
	5 MIN		15 MIN		30 MIN		1 HR		4 HR		1 DAY	

Instrument(s) Traded	Hard Shares		Options		Forex		Crypto			
Trade #	Entry Time	Exit Time	Time Elapsed	Buy/Call Sell/Put	Entry Price	Exit Price	Quantity	Profit/Loss	Total
1									
2									
3									
4									
5									
6									
7									
8									
9									
10									

Total Trades	Winning Trades	Losing Trades	Win Rate %
Notes			

DATE:_____   ACCOUNT BALANCE:_____

TRADING POWDER:_____   MAXIMUM RISK AMOUNT PER TRADE:_____

DAILY GOAL: _____

MARKET ANALYSIS

Check the momentum of the market based on Key Indices, Commodities, and ETFs.

Type of Market Day	Key Indices and Commodities					
	S&P 500	Dow 30	Nasdaq	Russell 2000	Crude Oil	Gold
GREEN						
RED						

INDICATORS OVERVIEW

	Ticker Symbol																	
Indicators	5M	15M	30M	1HR	4HR	1D	5M	15M	30M	1HR	4HR	1D	5M	15M	30M	1HR	4HR	1D
Moving Averages																		
5 day																		
9 day																		
50 day																		
100 day																		
200 day																		
Bollinger Bands																		
Upper Band																		
Lower Band																		
DMI																		
Bullish																		
Bearish																		
MACD																		
Bullish																		
Bearish																		
RSI																		
Overbought																		
Oversold																		
Stochastic																		
Overbought																		
Oversold																		

Company Ticker	Chart Momentum																
	5 MIN			15 MIN			30 MIN			1 HR			4 HR			1 DAY		

Instrument(s) Traded	Hard Shares		Options		Forex		Crypto		
Trade #	Entry Time	Exit Time	Time Elapsed	Buy/Call Sell/Put	Entry Price	Exit Price	Quantity	Profit/Loss	Total
1									
2									
3									
4									
5									
6									
7									
8									
9									
10									

Total Trades	Winning Trades	Losing Trades	Win Rate %
Notes			

DATE:_____   ACCOUNT BALANCE:_____

TRADING POWDER:_____   MAXIMUM RISK AMOUNT PER TRADE:_____

DAILY GOAL: _____

MARKET ANALYSIS

Check the momentum of the market based on Key Indices, Commodities, and ETFs.

Type of Market Day	Key Indices and Commodities					
	S&P 500	Dow 30	Nasdaq	Russell 2000	Crude Oil	Gold
GREEN						
RED						

INDICATORS OVERVIEW

	Ticker Symbol																	
Indicators	5M	15M	30M	1HR	4HR	1D	5M	15M	30M	1HR	4HR	1D	5M	15M	30M	1HR	4HR	1D
Moving Averages																		
5 day																		
9 day																		
50 day																		
100 day																		
200 day																		
Bollinger Bands																		
Upper Band																		
Lower Band																		
DMI																		
Bullish																		
Bearish																		
MACD																		
Bullish																		
Bearish																		
RSI																		
Overbought																		
Oversold																		
Stochastic																		
Overbought																		
Oversold																		

Company Ticker	Chart Momentum																	
	5 MIN			15 MIN			30 MIN			1 HR			4 HR			1 DAY		

Instrument(s) Traded	Hard Shares		Options		Forex		Crypto		
Trade #	Entry Time	Exit Time	Time Elapsed	Buy/Call Sell/Put	Entry Price	Exit Price	Quantity	Profit/Loss	Total
1									
2									
3									
4									
5									
6									
7									
8									
9									
10									

Total Trades	Winning Trades	Losing Trades	Win Rate %

Notes

DATE:_____   ACCOUNT BALANCE:_____

TRADING POWDER:_____   MAXIMUM RISK AMOUNT PER TRADE:_____

DAILY GOAL: _____

MARKET ANALYSIS

Check the momentum of the market based on Key Indices, Commodities, and ETFs.

Type of Market Day	Key Indices and Commodities					
	S&P 500	Dow 30	Nasdaq	Russell 2000	Crude Oil	Gold
GREEN						
RED						

INDICATORS OVERVIEW

	Ticker Symbol																	
Indicators	5M	15M	30M	1HR	4HR	1D	5M	15M	30M	1HR	4HR	1D	5M	15M	30M	1HR	4HR	1D
Moving Averages																		
5 day																		
9 day																		
50 day																		
100 day																		
200 day																		
Bollinger Bands																		
Upper Band																		
Lower Band																		
DMI																		
Bullish																		
Bearish																		
MACD																		
Bullish																		
Bearish																		
RSI																		
Overbought																		
Oversold																		
Stochastic																		
Overbought																		
Oversold																		

Company Ticker	Chart Momentum											
	5 MIN		15 MIN		30 MIN		1 HR		4 HR		1 DAY	

Instrument(s) Traded	Hard Shares			Options		Forex		Crypto		
Trade #	Entry Time	Exit Time	Time Elapsed	Buy/Call Sell/Put	Entry Price	Exit Price	Quantity	Profit/Loss	Total	
1										
2										
3										
4										
5										
6										
7										
8										
9										
10										

Total Trades	Winning Trades	Losing Trades	Win Rate %

Notes

DATE:_____   ACCOUNT BALANCE:_____

TRADING POWDER:_____   MAXIMUM RISK AMOUNT PER TRADE:_____

DAILY GOAL: _____

MARKET ANALYSIS

Check the momentum of the market based on Key Indices, Commodities, and ETFs.

Type of Market Day	Key Indices and Commodities					
	S&P 500	Dow 30	Nasdaq	Russell 2000	Crude Oil	Gold
GREEN						
RED						

INDICATORS OVERVIEW

	Ticker Symbol																	
Indicators	5M	15M	30M	1HR	4HR	1D	5M	15M	30M	1HR	4HR	1D	5M	15M	30M	1HR	4HR	1D
Moving Averages																		
5 day																		
9 day																		
50 day																		
100 day																		
200 day																		
Bollinger Bands																		
Upper Band																		
Lower Band																		
DMI																		
Bullish																		
Bearish																		
MACD																		
Bullish																		
Bearish																		
RSI																		
Overbought																		
Oversold																		
Stochastic																		
Overbought																		
Oversold																		

Company Ticker	Chart Momentum																	
	5 MIN			15 MIN			30 MIN			1 HR			4 HR			1 DAY		

Instrument(s) Traded	Hard Shares		Options		Forex		Crypto		
Trade #	Entry Time	Exit Time	Time Elapsed	Buy/Call Sell/Put	Entry Price	Exit Price	Quantity	Profit/Loss	Total
1									
2									
3									
4									
5									
6									
7									
8									
9									
10									

Total Trades	Winning Trades	Losing Trades	Win Rate %

Notes

DATE:_____   ACCOUNT BALANCE:_____

TRADING POWDER:_____   MAXIMUM RISK AMOUNT PER TRADE:_____

DAILY GOAL: _____

MARKET ANALYSIS

Check the momentum of the market based on Key Indices, Commodities, and ETFs.

Type of Market Day	Key Indices and Commodities					
	S&P 500	Dow 30	Nasdaq	Russell 2000	Crude Oil	Gold
GREEN						
RED						

INDICATORS OVERVIEW

	Ticker Symbol																	
Indicators	5M	15M	30M	1HR	4HR	1D	5M	15M	30M	1HR	4HR	1D	5M	15M	30M	1HR	4HR	1D
Moving Averages																		
5 day																		
9 day																		
50 day																		
100 day																		
200 day																		
Bollinger Bands																		
Upper Band																		
Lower Band																		
DMI																		
Bullish																		
Bearish																		
MACD																		
Bullish																		
Bearish																		
RSI																		
Overbought																		
Oversold																		
Stochastic																		
Overbought																		
Oversold																		

Company Ticker	Chart Momentum											
	5 MIN		15 MIN		30 MIN		1 HR		4 HR		1 DAY	

Instrument(s) Traded	Hard Shares		Options		Forex		Crypto		
Trade #	Entry Time	Exit Time	Time Elapsed	Buy/Call Sell/Put	Entry Price	Exit Price	Quantity	Profit/Loss	Total
1									
2									
3									
4									
5									
6									
7									
8									
9									
10									

Total Trades	Winning Trades	Losing Trades	Win Rate %

Notes

DATE:_____

ACCOUNT BALANCE:_____

TRADING POWDER:_____

MAXIMUM RISK AMOUNT PER TRADE:_____

DAILY GOAL: _____

MARKET ANALYSIS

Check the momentum of the market based on Key Indices, Commodities, and ETFs.

Type of Market Day	Key Indices and Commodities					
	S&P 500	Dow 30	Nasdaq	Russell 2000	Crude Oil	Gold
GREEN						
RED						

INDICATORS OVERVIEW

	Ticker Symbol																	
Indicators	5M	15M	30M	1HR	4HR	1D	5M	15M	30M	1HR	4HR	1D	5M	15M	30M	1HR	4HR	1D
Moving Averages																		
5 day																		
9 day																		
50 day																		
100 day																		
200 day																		
Bollinger Bands																		
Upper Band																		
Lower Band																		
DMI																		
Bullish																		
Bearish																		
MACD																		
Bullish																		
Bearish																		
RSI																		
Overbought																		
Oversold																		
Stochastic																		
Overbought																		
Oversold																		

Company Ticker	Chart Momentum																
	5 MIN			15 MIN			30 MIN			1 HR			4 HR			1 DAY		

Instrument(s) Traded	Hard Shares		Options		Forex		Crypto		
Trade #	Entry Time	Exit Time	Time Elapsed	Buy/Call Sell/Put	Entry Price	Exit Price	Quantity	Profit/Loss	Total
1									
2									
3									
4									
5									
6									
7									
8									
9									
10									

Total Trades	Winning Trades	Losing Trades	Win Rate %

Notes

DATE:_____   ACCOUNT BALANCE:_____

TRADING POWDER:_____   MAXIMUM RISK AMOUNT PER TRADE:_____

DAILY GOAL: _____

MARKET ANALYSIS

Check the momentum of the market based on Key Indices, Commodities, and ETFs.

Type of Market Day	Key Indices and Commodities					
	S&P 500	Dow 30	Nasdaq	Russell 2000	Crude Oil	Gold
GREEN						
RED						

INDICATORS OVERVIEW

	Ticker Symbol																	
Indicators	5M	15M	30M	1HR	4HR	1D	5M	15M	30M	1HR	4HR	1D	5M	15M	30M	1HR	4HR	1D
Moving Averages																		
5 day																		
9 day																		
50 day																		
100 day																		
200 day																		
Bollinger Bands																		
Upper Band																		
Lower Band																		
DMI																		
Bullish																		
Bearish																		
MACD																		
Bullish																		
Bearish																		
RSI																		
Overbought																		
Oversold																		
Stochastic																		
Overbought																		
Oversold																		

Company Ticker	Chart Momentum											
	5 MIN		15 MIN		30 MIN		1 HR		4 HR		1 DAY	

Instrument(s) Traded	Hard Shares		Options		Forex		Crypto			
Trade #	Entry Time	Exit Time	Time Elapsed	Buy/Call Sell/Put	Entry Price	Exit Price	Quantity	Profit/Loss	Total
1									
2									
3									
4									
5									
6									
7									
8									
9									
10									

Total Trades	Winning Trades	Losing Trades	Win Rate %

Notes

DATE:_____

ACCOUNT BALANCE:_____

TRADING POWDER:_____

MAXIMUM RISK AMOUNT PER TRADE:_____

DAILY GOAL: _____

MARKET ANALYSIS

Check the momentum of the market based on Key Indices, Commodities, and ETFs.

Type of Market Day	Key Indices and Commodities					
	S&P 500	Dow 30	Nasdaq	Russell 2000	Crude Oil	Gold
GREEN						
RED						

INDICATORS OVERVIEW

	Ticker Symbol																	
Indicators	5M	15M	30M	1HR	4HR	1D	5M	15M	30M	1HR	4HR	1D	5M	15M	30M	1HR	4HR	1D
Moving Averages																		
5 day																		
9 day																		
50 day																		
100 day																		
200 day																		
Bollinger Bands																		
Upper Band																		
Lower Band																		
DMI																		
Bullish																		
Bearish																		
MACD																		
Bullish																		
Bearish																		
RSI																		
Overbought																		
Oversold																		
Stochastic																		
Overbought																		
Oversold																		

Company Ticker	Chart Momentum																	
	5 MIN			15 MIN			30 MIN			1 HR			4 HR			1 DAY		

Instrument(s) Traded	Hard Shares		Options		Forex		Crypto		
Trade #	Entry Time	Exit Time	Time Elapsed	Buy/Call Sell/Put	Entry Price	Exit Price	Quantity	Profit/Loss	Total
1									
2									
3									
4									
5									
6									
7									
8									
9									
10									

Total Trades	Winning Trades	Losing Trades	Win Rate %

Notes

DATE:_____   ACCOUNT BALANCE:_____

TRADING POWDER:_____   MAXIMUM RISK AMOUNT PER TRADE:_____

DAILY GOAL: _____

MARKET ANALYSIS

Check the momentum of the market based on Key Indices, Commodities, and ETFs.

Type of Market Day	Key Indices and Commodities					
	S&P 500	Dow 30	Nasdaq	Russell 2000	Crude Oil	Gold
GREEN						
RED						

INDICATORS OVERVIEW

	Ticker Symbol																	
Indicators	5M	15M	30M	1HR	4HR	1D	5M	15M	30M	1HR	4HR	1D	5M	15M	30M	1HR	4HR	1D
Moving Averages																		
5 day																		
9 day																		
50 day																		
100 day																		
200 day																		
Bollinger Bands																		
Upper Band																		
Lower Band																		
DMI																		
Bullish																		
Bearish																		
MACD																		
Bullish																		
Bearish																		
RSI																		
Overbought																		
Oversold																		
Stochastic																		
Overbought																		
Oversold																		

Company Ticker	Chart Momentum																
	5 MIN			15 MIN			30 MIN			1 HR			4 HR			1 DAY		

Instrument(s) Traded	Hard Shares		Options		Forex		Crypto		
Trade #	Entry Time	Exit Time	Time Elapsed	Buy/Call Sell/Put	Entry Price	Exit Price	Quantity	Profit/Loss	Total
1									
2									
3									
4									
5									
6									
7									
8									
9									
10									

Total Trades	Winning Trades	Losing Trades	Win Rate %

Notes

DATE:_____   ACCOUNT BALANCE:_____

TRADING POWDER:_____   MAXIMUM RISK AMOUNT PER TRADE:_____

DAILY GOAL: _____

MARKET ANALYSIS

Check the momentum of the market based on Key Indices, Commodities, and ETFs.

Type of Market Day	Key Indices and Commodities					
	S&P 500	Dow 30	Nasdaq	Russell 2000	Crude Oil	Gold
GREEN						
RED						

INDICATORS OVERVIEW

	Ticker Symbol																	
Indicators	5M	15M	30M	1HR	4HR	1D	5M	15M	30M	1HR	4HR	1D	5M	15M	30M	1HR	4HR	1D
Moving Averages																		
5 day																		
9 day																		
50 day																		
100 day																		
200 day																		
Bollinger Bands																		
Upper Band																		
Lower Band																		
DMI																		
Bullish																		
Bearish																		
MACD																		
Bullish																		
Bearish																		
RSI																		
Overbought																		
Oversold																		
Stochastic																		
Overbought																		
Oversold																		

Company Ticker	Chart Momentum																
	5 MIN			15 MIN			30 MIN			1 HR			4 HR			1 DAY		

Instrument(s) Traded	Hard Shares		Options		Forex		Crypto		
Trade #	Entry Time	Exit Time	Time Elapsed	Buy/Call Sell/Put	Entry Price	Exit Price	Quantity	Profit/Loss	Total
1									
2									
3									
4									
5									
6									
7									
8									
9									
10									

Total Trades	Winning Trades	Losing Trades	Win Rate %

Notes

DATE:_____   ACCOUNT BALANCE:_____

TRADING POWDER:_____   MAXIMUM RISK AMOUNT PER TRADE:_____

DAILY GOAL: _____

MARKET ANALYSIS

Check the momentum of the market based on Key Indices, Commodities, and ETFs.

Type of Market Day	Key Indices and Commodities					
	S&P 500	Dow 30	Nasdaq	Russell 2000	Crude Oil	Gold
GREEN						
RED						

INDICATORS OVERVIEW

	Ticker Symbol																	
Indicators	5M	15M	30M	1HR	4HR	1D	5M	15M	30M	1HR	4HR	1D	5M	15M	30M	1HR	4HR	1D
Moving Averages																		
5 day																		
9 day																		
50 day																		
100 day																		
200 day																		
Bollinger Bands																		
Upper Band																		
Lower Band																		
DMI																		
Bullish																		
Bearish																		
MACD																		
Bullish																		
Bearish																		
RSI																		
Overbought																		
Oversold																		
Stochastic																		
Overbought																		
Oversold																		

Company Ticker	Chart Momentum																
	5 MIN			15 MIN			30 MIN			1 HR			4 HR			1 DAY		

Instrument(s) Traded	Hard Shares		Options		Forex		Crypto		
Trade #	Entry Time	Exit Time	Time Elapsed	Buy/Call Sell/Put	Entry Price	Exit Price	Quantity	Profit/Loss	Total
1									
2									
3									
4									
5									
6									
7									
8									
9									
10									

Total Trades	Winning Trades	Losing Trades	Win Rate %
Notes			

DATE:_____   ACCOUNT BALANCE:_____

TRADING POWDER:_____   MAXIMUM RISK AMOUNT PER TRADE:_____

DAILY GOAL: _____

MARKET ANALYSIS

Check the momentum of the market based on Key Indices, Commodities, and ETFs.

Type of Market Day	Key Indices and Commodities					
	S&P 500	Dow 30	Nasdaq	Russell 2000	Crude Oil	Gold
GREEN						
RED						

INDICATORS OVERVIEW

	Ticker Symbol																	
Indicators	5M	15M	30M	1HR	4HR	1D	5M	15M	30M	1HR	4HR	1D	5M	15M	30M	1HR	4HR	1D
Moving Averages																		
5 day																		
9 day																		
50 day																		
100 day																		
200 day																		
Bollinger Bands																		
Upper Band																		
Lower Band																		
DMI																		
Bullish																		
Bearish																		
MACD																		
Bullish																		
Bearish																		
RSI																		
Overbought																		
Oversold																		
Stochastic																		
Overbought																		
Oversold																		

Company Ticker	Chart Momentum												
	5 MIN		15 MIN		30 MIN		1 HR		4 HR		1 DAY		

Instrument(s) Traded	Hard Shares		Options		Forex		Crypto		
Trade #	Entry Time	Exit Time	Time Elapsed	Buy/Call Sell/Put	Entry Price	Exit Price	Quantity	Profit/Loss	Total
1									
2									
3									
4									
5									
6									
7									
8									
9									
10									

Total Trades	Winning Trades	Losing Trades	Win Rate %

Notes

DATE:_____   ACCOUNT BALANCE:_____

TRADING POWDER:_____   MAXIMUM RISK AMOUNT PER TRADE:_____

DAILY GOAL: _____

MARKET ANALYSIS

Check the momentum of the market based on Key Indices, Commodities, and ETFs.

Type of Market Day	Key Indices and Commodities					
	S&P 500	Dow 30	Nasdaq	Russell 2000	Crude Oil	Gold
GREEN						
RED						

INDICATORS OVERVIEW

| | Ticker Symbol | | | | | | | | | | | | | | | | | |
| | | | | | | | | | | | | | | | | | | |
Indicators	5M	15M	30M	1HR	4HR	1D	5M	15M	30M	1HR	4HR	1D	5M	15M	30M	1HR	4HR	1D
Moving Averages																		
5 day																		
9 day																		
50 day																		
100 day																		
200 day																		
Bollinger Bands																		
Upper Band																		
Lower Band																		
DMI																		
Bullish																		
Bearish																		
MACD																		
Bullish																		
Bearish																		
RSI																		
Overbought																		
Oversold																		
Stochastic																		
Overbought																		
Oversold																		

Company Ticker	Chart Momentum											
	5 MIN		15 MIN		30 MIN		1 HR		4 HR		1 DAY	

Instrument(s) Traded	Hard Shares		Options		Forex		Crypto		
Trade #	Entry Time	Exit Time	Time Elapsed	Buy/Call Sell/Put	Entry Price	Exit Price	Quantity	Profit/Loss	Total
1									
2									
3									
4									
5									
6									
7									
8									
9									
10									

Total Trades	Winning Trades	Losing Trades	Win Rate %

Notes

DATE:_____   ACCOUNT BALANCE:_____

TRADING POWDER:_____   MAXIMUM RISK AMOUNT PER TRADE:_____

DAILY GOAL: _____

MARKET ANALYSIS

Check the momentum of the market based on Key Indices, Commodities, and ETFs.

Type of Market Day	Key Indices and Commodities					
	S&P 500	Dow 30	Nasdaq	Russell 2000	Crude Oil	Gold
GREEN						
RED						

INDICATORS OVERVIEW

	Ticker Symbol																	
Indicators	5M	15M	30M	1HR	4HR	1D	5M	15M	30M	1HR	4HR	1D	5M	15M	30M	1HR	4HR	1D
Moving Averages																		
5 day																		
9 day																		
50 day																		
100 day																		
200 day																		
Bollinger Bands																		
Upper Band																		
Lower Band																		
DMI																		
Bullish																		
Bearish																		
MACD																		
Bullish																		
Bearish																		
RSI																		
Overbought																		
Oversold																		
Stochastic																		
Overbought																		
Oversold																		

Company Ticker	Chart Momentum																	
	5 MIN			15 MIN			30 MIN			1 HR			4 HR			1 DAY		

Instrument(s) Traded	Hard Shares		Options		Forex		Crypto		
Trade #	Entry Time	Exit Time	Time Elapsed	Buy/Call Sell/Put	Entry Price	Exit Price	Quantity	Profit/Loss	Total
1									
2									
3									
4									
5									
6									
7									
8									
9									
10									

Total Trades	Winning Trades	Losing Trades	Win Rate %

Notes

DATE:_____   ACCOUNT BALANCE:_____

TRADING POWDER:_____   MAXIMUM RISK AMOUNT PER TRADE:_____

DAILY GOAL: _____

MARKET ANALYSIS

Check the momentum of the market based on Key Indices, Commodities, and ETFs.

Type of Market Day	Key Indices and Commodities					
	S&P 500	Dow 30	Nasdaq	Russell 2000	Crude Oil	Gold
GREEN						
RED						

INDICATORS OVERVIEW

	Ticker Symbol																	
Indicators	5M	15M	30M	1HR	4HR	1D	5M	15M	30M	1HR	4HR	1D	5M	15M	30M	1HR	4HR	1D
Moving Averages																		
5 day																		
9 day																		
50 day																		
100 day																		
200 day																		
Bollinger Bands																		
Upper Band																		
Lower Band																		
DMI																		
Bullish																		
Bearish																		
MACD																		
Bullish																		
Bearish																		
RSI																		
Overbought																		
Oversold																		
Stochastic																		
Overbought																		
Oversold																		

Company Ticker	Chart Momentum											
	5 MIN		15 MIN		30 MIN		1 HR		4 HR		1 DAY	

Instrument(s) Traded	Hard Shares		Options		Forex		Crypto			
Trade #	Entry Time	Exit Time	Time Elapsed	Buy/Call Sell/Put	Entry Price	Exit Price	Quantity	Profit/Loss	Total	
1										
2										
3										
4										
5										
6										
7										
8										
9										
10										

Total Trades	Winning Trades	Losing Trades	Win Rate %

Notes

DATE:_____   ACCOUNT BALANCE:_____

TRADING POWDER:_____   MAXIMUM RISK AMOUNT PER TRADE:_____

DAILY GOAL: _____

MARKET ANALYSIS

Check the momentum of the market based on Key Indices, Commodities, and ETFs.

Type of Market Day	Key Indices and Commodities					
	S&P 500	Dow 30	Nasdaq	Russell 2000	Crude Oil	Gold
GREEN						
RED						

INDICATORS OVERVIEW

	Ticker Symbol																	
Indicators	5M	15M	30M	1HR	4HR	1D	5M	15M	30M	1HR	4HR	1D	5M	15M	30M	1HR	4HR	1D
Moving Averages																		
5 day																		
9 day																		
50 day																		
100 day																		
200 day																		
Bollinger Bands																		
Upper Band																		
Lower Band																		
DMI																		
Bullish																		
Bearish																		
MACD																		
Bullish																		
Bearish																		
RSI																		
Overbought																		
Oversold																		
Stochastic																		
Overbought																		
Oversold																		

Company Ticker	Chart Momentum												
	5 MIN		15 MIN		30 MIN		1 HR		4 HR		1 DAY		

Instrument(s) Traded	Hard Shares		Options		Forex		Crypto			
Trade #	Entry Time	Exit Time	Time Elapsed	Buy/Call Sell/Put	Entry Price	Exit Price	Quantity	Profit/Loss	Total
1									
2									
3									
4									
5									
6									
7									
8									
9									
10									

Total Trades	Winning Trades	Losing Trades	Win Rate %

Notes

DATE:_____   ACCOUNT BALANCE:_____

TRADING POWDER:_____   MAXIMUM RISK AMOUNT PER TRADE:_____

DAILY GOAL: _____

MARKET ANALYSIS

Check the momentum of the market based on Key Indices, Commodities, and ETFs.

Type of Market Day	Key Indices and Commodities					
	S&P 500	Dow 30	Nasdaq	Russell 2000	Crude Oil	Gold
GREEN						
RED						

INDICATORS OVERVIEW

	Ticker Symbol																	
Indicators	5M	15M	30M	1HR	4HR	1D	5M	15M	30M	1HR	4HR	1D	5M	15M	30M	1HR	4HR	1D
Moving Averages																		
5 day																		
9 day																		
50 day																		
100 day																		
200 day																		
Bollinger Bands																		
Upper Band																		
Lower Band																		
DMI																		
Bullish																		
Bearish																		
MACD																		
Bullish																		
Bearish																		
RSI																		
Overbought																		
Oversold																		
Stochastic																		
Overbought																		
Oversold																		

Company Ticker	Chart Momentum																
	5 MIN			15 MIN			30 MIN			1 HR			4 HR			1 DAY		

Instrument(s) Traded	Hard Shares		Options		Forex		Crypto		
Trade #	Entry Time	Exit Time	Time Elapsed	Buy/Call Sell/Put	Entry Price	Exit Price	Quantity	Profit/Loss	Total
1									
2									
3									
4									
5									
6									
7									
8									
9									
10									

Total Trades	Winning Trades	Losing Trades	Win Rate %

Notes

DATE:_____   ACCOUNT BALANCE:_____

TRADING POWDER:_____   MAXIMUM RISK AMOUNT PER TRADE:_____

DAILY GOAL: _____

MARKET ANALYSIS

Check the momentum of the market based on Key Indices, Commodities, and ETFs.

Type of Market Day	Key Indices and Commodities					
	S&P 500	Dow 30	Nasdaq	Russell 2000	Crude Oil	Gold
GREEN						
RED						

INDICATORS OVERVIEW

	Ticker Symbol																	
Indicators	5M	15M	30M	1HR	4HR	1D	5M	15M	30M	1HR	4HR	1D	5M	15M	30M	1HR	4HR	1D
Moving Averages																		
5 day																		
9 day																		
50 day																		
100 day																		
200 day																		
Bollinger Bands																		
Upper Band																		
Lower Band																		
DMI																		
Bullish																		
Bearish																		
MACD																		
Bullish																		
Bearish																		
RSI																		
Overbought																		
Oversold																		
Stochastic																		
Overbought																		
Oversold																		

Company Ticker	Chart Momentum																
	5 MIN			15 MIN			30 MIN			1 HR			4 HR			1 DAY		

Instrument(s) Traded	Hard Shares		Options		Forex		Crypto		
Trade #	Entry Time	Exit Time	Time Elapsed	Buy/Call Sell/Put	Entry Price	Exit Price	Quantity	Profit/Loss	Total
1									
2									
3									
4									
5									
6									
7									
8									
9									
10									

Total Trades	Winning Trades	Losing Trades	Win Rate %

Notes

DATE:_____   ACCOUNT BALANCE:_____

TRADING POWDER:_____   MAXIMUM RISK AMOUNT PER TRADE:_____

DAILY GOAL: _____

MARKET ANALYSIS

Check the momentum of the market based on Key Indices, Commodities, and ETFs.

Type of Market Day	Key Indices and Commodities					
	S&P 500	Dow 30	Nasdaq	Russell 2000	Crude Oil	Gold
GREEN						
RED						

INDICATORS OVERVIEW

	Ticker Symbol																	
Indicators	5M	15M	30M	1HR	4HR	1D	5M	15M	30M	1HR	4HR	1D	5M	15M	30M	1HR	4HR	1D
Moving Averages																		
5 day																		
9 day																		
50 day																		
100 day																		
200 day																		
Bollinger Bands																		
Upper Band																		
Lower Band																		
DMI																		
Bullish																		
Bearish																		
MACD																		
Bullish																		
Bearish																		
RSI																		
Overbought																		
Oversold																		
Stochastic																		
Overbought																		
Oversold																		

Company Ticker	Chart Momentum											
	5 MIN		15 MIN		30 MIN		1 HR		4 HR		1 DAY	

Instrument(s) Traded	Hard Shares		Options		Forex		Crypto			
Trade #	Entry Time	Exit Time	Time Elapsed	Buy/Call Sell/Put	Entry Price	Exit Price	Quantity	Profit/Loss	Total	
1										
2										
3										
4										
5										
6										
7										
8										
9										
10										

Total Trades	Winning Trades	Losing Trades	Win Rate %

Notes

DATE:_____   ACCOUNT BALANCE:_____

TRADING POWDER:_____   MAXIMUM RISK AMOUNT PER TRADE:_____

DAILY GOAL: _____

MARKET ANALYSIS

Check the momentum of the market based on Key Indices, Commodities, and ETFs.

Type of Market Day	Key Indices and Commodities					
	S&P 500	Dow 30	Nasdaq	Russell 2000	Crude Oil	Gold
GREEN						
RED						

INDICATORS OVERVIEW

	Ticker Symbol																	
Indicators	5M	15M	30M	1HR	4HR	1D	5M	15M	30M	1HR	4HR	1D	5M	15M	30M	1HR	4HR	1D
Moving Averages																		
5 day																		
9 day																		
50 day																		
100 day																		
200 day																		
Bollinger Bands																		
Upper Band																		
Lower Band																		
DMI																		
Bullish																		
Bearish																		
MACD																		
Bullish																		
Bearish																		
RSI																		
Overbought																		
Oversold																		
Stochastic																		
Overbought																		
Oversold																		

Company Ticker	Chart Momentum																
	5 MIN			15 MIN			30 MIN			1 HR			4 HR			1 DAY		

Instrument(s) Traded	Hard Shares		Options		Forex		Crypto			
Trade #	Entry Time	Exit Time	Time Elapsed	Buy/Call Sell/Put	Entry Price	Exit Price	Quantity	Profit/Loss	Total
1									
2									
3									
4									
5									
6									
7									
8									
9									
10									

Total Trades	Winning Trades	Losing Trades	Win Rate %

Notes

DATE:_____   ACCOUNT BALANCE:_____

TRADING POWDER:_____   MAXIMUM RISK AMOUNT PER TRADE:_____

DAILY GOAL: _____

MARKET ANALYSIS

Check the momentum of the market based on Key Indices, Commodities, and ETFs.

Type of Market Day	Key Indices and Commodities					
	S&P 500	Dow 30	Nasdaq	Russell 2000	Crude Oil	Gold
GREEN						
RED						

INDICATORS OVERVIEW

	Ticker Symbol																	
Indicators	5M	15M	30M	1HR	4HR	1D	5M	15M	30M	1HR	4HR	1D	5M	15M	30M	1HR	4HR	1D
Moving Averages																		
5 day																		
9 day																		
50 day																		
100 day																		
200 day																		
Bollinger Bands																		
Upper Band																		
Lower Band																		
DMI																		
Bullish																		
Bearish																		
MACD																		
Bullish																		
Bearish																		
RSI																		
Overbought																		
Oversold																		
Stochastic																		
Overbought																		
Oversold																		

Company Ticker	Chart Momentum											
	5 MIN		15 MIN		30 MIN		1 HR		4 HR		1 DAY	

Instrument(s) Traded	Hard Shares		Options		Forex		Crypto			
Trade #	Entry Time	Exit Time	Time Elapsed	Buy/Call Sell/Put	Entry Price	Exit Price	Quantity	Profit/Loss	Total	
1										
2										
3										
4										
5										
6										
7										
8										
9										
10										

Total Trades	Winning Trades	Losing Trades	Win Rate %

Notes

DATE:_____   ACCOUNT BALANCE:_____

TRADING POWDER:_____   MAXIMUM RISK AMOUNT PER TRADE:_____

DAILY GOAL: _____

MARKET ANALYSIS

Check the momentum of the market based on Key Indices, Commodities, and ETFs.

Type of Market Day	Key Indices and Commodities					
	S&P 500	Dow 30	Nasdaq	Russell 2000	Crude Oil	Gold
GREEN						
RED						

INDICATORS OVERVIEW

	Ticker Symbol																	
Indicators	5M	15M	30M	1HR	4HR	1D	5M	15M	30M	1HR	4HR	1D	5M	15M	30M	1HR	4HR	1D
Moving Averages																		
5 day																		
9 day																		
50 day																		
100 day																		
200 day																		
Bollinger Bands																		
Upper Band																		
Lower Band																		
DMI																		
Bullish																		
Bearish																		
MACD																		
Bullish																		
Bearish																		
RSI																		
Overbought																		
Oversold																		
Stochastic																		
Overbought																		
Oversold																		

Company Ticker	Chart Momentum																
	5 MIN			15 MIN			30 MIN			1 HR			4 HR			1 DAY		

Instrument(s) Traded	Hard Shares		Options		Forex		Crypto		
Trade #	Entry Time	Exit Time	Time Elapsed	Buy/Call Sell/Put	Entry Price	Exit Price	Quantity	Profit/Loss	Total
1									
2									
3									
4									
5									
6									
7									
8									
9									
10									

Total Trades	Winning Trades	Losing Trades	Win Rate %

Notes

DATE:_____   ACCOUNT BALANCE:_____

TRADING POWDER:_____   MAXIMUM RISK AMOUNT PER TRADE:_____

DAILY GOAL: _____

MARKET ANALYSIS

Check the momentum of the market based on Key Indices, Commodities, and ETFs.

Type of Market Day	Key Indices and Commodities					
	S&P 500	Dow 30	Nasdaq	Russell 2000	Crude Oil	Gold
GREEN						
RED						

INDICATORS OVERVIEW

	Ticker Symbol																	
Indicators	5M	15M	30M	1HR	4HR	1D	5M	15M	30M	1HR	4HR	1D	5M	15M	30M	1HR	4HR	1D
Moving Averages																		
5 day																		
9 day																		
50 day																		
100 day																		
200 day																		
Bollinger Bands																		
Upper Band																		
Lower Band																		
DMI																		
Bullish																		
Bearish																		
MACD																		
Bullish																		
Bearish																		
RSI																		
Overbought																		
Oversold																		
Stochastic																		
Overbought																		
Oversold																		

Company Ticker	Chart Momentum																
	5 MIN			15 MIN			30 MIN			1 HR			4 HR			1 DAY		

Instrument(s) Traded	Hard Shares		Options		Forex		Crypto		
Trade #	Entry Time	Exit Time	Time Elapsed	Buy/Call Sell/Put	Entry Price	Exit Price	Quantity	Profit/Loss	Total
1									
2									
3									
4									
5									
6									
7									
8									
9									
10									

Total Trades	Winning Trades	Losing Trades	Win Rate %

Notes

DATE:_____ ACCOUNT BALANCE:_____

TRADING POWDER:_____ MAXIMUM RISK AMOUNT PER TRADE:_____

DAILY GOAL: _____

MARKET ANALYSIS

Check the momentum of the market based on Key Indices, Commodities, and ETFs.

Type of Market Day	Key Indices and Commodities					
	S&P 500	Dow 30	Nasdaq	Russell 2000	Crude Oil	Gold
GREEN						
RED						

INDICATORS OVERVIEW

| | Ticker Symbol | | | | | | | | | | | | | | | | | |
| | | | | | | | | | | | | | | | | | | |
Indicators	5M	15M	30M	1HR	4HR	1D	5M	15M	30M	1HR	4HR	1D	5M	15M	30M	1HR	4HR	1D
Moving Averages																		
5 day																		
9 day																		
50 day																		
100 day																		
200 day																		
Bollinger Bands																		
Upper Band																		
Lower Band																		
DMI																		
Bullish																		
Bearish																		
MACD																		
Bullish																		
Bearish																		
RSI																		
Overbought																		
Oversold																		
Stochastic																		
Overbought																		
Oversold																		

Company Ticker	Chart Momentum											
	5 MIN			15 MIN			30 MIN			1 HR		

(continued columns: 4 HR, 1 DAY)

Instrument(s) Traded	Hard Shares		Options		Forex		Crypto		
Trade #	Entry Time	Exit Time	Time Elapsed	Buy/Call Sell/Put	Entry Price	Exit Price	Quantity	Profit/Loss	Total
1									
2									
3									
4									
5									
6									
7									
8									
9									
10									

Total Trades	Winning Trades	Losing Trades	Win Rate %

Notes

DATE:_____   ACCOUNT BALANCE:_____

TRADING POWDER:_____   MAXIMUM RISK AMOUNT PER TRADE:_____

DAILY GOAL: _____

MARKET ANALYSIS

Check the momentum of the market based on Key Indices, Commodities, and ETFs.

Type of Market Day	Key Indices and Commodities					
	S&P 500	Dow 30	Nasdaq	Russell 2000	Crude Oil	Gold
GREEN						
RED						

INDICATORS OVERVIEW

	Ticker Symbol																	
Indicators	5M	15M	30M	1HR	4HR	1D	5M	15M	30M	1HR	4HR	1D	5M	15M	30M	1HR	4HR	1D
Moving Averages																		
5 day																		
9 day																		
50 day																		
100 day																		
200 day																		
Bollinger Bands																		
Upper Band																		
Lower Band																		
DMI																		
Bullish																		
Bearish																		
MACD																		
Bullish																		
Bearish																		
RSI																		
Overbought																		
Oversold																		
Stochastic																		
Overbought																		
Oversold																		

Company Ticker	Chart Momentum																
	5 MIN			15 MIN			30 MIN			1 HR			4 HR			1 DAY		

Instrument(s) Traded	Hard Shares		Options		Forex		Crypto		
Trade #	Entry Time	Exit Time	Time Elapsed	Buy/Call Sell/Put	Entry Price	Exit Price	Quantity	Profit/Loss	Total
1									
2									
3									
4									
5									
6									
7									
8									
9									
10									

Total Trades	Winning Trades	Losing Trades	Win Rate %

Notes

DATE:_____ ACCOUNT BALANCE:_____

TRADING POWDER:_____ MAXIMUM RISK AMOUNT PER TRADE:_____

DAILY GOAL: _____

MARKET ANALYSIS

Check the momentum of the market based on Key Indices, Commodities, and ETFs.

Type of Market Day	Key Indices and Commodities					
	S&P 500	Dow 30	Nasdaq	Russell 2000	Crude Oil	Gold
GREEN						
RED						

INDICATORS OVERVIEW

	Ticker Symbol																	
Indicators	5M	15M	30M	1HR	4HR	1D	5M	15M	30M	1HR	4HR	1D	5M	15M	30M	1HR	4HR	1D
Moving Averages																		
5 day																		
9 day																		
50 day																		
100 day																		
200 day																		
Bollinger Bands																		
Upper Band																		
Lower Band																		
DMI																		
Bullish																		
Bearish																		
MACD																		
Bullish																		
Bearish																		
RSI																		
Overbought																		
Oversold																		
Stochastic																		
Overbought																		
Oversold																		

Company Ticker	Chart Momentum																
	5 MIN			15 MIN			30 MIN			1 HR			4 HR			1 DAY		

Instrument(s) Traded	Hard Shares		Options		Forex		Crypto		
Trade #	Entry Time	Exit Time	Time Elapsed	Buy/Call Sell/Put	Entry Price	Exit Price	Quantity	Profit/Loss	Total
1									
2									
3									
4									
5									
6									
7									
8									
9									
10									

Total Trades	Winning Trades	Losing Trades	Win Rate %

Notes

DATE:_____   ACCOUNT BALANCE:_____

TRADING POWDER:_____   MAXIMUM RISK AMOUNT PER TRADE:_____

DAILY GOAL: _____

MARKET ANALYSIS

Check the momentum of the market based on Key Indices, Commodities, and ETFs.

Type of Market Day	Key Indices and Commodities					
	S&P 500	Dow 30	Nasdaq	Russell 2000	Crude Oil	Gold
GREEN						
RED						

INDICATORS OVERVIEW

	Ticker Symbol																	
Indicators	5M	15M	30M	1HR	4HR	1D	5M	15M	30M	1HR	4HR	1D	5M	15M	30M	1HR	4HR	1D
Moving Averages																		
5 day																		
9 day																		
50 day																		
100 day																		
200 day																		
Bollinger Bands																		
Upper Band																		
Lower Band																		
DMI																		
Bullish																		
Bearish																		
MACD																		
Bullish																		
Bearish																		
RSI																		
Overbought																		
Oversold																		
Stochastic																		
Overbought																		
Oversold																		

Company Ticker	Chart Momentum											
	5 MIN		15 MIN		30 MIN		1 HR		4 HR		1 DAY	

Instrument(s) Traded	Hard Shares		Options		Forex		Crypto		
Trade #	Entry Time	Exit Time	Time Elapsed	Buy/Call Sell/Put	Entry Price	Exit Price	Quantity	Profit/Loss	Total
1									
2									
3									
4									
5									
6									
7									
8									
9									
10									

Total Trades	Winning Trades	Losing Trades	Win Rate %

Notes

DATE:_____   **ACCOUNT BALANCE:**_____

TRADING POWDER:_____   **MAXIMUM RISK AMOUNT PER TRADE:**_____

DAILY GOAL: _____

MARKET ANALYSIS

Check the momentum of the market based on Key Indices, Commodities, and ETFs.

Type of Market Day	Key Indices and Commodities					
	S&P 500	Dow 30	Nasdaq	Russell 2000	Crude Oil	Gold
GREEN						
RED						

INDICATORS OVERVIEW

	Ticker Symbol																	
Indicators	5M	15M	30M	1HR	4HR	1D	5M	15M	30M	1HR	4HR	1D	5M	15M	30M	1HR	4HR	1D
Moving Averages																		
5 day																		
9 day																		
50 day																		
100 day																		
200 day																		
Bollinger Bands																		
Upper Band																		
Lower Band																		
DMI																		
Bullish																		
Bearish																		
MACD																		
Bullish																		
Bearish																		
RSI																		
Overbought																		
Oversold																		
Stochastic																		
Overbought																		
Oversold																		

Company Ticker	Chart Momentum																
	5 MIN			15 MIN			30 MIN			1 HR			4 HR			1 DAY		

Instrument(s) Traded	Hard Shares		Options		Forex		Crypto			
Trade #	Entry Time	Exit Time	Time Elapsed	Buy/Call Sell/Put	Entry Price	Exit Price	Quantity	Profit/Loss	Total
1									
2									
3									
4									
5									
6									
7									
8									
9									
10									

Total Trades	Winning Trades	Losing Trades	Win Rate %

Notes

DATE:_____   **ACCOUNT BALANCE:**_____

TRADING POWDER:_____   **MAXIMUM RISK AMOUNT PER TRADE:**_____

DAILY GOAL: _____

MARKET ANALYSIS

Check the momentum of the market based on Key Indices, Commodities, and ETFs.

Type of Market Day	Key Indices and Commodities					
	S&P 500	Dow 30	Nasdaq	Russell 2000	Crude Oil	Gold
GREEN						
RED						

INDICATORS OVERVIEW

	Ticker Symbol																	
Indicators	5M	15M	30M	1HR	4HR	1D	5M	15M	30M	1HR	4HR	1D	5M	15M	30M	1HR	4HR	1D
Moving Averages																		
5 day																		
9 day																		
50 day																		
100 day																		
200 day																		
Bollinger Bands																		
Upper Band																		
Lower Band																		
DMI																		
Bullish																		
Bearish																		
MACD																		
Bullish																		
Bearish																		
RSI																		
Overbought																		
Oversold																		
Stochastic																		
Overbought																		
Oversold																		

Company Ticker	Chart Momentum												
	5 MIN		15 MIN		30 MIN		1 HR		4 HR		1 DAY		

Instrument(s) Traded	Hard Shares		Options		Forex		Crypto			
Trade #	Entry Time	Exit Time	Time Elapsed	Buy/Call Sell/Put	Entry Price	Exit Price	Quantity	Profit/Loss	Total	
1										
2										
3										
4										
5										
6										
7										
8										
9										
10										

Total Trades	Winning Trades	Losing Trades	Win Rate %

Notes

DATE:_____   ACCOUNT BALANCE:_____

TRADING POWDER:_____   MAXIMUM RISK AMOUNT PER TRADE:_____

DAILY GOAL: _____

MARKET ANALYSIS

Check the momentum of the market based on Key Indices, Commodities, and ETFs.

Type of Market Day	Key Indices and Commodities					
	S&P 500	Dow 30	Nasdaq	Russell 2000	Crude Oil	Gold
GREEN						
RED						

INDICATORS OVERVIEW

	Ticker Symbol																	
Indicators	5M	15M	30M	1HR	4HR	1D	5M	15M	30M	1HR	4HR	1D	5M	15M	30M	1HR	4HR	1D
Moving Averages																		
5 day																		
9 day																		
50 day																		
100 day																		
200 day																		
Bollinger Bands																		
Upper Band																		
Lower Band																		
DMI																		
Bullish																		
Bearish																		
MACD																		
Bullish																		
Bearish																		
RSI																		
Overbought																		
Oversold																		
Stochastic																		
Overbought																		
Oversold																		

Company Ticker	Chart Momentum											
	5 MIN			15 MIN			30 MIN			1 HR	4 HR	1 DAY

Instrument(s) Traded	Hard Shares		Options		Forex		Crypto		
Trade #	Entry Time	Exit Time	Time Elapsed	Buy/Call Sell/Put	Entry Price	Exit Price	Quantity	Profit/Loss	Total
1									
2									
3									
4									
5									
6									
7									
8									
9									
10									

Total Trades	Winning Trades	Losing Trades	Win Rate %

Notes

DATE:_____   ACCOUNT BALANCE:_____

TRADING POWDER:_____   MAXIMUM RISK AMOUNT PER TRADE:_____

DAILY GOAL: _____

MARKET ANALYSIS

Check the momentum of the market based on Key Indices, Commodities, and ETFs.

Type of Market Day	Key Indices and Commodities					
	S&P 500	Dow 30	Nasdaq	Russell 2000	Crude Oil	Gold
GREEN						
RED						

INDICATORS OVERVIEW

	Ticker Symbol																	
Indicators	5M	15M	30M	1HR	4HR	1D	5M	15M	30M	1HR	4HR	1D	5M	15M	30M	1HR	4HR	1D
Moving Averages																		
5 day																		
9 day																		
50 day																		
100 day																		
200 day																		
Bollinger Bands																		
Upper Band																		
Lower Band																		
DMI																		
Bullish																		
Bearish																		
MACD																		
Bullish																		
Bearish																		
RSI																		
Overbought																		
Oversold																		
Stochastic																		
Overbought																		
Oversold																		

Company Ticker	Chart Momentum												
	5 MIN		15 MIN		30 MIN		1 HR		4 HR		1 DAY		

Instrument(s) Traded	Hard Shares		Options		Forex		Crypto		
Trade #	Entry Time	Exit Time	Time Elapsed	Buy/Call Sell/Put	Entry Price	Exit Price	Quantity	Profit/Loss	Total
1									
2									
3									
4									
5									
6									
7									
8									
9									
10									

Total Trades	Winning Trades	Losing Trades	Win Rate %

Notes

DATE:_____   ACCOUNT BALANCE:_____

TRADING POWDER:_____   MAXIMUM RISK AMOUNT PER TRADE:_____

DAILY GOAL: _____

MARKET ANALYSIS

Check the momentum of the market based on Key Indices, Commodities, and ETFs.

Type of Market Day	Key Indices and Commodities					
	S&P 500	Dow 30	Nasdaq	Russell 2000	Crude Oil	Gold
GREEN						
RED						

INDICATORS OVERVIEW

	Ticker Symbol																	
Indicators	5M	15M	30M	1HR	4HR	1D	5M	15M	30M	1HR	4HR	1D	5M	15M	30M	1HR	4HR	1D
Moving Averages																		
5 day																		
9 day																		
50 day																		
100 day																		
200 day																		
Bollinger Bands																		
Upper Band																		
Lower Band																		
DMI																		
Bullish																		
Bearish																		
MACD																		
Bullish																		
Bearish																		
RSI																		
Overbought																		
Oversold																		
Stochastic																		
Overbought																		
Oversold																		

Company Ticker	Chart Momentum																
	5 MIN			15 MIN			30 MIN			1 HR			4 HR			1 DAY		

Instrument(s) Traded	Hard Shares		Options		Forex		Crypto		
Trade #	Entry Time	Exit Time	Time Elapsed	Buy/Call Sell/Put	Entry Price	Exit Price	Quantity	Profit/Loss	Total
1									
2									
3									
4									
5									
6									
7									
8									
9									
10									

Total Trades	Winning Trades	Losing Trades	Win Rate %

Notes

DATE:_____   ACCOUNT BALANCE:_____

TRADING POWDER:_____   MAXIMUM RISK AMOUNT PER TRADE:_____

DAILY GOAL: _____

MARKET ANALYSIS

Check the momentum of the market based on Key Indices, Commodities, and ETFs.

Type of Market Day	Key Indices and Commodities					
	S&P 500	Dow 30	Nasdaq	Russell 2000	Crude Oil	Gold
GREEN						
RED						

INDICATORS OVERVIEW

	Ticker Symbol																	
Indicators	5M	15M	30M	1HR	4HR	1D	5M	15M	30M	1HR	4HR	1D	5M	15M	30M	1HR	4HR	1D
Moving Averages																		
5 day																		
9 day																		
50 day																		
100 day																		
200 day																		
Bollinger Bands																		
Upper Band																		
Lower Band																		
DMI																		
Bullish																		
Bearish																		
MACD																		
Bullish																		
Bearish																		
RSI																		
Overbought																		
Oversold																		
Stochastic																		
Overbought																		
Oversold																		

Company Ticker	Chart Momentum																
	5 MIN			15 MIN			30 MIN			1 HR			4 HR			1 DAY		

Instrument(s) Traded	Hard Shares		Options		Forex		Crypto		
Trade #	Entry Time	Exit Time	Time Elapsed	Buy/Call Sell/Put	Entry Price	Exit Price	Quantity	Profit/Loss	Total
1									
2									
3									
4									
5									
6									
7									
8									
9									
10									

Total Trades	Winning Trades	Losing Trades	Win Rate %

Notes

DATE:_____   ACCOUNT BALANCE:_____

TRADING POWDER:_____   MAXIMUM RISK AMOUNT PER TRADE:_____

DAILY GOAL: _____

MARKET ANALYSIS

Check the momentum of the market based on Key Indices, Commodities, and ETFs.

Type of Market Day	Key Indices and Commodities					
	S&P 500	Dow 30	Nasdaq	Russell 2000	Crude Oil	Gold
GREEN						
RED						

INDICATORS OVERVIEW

	Ticker Symbol																	
Indicators	5M	15M	30M	1HR	4HR	1D	5M	15M	30M	1HR	4HR	1D	5M	15M	30M	1HR	4HR	1D
Moving Averages																		
5 day																		
9 day																		
50 day																		
100 day																		
200 day																		
Bollinger Bands																		
Upper Band																		
Lower Band																		
DMI																		
Bullish																		
Bearish																		
MACD																		
Bullish																		
Bearish																		
RSI																		
Overbought																		
Oversold																		
Stochastic																		
Overbought																		
Oversold																		

Company Ticker	Chart Momentum											
	5 MIN			15 MIN			30 MIN			1 HR	4 HR	1 DAY

Instrument(s) Traded	Hard Shares		Options		Forex		Crypto		
Trade #	Entry Time	Exit Time	Time Elapsed	Buy/Call Sell/Put	Entry Price	Exit Price	Quantity	Profit/Loss	Total
1									
2									
3									
4									
5									
6									
7									
8									
9									
10									

Total Trades	Winning Trades	Losing Trades	Win Rate %

Notes

DATE:_____ ACCOUNT BALANCE:_____

TRADING POWDER:_____ MAXIMUM RISK AMOUNT PER TRADE:_____

DAILY GOAL: _____

MARKET ANALYSIS

Check the momentum of the market based on Key Indices, Commodities, and ETFs.

Type of Market Day	Key Indices and Commodities					
	S&P 500	Dow 30	Nasdaq	Russell 2000	Crude Oil	Gold
GREEN						
RED						

INDICATORS OVERVIEW

	Ticker Symbol																	
Indicators	5M	15M	30M	1HR	4HR	1D	5M	15M	30M	1HR	4HR	1D	5M	15M	30M	1HR	4HR	1D
Moving Averages																		
5 day																		
9 day																		
50 day																		
100 day																		
200 day																		
Bollinger Bands																		
Upper Band																		
Lower Band																		
DMI																		
Bullish																		
Bearish																		
MACD																		
Bullish																		
Bearish																		
RSI																		
Overbought																		
Oversold																		
Stochastic																		
Overbought																		
Oversold																		

Company Ticker	Chart Momentum																	
	5 MIN			15 MIN			30 MIN			1 HR			4 HR			1 DAY		

Instrument(s) Traded	Hard Shares		Options		Forex		Crypto		
Trade #	Entry Time	Exit Time	Time Elapsed	Buy/Call Sell/Put	Entry Price	Exit Price	Quantity	Profit/Loss	Total
1									
2									
3									
4									
5									
6									
7									
8									
9									
10									

Total Trades	Winning Trades	Losing Trades	Win Rate %

Notes

DATE:_____   **ACCOUNT BALANCE:**_____

TRADING POWDER:_____   **MAXIMUM RISK AMOUNT PER TRADE:**_____

DAILY GOAL: _____

MARKET ANALYSIS

Check the momentum of the market based on Key Indices, Commodities, and ETFs.

Type of Market Day	Key Indices and Commodities					
	S&P 500	Dow 30	Nasdaq	Russell 2000	Crude Oil	Gold
GREEN						
RED						

INDICATORS OVERVIEW

	Ticker Symbol																	
Indicators	5M	15M	30M	1HR	4HR	1D	5M	15M	30M	1HR	4HR	1D	5M	15M	30M	1HR	4HR	1D
Moving Averages																		
5 day																		
9 day																		
50 day																		
100 day																		
200 day																		
Bollinger Bands																		
Upper Band																		
Lower Band																		
DMI																		
Bullish																		
Bearish																		
MACD																		
Bullish																		
Bearish																		
RSI																		
Overbought																		
Oversold																		
Stochastic																		
Overbought																		
Oversold																		

Company Ticker	Chart Momentum																
	5 MIN			15 MIN			30 MIN			1 HR			4 HR			1 DAY		

Instrument(s) Traded	Hard Shares		Options		Forex		Crypto		
Trade #	Entry Time	Exit Time	Time Elapsed	Buy/Call Sell/Put	Entry Price	Exit Price	Quantity	Profit/Loss	Total
1									
2									
3									
4									
5									
6									
7									
8									
9									
10									

Total Trades	Winning Trades	Losing Trades	Win Rate %

Notes

DATE:_____   ACCOUNT BALANCE:_____

TRADING POWDER:_____   MAXIMUM RISK AMOUNT PER TRADE:_____

DAILY GOAL: _____

MARKET ANALYSIS

Check the momentum of the market based on Key Indices, Commodities, and ETFs.

Type of Market Day	Key Indices and Commodities					
	S&P 500	Dow 30	Nasdaq	Russell 2000	Crude Oil	Gold
GREEN						
RED						

INDICATORS OVERVIEW

	Ticker Symbol																	
Indicators	5M	15M	30M	1HR	4HR	1D	5M	15M	30M	1HR	4HR	1D	5M	15M	30M	1HR	4HR	1D
Moving Averages																		
5 day																		
9 day																		
50 day																		
100 day																		
200 day																		
Bollinger Bands																		
Upper Band																		
Lower Band																		
DMI																		
Bullish																		
Bearish																		
MACD																		
Bullish																		
Bearish																		
RSI																		
Overbought																		
Oversold																		
Stochastic																		
Overbought																		
Oversold																		

Company Ticker	Chart Momentum																
	5 MIN			15 MIN			30 MIN			1 HR			4 HR			1 DAY		

Instrument(s) Traded	Hard Shares		Options		Forex		Crypto		
Trade #	Entry Time	Exit Time	Time Elapsed	Buy/Call Sell/Put	Entry Price	Exit Price	Quantity	Profit/Loss	Total
1									
2									
3									
4									
5									
6									
7									
8									
9									
10									

Total Trades	Winning Trades	Losing Trades	Win Rate %

Notes

DATE:_____   ACCOUNT BALANCE:_____

TRADING POWDER:_____   MAXIMUM RISK AMOUNT PER TRADE:_____

DAILY GOAL: _____

MARKET ANALYSIS

Check the momentum of the market based on Key Indices, Commodities, and ETFs.

Type of Market Day	Key Indices and Commodities					
	S&P 500	Dow 30	Nasdaq	Russell 2000	Crude Oil	Gold
GREEN						
RED						

INDICATORS OVERVIEW

	Ticker Symbol																	
Indicators	5M	15M	30M	1HR	4HR	1D	5M	15M	30M	1HR	4HR	1D	5M	15M	30M	1HR	4HR	1D
Moving Averages																		
5 day																		
9 day																		
50 day																		
100 day																		
200 day																		
Bollinger Bands																		
Upper Band																		
Lower Band																		
DMI																		
Bullish																		
Bearish																		
MACD																		
Bullish																		
Bearish																		
RSI																		
Overbought																		
Oversold																		
Stochastic																		
Overbought																		
Oversold																		

Company Ticker	Chart Momentum											
	5 MIN		15 MIN		30 MIN		1 HR		4 HR		1 DAY	

Instrument(s) Traded	Hard Shares		Options		Forex		Crypto		
Trade #	Entry Time	Exit TIme	Time Elapsed	Buy/Call Sell/Put	Entry Price	Exit Price	Quantity	Profit/Loss	Total
1									
2									
3									
4									
5									
6									
7									
8									
9									
10									

Total Trades	Winning Trades	Losing Trades	Win Rate %

Notes

DATE:_____   ACCOUNT BALANCE:_____

TRADING POWDER:_____   MAXIMUM RISK AMOUNT PER TRADE:_____

DAILY GOAL: _____

MARKET ANALYSIS

Check the momentum of the market based on Key Indices, Commodities, and ETFs.

Type of Market Day	Key Indices and Commodities					
	S&P 500	Dow 30	Nasdaq	Russell 2000	Crude Oil	Gold
GREEN						
RED						

INDICATORS OVERVIEW

	Ticker Symbol																	
Indicators	5M	15M	30M	1HR	4HR	1D	5M	15M	30M	1HR	4HR	1D	5M	15M	30M	1HR	4HR	1D
Moving Averages																		
5 day																		
9 day																		
50 day																		
100 day																		
200 day																		
Bollinger Bands																		
Upper Band																		
Lower Band																		
DMI																		
Bullish																		
Bearish																		
MACD																		
Bullish																		
Bearish																		
RSI																		
Overbought																		
Oversold																		
Stochastic																		
Overbought																		
Oversold																		

Company Ticker	Chart Momentum											
	5 MIN		15 MIN		30 MIN		1 HR		4 HR		1 DAY	

Instrument(s) Traded	Hard Shares		Options		Forex		Crypto		
Trade #	Entry Time	Exit Time	Time Elapsed	Buy/Call Sell/Put	Entry Price	Exit Price	Quantity	Profit/Loss	Total
1									
2									
3									
4									
5									
6									
7									
8									
9									
10									

Total Trades	Winning Trades	Losing Trades	Win Rate %

Notes

DATE:_____ **ACCOUNT BALANCE:**_____

TRADING POWDER:_____ **MAXIMUM RISK AMOUNT PER TRADE:**_____

DAILY GOAL:_____

MARKET ANALYSIS

Check the momentum of the market based on Key Indices, Commodities, and ETFs.

Type of Market Day	Key Indices and Commodities					
	S&P 500	Dow 30	Nasdaq	Russell 2000	Crude Oil	Gold
GREEN						
RED						

INDICATORS OVERVIEW

	Ticker Symbol																	
Indicators	5M	15M	30M	1HR	4HR	1D	5M	15M	30M	1HR	4HR	1D	5M	15M	30M	1HR	4HR	1D
Moving Averages																		
5 day																		
9 day																		
50 day																		
100 day																		
200 day																		
Bollinger Bands																		
Upper Band																		
Lower Band																		
DMI																		
Bullish																		
Bearish																		
MACD																		
Bullish																		
Bearish																		
RSI																		
Overbought																		
Oversold																		
Stochastic																		
Overbought																		
Oversold																		

Company Ticker	Chart Momentum											
	5 MIN		15 MIN		30 MIN		1 HR		4 HR		1 DAY	

Instrument(s) Traded	Hard Shares		Options		Forex		Crypto		
Trade #	Entry Time	Exit Time	Time Elapsed	Buy/Call Sell/Put	Entry Price	Exit Price	Quantity	Profit/Loss	Total
1									
2									
3									
4									
5									
6									
7									
8									
9									
10									

Total Trades	Winning Trades	Losing Trades	Win Rate %

Notes

DATE:_____   ACCOUNT BALANCE:_____

TRADING POWDER:_____   MAXIMUM RISK AMOUNT PER TRADE:_____

DAILY GOAL: _____

MARKET ANALYSIS

Check the momentum of the market based on Key Indices, Commodities, and ETFs.

Type of Market Day	Key Indices and Commodities					
	S&P 500	Dow 30	Nasdaq	Russell 2000	Crude Oil	Gold
GREEN						
RED						

INDICATORS OVERVIEW

	Ticker Symbol																	
Indicators	5M	15M	30M	1HR	4HR	1D	5M	15M	30M	1HR	4HR	1D	5M	15M	30M	1HR	4HR	1D
Moving Averages																		
5 day																		
9 day																		
50 day																		
100 day																		
200 day																		
Bollinger Bands																		
Upper Band																		
Lower Band																		
DMI																		
Bullish																		
Bearish																		
MACD																		
Bullish																		
Bearish																		
RSI																		
Overbought																		
Oversold																		
Stochastic																		
Overbought																		
Oversold																		

Company Ticker	Chart Momentum												
	5 MIN		15 MIN		30 MIN		1 HR		4 HR		1 DAY		

Instrument(s) Traded	Hard Shares		Options		Forex		Crypto		
Trade #	Entry Time	Exit Time	Time Elapsed	Buy/Call Sell/Put	Entry Price	Exit Price	Quantity	Profit/Loss	Total
1									
2									
3									
4									
5									
6									
7									
8									
9									
10									

Total Trades	Winning Trades	Losing Trades	Win Rate %

Notes

DATE:_____   ACCOUNT BALANCE:_____

TRADING POWDER:_____   MAXIMUM RISK AMOUNT PER TRADE:_____

DAILY GOAL: _____

MARKET ANALYSIS

Check the momentum of the market based on Key Indices, Commodities, and ETFs.

Type of Market Day	Key Indices and Commodities					
	S&P 500	Dow 30	Nasdaq	Russell 2000	Crude Oil	Gold
GREEN						
RED						

INDICATORS OVERVIEW

	Ticker Symbol																	
Indicators	5M	15M	30M	1HR	4HR	1D	5M	15M	30M	1HR	4HR	1D	5M	15M	30M	1HR	4HR	1D
Moving Averages																		
5 day																		
9 day																		
50 day																		
100 day																		
200 day																		
Bollinger Bands																		
Upper Band																		
Lower Band																		
DMI																		
Bullish																		
Bearish																		
MACD																		
Bullish																		
Bearish																		
RSI																		
Overbought																		
Oversold																		
Stochastic																		
Overbought																		
Oversold																		

Company Ticker	Chart Momentum																
	5 MIN			15 MIN			30 MIN			1 HR			4 HR			1 DAY		

Instrument(s) Traded	Hard Shares		Options		Forex		Crypto		
Trade #	Entry Time	Exit TIme	Time Elapsed	Buy/Call Sell/Put	Entry Price	Exit Price	Quantity	Profit/Loss	Total
1									
2									
3									
4									
5									
6									
7									
8									
9									
10									

Total Trades	Winning Trades	Losing Trades	Win Rate %

Notes

DATE:_____   ACCOUNT BALANCE:_____

TRADING POWDER:_____   MAXIMUM RISK AMOUNT PER TRADE:_____

DAILY GOAL: _____

MARKET ANALYSIS

Check the momentum of the market based on Key Indices, Commodities, and ETFs.

Type of Market Day	Key Indices and Commodities					
	S&P 500	Dow 30	Nasdaq	Russell 2000	Crude Oil	Gold
GREEN						
RED						

INDICATORS OVERVIEW

	Ticker Symbol																	
Indicators	5M	15M	30M	1HR	4HR	1D	5M	15M	30M	1HR	4HR	1D	5M	15M	30M	1HR	4HR	1D
Moving Averages																		
5 day																		
9 day																		
50 day																		
100 day																		
200 day																		
Bollinger Bands																		
Upper Band																		
Lower Band																		
DMI																		
Bullish																		
Bearish																		
MACD																		
Bullish																		
Bearish																		
RSI																		
Overbought																		
Oversold																		
Stochastic																		
Overbought																		
Oversold																		

Company Ticker	Chart Momentum											
	5 MIN		15 MIN		30 MIN		1 HR		4 HR		1 DAY	

Instrument(s) Traded	Hard Shares		Options		Forex		Crypto			
Trade #	Entry Time	Exit Time	Time Elapsed	Buy/Call Sell/Put	Entry Price	Exit Price	Quantity	Profit/Loss	Total
1									
2									
3									
4									
5									
6									
7									
8									
9									
10									

Total Trades	Winning Trades	Losing Trades	Win Rate %

Notes

DATE:_____   ACCOUNT BALANCE:_____

TRADING POWDER:_____   MAXIMUM RISK AMOUNT PER TRADE:_____

DAILY GOAL: _____

MARKET ANALYSIS

Check the momentum of the market based on Key Indices, Commodities, and ETFs.

Type of Market Day	Key Indices and Commodities					
	S&P 500	Dow 30	Nasdaq	Russell 2000	Crude Oil	Gold
GREEN						
RED						

INDICATORS OVERVIEW

	Ticker Symbol																	
Indicators	5M	15M	30M	1HR	4HR	1D	5M	15M	30M	1HR	4HR	1D	5M	15M	30M	1HR	4HR	1D
Moving Averages																		
5 day																		
9 day																		
50 day																		
100 day																		
200 day																		
Bollinger Bands																		
Upper Band																		
Lower Band																		
DMI																		
Bullish																		
Bearish																		
MACD																		
Bullish																		
Bearish																		
RSI																		
Overbought																		
Oversold																		
Stochastic																		
Overbought																		
Oversold																		

Company Ticker	Chart Momentum																
	5 MIN			15 MIN			30 MIN			1 HR			4 HR			1 DAY		

Instrument(s) Traded	Hard Shares		Options		Forex		Crypto		
Trade #	Entry Time	Exit Time	Time Elapsed	Buy/Call Sell/Put	Entry Price	Exit Price	Quantity	Profit/Loss	Total
1									
2									
3									
4									
5									
6									
7									
8									
9									
10									

Total Trades	Winning Trades	Losing Trades	Win Rate %

Notes

DATE:_____   ACCOUNT BALANCE:_____

TRADING POWDER:_____   MAXIMUM RISK AMOUNT PER TRADE:_____

DAILY GOAL: _____

MARKET ANALYSIS

Check the momentum of the market based on Key Indices, Commodities, and ETFs.

Type of Market Day	Key Indices and Commodities					
	S&P 500	Dow 30	Nasdaq	Russell 2000	Crude Oil	Gold
GREEN						
RED						

INDICATORS OVERVIEW

	Ticker Symbol																	
Indicators	5M	15M	30M	1HR	4HR	1D	5M	15M	30M	1HR	4HR	1D	5M	15M	30M	1HR	4HR	1D
Moving Averages																		
5 day																		
9 day																		
50 day																		
100 day																		
200 day																		
Bollinger Bands																		
Upper Band																		
Lower Band																		
DMI																		
Bullish																		
Bearish																		
MACD																		
Bullish																		
Bearish																		
RSI																		
Overbought																		
Oversold																		
Stochastic																		
Overbought																		
Oversold																		

Company Ticker	Chart Momentum											
	5 MIN		15 MIN		30 MIN		1 HR		4 HR		1 DAY	

Instrument(s) Traded	Hard Shares		Options		Forex		Crypto		
Trade #	Entry Time	Exit Time	Time Elapsed	Buy/Call Sell/Put	Entry Price	Exit Price	Quantity	Profit/Loss	Total
1									
2									
3									
4									
5									
6									
7									
8									
9									
10									

Total Trades	Winning Trades	Losing Trades	Win Rate %

Notes

DATE:_____   ACCOUNT BALANCE:_____

TRADING POWDER:_____   MAXIMUM RISK AMOUNT PER TRADE:_____

DAILY GOAL: _____

MARKET ANALYSIS

Check the momentum of the market based on Key Indices, Commodities, and ETFs.

Type of Market Day	Key Indices and Commodities					
	S&P 500	Dow 30	Nasdaq	Russell 2000	Crude Oil	Gold
GREEN						
RED						

INDICATORS OVERVIEW

	Ticker Symbol																	
Indicators	5M	15M	30M	1HR	4HR	1D	5M	15M	30M	1HR	4HR	1D	5M	15M	30M	1HR	4HR	1D
Moving Averages																		
5 day																		
9 day																		
50 day																		
100 day																		
200 day																		
Bollinger Bands																		
Upper Band																		
Lower Band																		
DMI																		
Bullish																		
Bearish																		
MACD																		
Bullish																		
Bearish																		
RSI																		
Overbought																		
Oversold																		
Stochastic																		
Overbought																		
Oversold																		

Company Ticker	Chart Momentum																
	5 MIN			15 MIN			30 MIN			1 HR			4 HR			1 DAY		

Instrument(s) Traded	Hard Shares		Options		Forex		Crypto		
Trade #	Entry Time	Exit Time	Time Elapsed	Buy/Call Sell/Put	Entry Price	Exit Price	Quantity	Profit/Loss	Total
1									
2									
3									
4									
5									
6									
7									
8									
9									
10									

Total Trades	Winning Trades	Losing Trades	Win Rate %

Notes

DATE:_____   ACCOUNT BALANCE:_____

TRADING POWDER:_____   MAXIMUM RISK AMOUNT PER TRADE:_____

DAILY GOAL: _____

MARKET ANALYSIS

Check the momentum of the market based on Key Indices, Commodities, and ETFs.

Type of Market Day	Key Indices and Commodities					
	S&P 500	Dow 30	Nasdaq	Russell 2000	Crude Oil	Gold
GREEN						
RED						

INDICATORS OVERVIEW

	Ticker Symbol																	
Indicators	5M	15M	30M	1HR	4HR	1D	5M	15M	30M	1HR	4HR	1D	5M	15M	30M	1HR	4HR	1D
Moving Averages																		
5 day																		
9 day																		
50 day																		
100 day																		
200 day																		
Bollinger Bands																		
Upper Band																		
Lower Band																		
DMI																		
Bullish																		
Bearish																		
MACD																		
Bullish																		
Bearish																		
RSI																		
Overbought																		
Oversold																		
Stochastic																		
Overbought																		
Oversold																		

Company Ticker	Chart Momentum												
	5 MIN		15 MIN		30 MIN		1 HR		4 HR		1 DAY		

Instrument(s) Traded	Hard Shares		Options		Forex		Crypto		
Trade #	Entry Time	Exit Time	Time Elapsed	Buy/Call Sell/Put	Entry Price	Exit Price	Quantity	Profit/Loss	Total
1									
2									
3									
4									
5									
6									
7									
8									
9									
10									

Total Trades	Winning Trades	Losing Trades	Win Rate %

Notes

DATE:_____   ACCOUNT BALANCE:_____

TRADING POWDER:_____   MAXIMUM RISK AMOUNT PER TRADE:_____

DAILY GOAL: _____

MARKET ANALYSIS

Check the momentum of the market based on Key Indices, Commodities, and ETFs.

Type of Market Day	Key Indices and Commodities					
	S&P 500	Dow 30	Nasdaq	Russell 2000	Crude Oil	Gold
GREEN						
RED						

INDICATORS OVERVIEW

	Ticker Symbol																	
Indicators	5M	15M	30M	1HR	4HR	1D	5M	15M	30M	1HR	4HR	1D	5M	15M	30M	1HR	4HR	1D
Moving Averages																		
5 day																		
9 day																		
50 day																		
100 day																		
200 day																		
Bollinger Bands																		
Upper Band																		
Lower Band																		
DMI																		
Bullish																		
Bearish																		
MACD																		
Bullish																		
Bearish																		
RSI																		
Overbought																		
Oversold																		
Stochastic																		
Overbought																		
Oversold																		

Company Ticker	Chart Momentum												
	5 MIN			15 MIN			30 MIN			1 HR		4 HR	1 DAY

Instrument(s) Traded	Hard Shares		Options		Forex		Crypto		
Trade #	Entry Time	Exit Time	Time Elapsed	Buy/Call Sell/Put	Entry Price	Exit Price	Quantity	Profit/Loss	Total
1									
2									
3									
4									
5									
6									
7									
8									
9									
10									

Total Trades	Winning Trades	Losing Trades	Win Rate %

Notes

DATE:_____   ACCOUNT BALANCE:_____

TRADING POWDER:_____   MAXIMUM RISK AMOUNT PER TRADE:_____

DAILY GOAL: _____

MARKET ANALYSIS

Check the momentum of the market based on Key Indices, Commodities, and ETFs.

Type of Market Day	Key Indices and Commodities					
	S&P 500	Dow 30	Nasdaq	Russell 2000	Crude Oil	Gold
GREEN						
RED						

INDICATORS OVERVIEW

	Ticker Symbol																	
Indicators	5M	15M	30M	1HR	4HR	1D	5M	15M	30M	1HR	4HR	1D	5M	15M	30M	1HR	4HR	1D
Moving Averages																		
5 day																		
9 day																		
50 day																		
100 day																		
200 day																		
Bollinger Bands																		
Upper Band																		
Lower Band																		
DMI																		
Bullish																		
Bearish																		
MACD																		
Bullish																		
Bearish																		
RSI																		
Overbought																		
Oversold																		
Stochastic																		
Overbought																		
Oversold																		

Company Ticker	Chart Momentum											
	5 MIN		15 MIN		30 MIN		1 HR		4 HR		1 DAY	

Instrument(s) Traded	Hard Shares		Options		Forex		Crypto			
Trade #	Entry Time	Exit Time	Time Elapsed	Buy/Call Sell/Put	Entry Price	Exit Price	Quantity	Profit/Loss	Total
1									
2									
3									
4									
5									
6									
7									
8									
9									
10									

Total Trades	Winning Trades	Losing Trades	Win Rate %

Notes

DATE:_____   ACCOUNT BALANCE:_____

TRADING POWDER:_____   MAXIMUM RISK AMOUNT PER TRADE:_____

DAILY GOAL: _____

MARKET ANALYSIS

Check the momentum of the market based on Key Indices, Commodities, and ETFs.

Type of Market Day	Key Indices and Commodities					
	S&P 500	Dow 30	Nasdaq	Russell 2000	Crude Oil	Gold
GREEN						
RED						

INDICATORS OVERVIEW

	Ticker Symbol																	
Indicators	5M	15M	30M	1HR	4HR	1D	5M	15M	30M	1HR	4HR	1D	5M	15M	30M	1HR	4HR	1D
Moving Averages																		
5 day																		
9 day																		
50 day																		
100 day																		
200 day																		
Bollinger Bands																		
Upper Band																		
Lower Band																		
DMI																		
Bullish																		
Bearish																		
MACD																		
Bullish																		
Bearish																		
RSI																		
Overbought																		
Oversold																		
Stochastic																		
Overbought																		
Oversold																		

Company Ticker	Chart Momentum																	
	5 MIN			15 MIN			30 MIN			1 HR			4 HR			1 DAY		

Instrument(s) Traded	Hard Shares		Options		Forex		Crypto		
Trade #	Entry Time	Exit Time	Time Elapsed	Buy/Call Sell/Put	Entry Price	Exit Price	Quantity	Profit/Loss	Total
1									
2									
3									
4									
5									
6									
7									
8									
9									
10									

Total Trades	Winning Trades	Losing Trades	Win Rate %
Notes			

Notes

DATE:_____   ACCOUNT BALANCE:_____

TRADING POWDER:_____   MAXIMUM RISK AMOUNT PER TRADE:_____

DAILY GOAL: _____

MARKET ANALYSIS

Check the momentum of the market based on Key Indices, Commodities, and ETFs.

Type of Market Day	Key Indices and Commodities					
	S&P 500	Dow 30	Nasdaq	Russell 2000	Crude Oil	Gold
GREEN						
RED						

INDICATORS OVERVIEW

	Ticker Symbol																	
Indicators	5M	15M	30M	1HR	4HR	1D	5M	15M	30M	1HR	4HR	1D	5M	15M	30M	1HR	4HR	1D
Moving Averages																		
5 day																		
9 day																		
50 day																		
100 day																		
200 day																		
Bollinger Bands																		
Upper Band																		
Lower Band																		
DMI																		
Bullish																		
Bearish																		
MACD																		
Bullish																		
Bearish																		
RSI																		
Overbought																		
Oversold																		
Stochastic																		
Overbought																		
Oversold																		

Company Ticker	Chart Momentum											
	5 MIN		15 MIN		30 MIN		1 HR		4 HR		1 DAY	

Instrument(s) Traded	Hard Shares		Options		Forex		Crypto			
Trade #	Entry Time	Exit Time	Time Elapsed	Buy/Call Sell/Put	Entry Price	Exit Price	Quantity	Profit/Loss	Total
1									
2									
3									
4									
5									
6									
7									
8									
9									
10									

Total Trades	Winning Trades	Losing Trades	Win Rate %

Notes

DATE:_____   ACCOUNT BALANCE:_____

TRADING POWDER:_____   MAXIMUM RISK AMOUNT PER TRADE:_____

DAILY GOAL:_____

MARKET ANALYSIS

Check the momentum of the market based on Key Indices, Commodities, and ETFs.

Type of Market Day	Key Indices and Commodities					
	S&P 500	Dow 30	Nasdaq	Russell 2000	Crude Oil	Gold
GREEN						
RED						

INDICATORS OVERVIEW

	Ticker Symbol																	
Indicators	5M	15M	30M	1HR	4HR	1D	5M	15M	30M	1HR	4HR	1D	5M	15M	30M	1HR	4HR	1D
Moving Averages																		
5 day																		
9 day																		
50 day																		
100 day																		
200 day																		
Bollinger Bands																		
Upper Band																		
Lower Band																		
DMI																		
Bullish																		
Bearish																		
MACD																		
Bullish																		
Bearish																		
RSI																		
Overbought																		
Oversold																		
Stochastic																		
Overbought																		
Oversold																		

Company Ticker	Chart Momentum																
	5 MIN			15 MIN			30 MIN			1 HR			4 HR			1 DAY		

Instrument(s) Traded	Hard Shares		Options			Forex		Crypto		
Trade #	Entry Time	Exit Time	Time Elapsed	Buy/Call Sell/Put	Entry Price	Exit Price	Quantity	Profit/Loss	Total
1									
2									
3									
4									
5									
6									
7									
8									
9									
10									

Total Trades	Winning Trades	Losing Trades	Win Rate %

Notes

DATE:_____   ACCOUNT BALANCE:_____

TRADING POWDER:_____   MAXIMUM RISK AMOUNT PER TRADE:_____

DAILY GOAL: _____

MARKET ANALYSIS

Check the momentum of the market based on Key Indices, Commodities, and ETFs.

Type of Market Day	Key Indices and Commodities					
	S&P 500	Dow 30	Nasdaq	Russell 2000	Crude Oil	Gold
GREEN						
RED						

INDICATORS OVERVIEW

	Ticker Symbol																	
Indicators	5M	15M	30M	1HR	4HR	1D	5M	15M	30M	1HR	4HR	1D	5M	15M	30M	1HR	4HR	1D
Moving Averages																		
5 day																		
9 day																		
50 day																		
100 day																		
200 day																		
Bollinger Bands																		
Upper Band																		
Lower Band																		
DMI																		
Bullish																		
Bearish																		
MACD																		
Bullish																		
Bearish																		
RSI																		
Overbought																		
Oversold																		
Stochastic																		
Overbought																		
Oversold																		

Company Ticker	Chart Momentum																
	5 MIN			15 MIN			30 MIN			1 HR			4 HR			1 DAY		

Instrument(s) Traded	Hard Shares		Options		Forex		Crypto		
Trade #	Entry Time	Exit Time	Time Elapsed	Buy/Call Sell/Put	Entry Price	Exit Price	Quantity	Profit/Loss	Total
1									
2									
3									
4									
5									
6									
7									
8									
9									
10									

Total Trades	Winning Trades	Losing Trades	Win Rate %

Notes

DATE:_____   ACCOUNT BALANCE:_____

TRADING POWDER:_____   MAXIMUM RISK AMOUNT PER TRADE:_____

DAILY GOAL: _____

MARKET ANALYSIS

Check the momentum of the market based on Key Indices, Commodities, and ETFs.

Type of Market Day	Key Indices and Commodities					
	S&P 500	Dow 30	Nasdaq	Russell 2000	Crude Oil	Gold
GREEN						
RED						

INDICATORS OVERVIEW

	Ticker Symbol																	
Indicators	5M	15M	30M	1HR	4HR	1D	5M	15M	30M	1HR	4HR	1D	5M	15M	30M	1HR	4HR	1D
Moving Averages																		
5 day																		
9 day																		
50 day																		
100 day																		
200 day																		
Bollinger Bands																		
Upper Band																		
Lower Band																		
DMI																		
Bullish																		
Bearish																		
MACD																		
Bullish																		
Bearish																		
RSI																		
Overbought																		
Oversold																		
Stochastic																		
Overbought																		
Oversold																		

Company Ticker	Chart Momentum											
	5 MIN		15 MIN		30 MIN		1 HR		4 HR		1 DAY	

Instrument(s) Traded	Hard Shares		Options		Forex		Crypto		
Trade #	Entry Time	Exit Time	Time Elapsed	Buy/Call Sell/Put	Entry Price	Exit Price	Quantity	Profit/Loss	Total
1									
2									
3									
4									
5									
6									
7									
8									
9									
10									

Total Trades	Winning Trades	Losing Trades	Win Rate %

Notes

DATE:_____   ACCOUNT BALANCE:_____

TRADING POWDER:_____   MAXIMUM RISK AMOUNT PER TRADE:_____

DAILY GOAL: _____

MARKET ANALYSIS

Check the momentum of the market based on Key Indices, Commodities, and ETFs.

Type of Market Day	Key Indices and Commodities					
	S&P 500	Dow 30	Nasdaq	Russell 2000	Crude Oil	Gold
GREEN						
RED						

INDICATORS OVERVIEW

	Ticker Symbol																	
Indicators	5M	15M	30M	1HR	4HR	1D	5M	15M	30M	1HR	4HR	1D	5M	15M	30M	1HR	4HR	1D
Moving Averages																		
5 day																		
9 day																		
50 day																		
100 day																		
200 day																		
Bollinger Bands																		
Upper Band																		
Lower Band																		
DMI																		
Bullish																		
Bearish																		
MACD																		
Bullish																		
Bearish																		
RSI																		
Overbought																		
Oversold																		
Stochastic																		
Overbought																		
Oversold																		

Company Ticker	Chart Momentum											
	5 MIN		15 MIN		30 MIN		1 HR		4 HR		1 DAY	

Instrument(s) Traded	Hard Shares		Options		Forex		Crypto			
Trade #	Entry Time	Exit Time	Time Elapsed	Buy/Call Sell/Put	Entry Price	Exit Price	Quantity	Profit/Loss	Total	
1										
2										
3										
4										
5										
6										
7										
8										
9										
10										

Total Trades	Winning Trades	Losing Trades	Win Rate %

Notes

DATE:_____   ACCOUNT BALANCE:_____

TRADING POWDER:_____   MAXIMUM RISK AMOUNT PER TRADE:_____

DAILY GOAL: _____

MARKET ANALYSIS

Check the momentum of the market based on Key Indices, Commodities, and ETFs.

Type of Market Day	Key Indices and Commodities					
	S&P 500	Dow 30	Nasdaq	Russell 2000	Crude Oil	Gold
GREEN						
RED						

INDICATORS OVERVIEW

	Ticker Symbol																	
Indicators	5M	15M	30M	1HR	4HR	1D	5M	15M	30M	1HR	4HR	1D	5M	15M	30M	1HR	4HR	1D
Moving Averages																		
5 day																		
9 day																		
50 day																		
100 day																		
200 day																		
Bollinger Bands																		
Upper Band																		
Lower Band																		
DMI																		
Bullish																		
Bearish																		
MACD																		
Bullish																		
Bearish																		
RSI																		
Overbought																		
Oversold																		
Stochastic																		
Overbought																		
Oversold																		

Company Ticker	Chart Momentum												
	5 MIN			15 MIN			30 MIN			1 HR		4 HR	1 DAY

Instrument(s) Traded	Hard Shares		Options		Forex		Crypto		
Trade #	Entry Time	Exit Time	Time Elapsed	Buy/Call Sell/Put	Entry Price	Exit Price	Quantity	Profit/Loss	Total
1									
2									
3									
4									
5									
6									
7									
8									
9									
10									

Total Trades	Winning Trades	Losing Trades	Win Rate %

Notes

DATE:_____ ACCOUNT BALANCE:_____

TRADING POWDER:_____ MAXIMUM RISK AMOUNT PER TRADE:_____

DAILY GOAL: _____

MARKET ANALYSIS

Check the momentum of the market based on Key Indices, Commodities, and ETFs.

Type of Market Day	Key Indices and Commodities					
	S&P 500	Dow 30	Nasdaq	Russell 2000	Crude Oil	Gold
GREEN						
RED						

INDICATORS OVERVIEW

	Ticker Symbol																	
Indicators	5M	15M	30M	1HR	4HR	1D	5M	15M	30M	1HR	4HR	1D	5M	15M	30M	1HR	4HR	1D
Moving Averages																		
5 day																		
9 day																		
50 day																		
100 day																		
200 day																		
Bollinger Bands																		
Upper Band																		
Lower Band																		
DMI																		
Bullish																		
Bearish																		
MACD																		
Bullish																		
Bearish																		
RSI																		
Overbought																		
Oversold																		
Stochastic																		
Overbought																		
Oversold																		

Company Ticker	Chart Momentum																
	5 MIN			15 MIN			30 MIN			1 HR			4 HR			1 DAY		

Instrument(s) Traded	Hard Shares		Options		Forex		Crypto		
Trade #	Entry Time	Exit Time	Time Elapsed	Buy/Call Sell/Put	Entry Price	Exit Price	Quantity	Profit/Loss	Total
1									
2									
3									
4									
5									
6									
7									
8									
9									
10									

Total Trades	Winning Trades	Losing Trades	Win Rate %

Notes

DATE:_____   ACCOUNT BALANCE:_____

TRADING POWDER:_____   MAXIMUM RISK AMOUNT PER TRADE:_____

DAILY GOAL: _____

MARKET ANALYSIS

Check the momentum of the market based on Key Indices, Commodities, and ETFs.

Type of Market Day	Key Indices and Commodities					
	S&P 500	Dow 30	Nasdaq	Russell 2000	Crude Oil	Gold
GREEN						
RED						

INDICATORS OVERVIEW

	Ticker Symbol																	
Indicators	5M	15M	30M	1HR	4HR	1D	5M	15M	30M	1HR	4HR	1D	5M	15M	30M	1HR	4HR	1D
Moving Averages																		
5 day																		
9 day																		
50 day																		
100 day																		
200 day																		
Bollinger Bands																		
Upper Band																		
Lower Band																		
DMI																		
Bullish																		
Bearish																		
MACD																		
Bullish																		
Bearish																		
RSI																		
Overbought																		
Oversold																		
Stochastic																		
Overbought																		
Oversold																		

Company Ticker	Chart Momentum											
	5 MIN		15 MIN		30 MIN		1 HR		4 HR		1 DAY	

Instrument(s) Traded	Hard Shares		Options		Forex		Crypto			
Trade #	Entry Time	Exit Time	Time Elapsed	Buy/Call Sell/Put	Entry Price	Exit Price	Quantity	Profit/Loss	Total
1									
2									
3									
4									
5									
6									
7									
8									
9									
10									

Total Trades	Winning Trades	Losing Trades	Win Rate %

Notes

DATE:_____   ACCOUNT BALANCE:_____

TRADING POWDER:_____   MAXIMUM RISK AMOUNT PER TRADE:_____

DAILY GOAL: _____

MARKET ANALYSIS

Check the momentum of the market based on Key Indices, Commodities, and ETFs.

Type of Market Day	Key Indices and Commodities					
	S&P 500	Dow 30	Nasdaq	Russell 2000	Crude Oil	Gold
GREEN						
RED						

INDICATORS OVERVIEW

Indicators	Ticker Symbol																	
	5M	15M	30M	1HR	4HR	1D	5M	15M	30M	1HR	4HR	1D	5M	15M	30M	1HR	4HR	1D
Moving Averages																		
5 day																		
9 day																		
50 day																		
100 day																		
200 day																		
Bollinger Bands																		
Upper Band																		
Lower Band																		
DMI																		
Bullish																		
Bearish																		
MACD																		
Bullish																		
Bearish																		
RSI																		
Overbought																		
Oversold																		
Stochastic																		
Overbought																		
Oversold																		

Company Ticker	Chart Momentum																
	5 MIN			15 MIN			30 MIN			1 HR			4 HR			1 DAY		

Instrument(s) Traded	Hard Shares		Options		Forex		Crypto		
Trade #	Entry Time	Exit Time	Time Elapsed	Buy/Call Sell/Put	Entry Price	Exit Price	Quantity	Profit/Loss	Total
1									
2									
3									
4									
5									
6									
7									
8									
9									
10									

Total Trades	Winning Trades	Losing Trades	Win Rate %
Notes			

DATE:_____   ACCOUNT BALANCE:_____

TRADING POWDER:_____   MAXIMUM RISK AMOUNT PER TRADE:_____

DAILY GOAL: _____

MARKET ANALYSIS

Check the momentum of the market based on Key Indices, Commodities, and ETFs.

Type of Market Day	Key Indices and Commodities					
	S&P 500	Dow 30	Nasdaq	Russell 2000	Crude Oil	Gold
GREEN						
RED						

INDICATORS OVERVIEW

	Ticker Symbol																	
Indicators	5M	15M	30M	1HR	4HR	1D	5M	15M	30M	1HR	4HR	1D	5M	15M	30M	1HR	4HR	1D
Moving Averages																		
5 day																		
9 day																		
50 day																		
100 day																		
200 day																		
Bollinger Bands																		
Upper Band																		
Lower Band																		
DMI																		
Bullish																		
Bearish																		
MACD																		
Bullish																		
Bearish																		
RSI																		
Overbought																		
Oversold																		
Stochastic																		
Overbought																		
Oversold																		

Company Ticker	Chart Momentum											
	5 MIN		15 MIN		30 MIN		1 HR		4 HR		1 DAY	

Instrument(s) Traded	Hard Shares		Options		Forex		Crypto		
Trade #	Entry Time	Exit Time	Time Elapsed	Buy/Call Sell/Put	Entry Price	Exit Price	Quantity	Profit/Loss	Total
1									
2									
3									
4									
5									
6									
7									
8									
9									
10									

Total Trades	Winning Trades	Losing Trades	Win Rate %

Notes

DATE:_____ ACCOUNT BALANCE:_____

TRADING POWDER:_____ MAXIMUM RISK AMOUNT PER TRADE:_____

DAILY GOAL: _____

MARKET ANALYSIS

Check the momentum of the market based on Key Indices, Commodities, and ETFs.

Type of Market Day	Key Indices and Commodities					
	S&P 500	Dow 30	Nasdaq	Russell 2000	Crude Oil	Gold
GREEN						
RED						

INDICATORS OVERVIEW

	Ticker Symbol																	
Indicators	5M	15M	30M	1HR	4HR	1D	5M	15M	30M	1HR	4HR	1D	5M	15M	30M	1HR	4HR	1D
Moving Averages																		
5 day																		
9 day																		
50 day																		
100 day																		
200 day																		
Bollinger Bands																		
Upper Band																		
Lower Band																		
DMI																		
Bullish																		
Bearish																		
MACD																		
Bullish																		
Bearish																		
RSI																		
Overbought																		
Oversold																		
Stochastic																		
Overbought																		
Oversold																		

Company Ticker	Chart Momentum																
	5 MIN			15 MIN			30 MIN			1 HR			4 HR			1 DAY		

Instrument(s) Traded	Hard Shares		Options		Forex		Crypto		
Trade #	Entry Time	Exit Time	Time Elapsed	Buy/Call Sell/Put	Entry Price	Exit Price	Quantity	Profit/Loss	Total
1									
2									
3									
4									
5									
6									
7									
8									
9									
10									

Total Trades	Winning Trades	Losing Trades	Win Rate %

Notes

DATE:_____   ACCOUNT BALANCE:_____

TRADING POWDER:_____   MAXIMUM RISK AMOUNT PER TRADE:_____

DAILY GOAL: _____

MARKET ANALYSIS

Check the momentum of the market based on Key Indices, Commodities, and ETFs.

Type of Market Day	Key Indices and Commodities					
	S&P 500	Dow 30	Nasdaq	Russell 2000	Crude Oil	Gold
GREEN						
RED						

INDICATORS OVERVIEW

	Ticker Symbol																	
Indicators	5M	15M	30M	1HR	4HR	1D	5M	15M	30M	1HR	4HR	1D	5M	15M	30M	1HR	4HR	1D
Moving Averages																		
5 day																		
9 day																		
50 day																		
100 day																		
200 day																		
Bollinger Bands																		
Upper Band																		
Lower Band																		
DMI																		
Bullish																		
Bearish																		
MACD																		
Bullish																		
Bearish																		
RSI																		
Overbought																		
Oversold																		
Stochastic																		
Overbought																		
Oversold																		

Company Ticker	Chart Momentum													
	5 MIN			15 MIN			30 MIN			1 HR		4 HR		1 DAY

Instrument(s) Traded	Hard Shares		Options		Forex		Crypto		
Trade #	Entry Time	Exit Time	Time Elapsed	Buy/Call Sell/Put	Entry Price	Exit Price	Quantity	Profit/Loss	Total
1									
2									
3									
4									
5									
6									
7									
8									
9									
10									

Total Trades	Winning Trades	Losing Trades	Win Rate %

Notes

DATE:_____   ACCOUNT BALANCE:_____

TRADING POWDER:_____   MAXIMUM RISK AMOUNT PER TRADE:_____

DAILY GOAL:_____

MARKET ANALYSIS

Check the momentum of the market based on Key Indices, Commodities, and ETFs.

Type of Market Day	Key Indices and Commodities					
	S&P 500	Dow 30	Nasdaq	Russell 2000	Crude Oil	Gold
GREEN						
RED						

INDICATORS OVERVIEW

	Ticker Symbol																	
Indicators	5M	15M	30M	1HR	4HR	1D	5M	15M	30M	1HR	4HR	1D	5M	15M	30M	1HR	4HR	1D
Moving Averages																		
5 day																		
9 day																		
50 day																		
100 day																		
200 day																		
Bollinger Bands																		
Upper Band																		
Lower Band																		
DMI																		
Bullish																		
Bearish																		
MACD																		
Bullish																		
Bearish																		
RSI																		
Overbought																		
Oversold																		
Stochastic																		
Overbought																		
Oversold																		

Company Ticker	Chart Momentum													
	5 MIN		15 MIN		30 MIN		1 HR		4 HR		1 DAY			

Instrument(s) Traded	Hard Shares		Options		Forex		Crypto		
Trade #	Entry Time	Exit Time	Time Elapsed	Buy/Call Sell/Put	Entry Price	Exit Price	Quantity	Profit/Loss	Total
1									
2									
3									
4									
5									
6									
7									
8									
9									
10									

Total Trades	Winning Trades	Losing Trades	Win Rate %

Notes

DATE:_____   ACCOUNT BALANCE:_____

TRADING POWDER:_____   MAXIMUM RISK AMOUNT PER TRADE:_____

DAILY GOAL: _____

MARKET ANALYSIS

Check the momentum of the market based on Key Indices, Commodities, and ETFs.

Type of Market Day	Key Indices and Commodities					
	S&P 500	Dow 30	Nasdaq	Russell 2000	Crude Oil	Gold
GREEN						
RED						

INDICATORS OVERVIEW

| | Ticker Symbol | | | | | | | | | | | | | | | | | |
| | | | | | | | | | | | | | | | | | |
Indicators	5M	15M	30M	1HR	4HR	1D	5M	15M	30M	1HR	4HR	1D	5M	15M	30M	1HR	4HR	1D
Moving Averages																		
5 day																		
9 day																		
50 day																		
100 day																		
200 day																		
Bollinger Bands																		
Upper Band																		
Lower Band																		
DMI																		
Bullish																		
Bearish																		
MACD																		
Bullish																		
Bearish																		
RSI																		
Overbought																		
Oversold																		
Stochastic																		
Overbought																		
Oversold																		

Company Ticker	Chart Momentum																
	5 MIN			15 MIN			30 MIN			1 HR			4 HR			1 DAY		

Instrument(s) Traded	Hard Shares		Options		Forex		Crypto		
Trade #	Entry Time	Exit Time	Time Elapsed	Buy/Call Sell/Put	Entry Price	Exit Price	Quantity	Profit/Loss	Total
1									
2									
3									
4									
5									
6									
7									
8									
9									
10									

Total Trades	Winning Trades	Losing Trades	Win Rate %

Notes

DATE:_____   ACCOUNT BALANCE:_____

TRADING POWDER:_____   MAXIMUM RISK AMOUNT PER TRADE:_____

DAILY GOAL: _____

MARKET ANALYSIS

Check the momentum of the market based on Key Indices, Commodities, and ETFs.

Type of Market Day	Key Indices and Commodities					
	S&P 500	Dow 30	Nasdaq	Russell 2000	Crude Oil	Gold
GREEN						
RED						

INDICATORS OVERVIEW

	Ticker Symbol																	
Indicators	5M	15M	30M	1HR	4HR	1D	5M	15M	30M	1HR	4HR	1D	5M	15M	30M	1HR	4HR	1D
Moving Averages																		
5 day																		
9 day																		
50 day																		
100 day																		
200 day																		
Bollinger Bands																		
Upper Band																		
Lower Band																		
DMI																		
Bullish																		
Bearish																		
MACD																		
Bullish																		
Bearish																		
RSI																		
Overbought																		
Oversold																		
Stochastic																		
Overbought																		
Oversold																		

Company Ticker	Chart Momentum											
	5 MIN		15 MIN		30 MIN		1 HR		4 HR		1 DAY	

Instrument(s) Traded	Hard Shares		Options		Forex		Crypto			
Trade #	Entry Time	Exit Time	Time Elapsed	Buy/Call Sell/Put	Entry Price	Exit Price	Quantity	Profit/Loss	Total
1									
2									
3									
4									
5									
6									
7									
8									
9									
10									

Total Trades	Winning Trades	Losing Trades	Win Rate %

Notes

DATE:_____

ACCOUNT BALANCE:_____

TRADING POWDER:_____

MAXIMUM RISK AMOUNT PER TRADE:_____

DAILY GOAL: _____

MARKET ANALYSIS

Check the momentum of the market based on Key Indices, Commodities, and ETFs.

Type of Market Day	Key Indices and Commodities					
	S&P 500	Dow 30	Nasdaq	Russell 2000	Crude Oil	Gold
GREEN						
RED						

INDICATORS OVERVIEW

	Ticker Symbol																	
Indicators	5M	15M	30M	1HR	4HR	1D	5M	15M	30M	1HR	4HR	1D	5M	15M	30M	1HR	4HR	1D
Moving Averages																		
5 day																		
9 day																		
50 day																		
100 day																		
200 day																		
Bollinger Bands																		
Upper Band																		
Lower Band																		
DMI																		
Bullish																		
Bearish																		
MACD																		
Bullish																		
Bearish																		
RSI																		
Overbought																		
Oversold																		
Stochastic																		
Overbought																		
Oversold																		

Company Ticker	Chart Momentum																
	5 MIN			15 MIN			30 MIN			1 HR			4 HR			1 DAY		

Instrument(s) Traded	Hard Shares		Options		Forex		Crypto		
Trade #	Entry Time	Exit Time	Time Elapsed	Buy/Call Sell/Put	Entry Price	Exit Price	Quantity	Profit/Loss	Total
1									
2									
3									
4									
5									
6									
7									
8									
9									
10									

Total Trades	Winning Trades	Losing Trades	Win Rate %

Notes

DATE:_____   ACCOUNT BALANCE:_____

TRADING POWDER:_____   MAXIMUM RISK AMOUNT PER TRADE:_____

DAILY GOAL: _____

MARKET ANALYSIS

Check the momentum of the market based on Key Indices, Commodities, and ETFs.

Type of Market Day	Key Indices and Commodities					
	S&P 500	Dow 30	Nasdaq	Russell 2000	Crude Oil	Gold
GREEN						
RED						

INDICATORS OVERVIEW

	Ticker Symbol																	
Indicators	5M	15M	30M	1HR	4HR	1D	5M	15M	30M	1HR	4HR	1D	5M	15M	30M	1HR	4HR	1D
Moving Averages																		
5 day																		
9 day																		
50 day																		
100 day																		
200 day																		
Bollinger Bands																		
Upper Band																		
Lower Band																		
DMI																		
Bullish																		
Bearish																		
MACD																		
Bullish																		
Bearish																		
RSI																		
Overbought																		
Oversold																		
Stochastic																		
Overbought																		
Oversold																		

Company Ticker	Chart Momentum											
	5 MIN		15 MIN		30 MIN		1 HR		4 HR		1 DAY	

Instrument(s) Traded	Hard Shares		Options		Forex		Crypto		
Trade #	Entry Time	Exit Time	Time Elapsed	Buy/Call Sell/Put	Entry Price	Exit Price	Quantity	Profit/Loss	Total
1									
2									
3									
4									
5									
6									
7									
8									
9									
10									

Total Trades	Winning Trades	Losing Trades	Win Rate %

Notes

DATE:_____   **ACCOUNT BALANCE:**_____

TRADING POWDER:_____   **MAXIMUM RISK AMOUNT PER TRADE:**_____

DAILY GOAL: _____

MARKET ANALYSIS

Check the momentum of the market based on Key Indices, Commodities, and ETFs.

Type of Market Day	Key Indices and Commodities					
	S&P 500	Dow 30	Nasdaq	Russell 2000	Crude Oil	Gold
GREEN						
RED						

INDICATORS OVERVIEW

	Ticker Symbol																	
Indicators	5M	15M	30M	1HR	4HR	1D	5M	15M	30M	1HR	4HR	1D	5M	15M	30M	1HR	4HR	1D
Moving Averages																		
5 day																		
9 day																		
50 day																		
100 day																		
200 day																		
Bollinger Bands																		
Upper Band																		
Lower Band																		
DMI																		
Bullish																		
Bearish																		
MACD																		
Bullish																		
Bearish																		
RSI																		
Overbought																		
Oversold																		
Stochastic																		
Overbought																		
Oversold																		

Company Ticker	Chart Momentum												
	5 MIN			15 MIN			30 MIN			1 HR		4 HR	1 DAY

Instrument(s) Traded	Hard Shares		Options		Forex		Crypto		
Trade #	Entry Time	Exit TIme	Time Elapsed	Buy/Call Sell/Put	Entry Price	Exit Price	Quantity	Profit/Loss	Total
1									
2									
3									
4									
5									
6									
7									
8									
9									
10									

Total Trades	Winning Trades	Losing Trades	Win Rate %

Notes

DATE:_____   ACCOUNT BALANCE:_____

TRADING POWDER:_____   MAXIMUM RISK AMOUNT PER TRADE:_____

DAILY GOAL: _____

MARKET ANALYSIS

Check the momentum of the market based on Key Indices, Commodities, and ETFs.

Type of Market Day	Key Indices and Commodities					
	S&P 500	Dow 30	Nasdaq	Russell 2000	Crude Oil	Gold
GREEN						
RED						

INDICATORS OVERVIEW

	Ticker Symbol																	
Indicators	5M	15M	30M	1HR	4HR	1D	5M	15M	30M	1HR	4HR	1D	5M	15M	30M	1HR	4HR	1D
Moving Averages																		
5 day																		
9 day																		
50 day																		
100 day																		
200 day																		
Bollinger Bands																		
Upper Band																		
Lower Band																		
DMI																		
Bullish																		
Bearish																		
MACD																		
Bullish																		
Bearish																		
RSI																		
Overbought																		
Oversold																		
Stochastic																		
Overbought																		
Oversold																		

Company Ticker	Chart Momentum												
	5 MIN		15 MIN		30 MIN		1 HR		4 HR		1 DAY		

Instrument(s) Traded	Hard Shares		Options		Forex		Crypto		
Trade #	Entry Time	Exit Time	Time Elapsed	Buy/Call Sell/Put	Entry Price	Exit Price	Quantity	Profit/Loss	Total
1									
2									
3									
4									
5									
6									
7									
8									
9									
10									

Total Trades	Winning Trades	Losing Trades	Win Rate %

Notes

DATE:_____   ACCOUNT BALANCE:_____

TRADING POWDER:_____   MAXIMUM RISK AMOUNT PER TRADE:_____

DAILY GOAL: _____

MARKET ANALYSIS

Check the momentum of the market based on Key Indices, Commodities, and ETFs.

Type of Market Day	Key Indices and Commodities					
	S&P 500	Dow 30	Nasdaq	Russell 2000	Crude Oil	Gold
GREEN						
RED						

INDICATORS OVERVIEW

	Ticker Symbol																	
Indicators	5M	15M	30M	1HR	4HR	1D	5M	15M	30M	1HR	4HR	1D	5M	15M	30M	1HR	4HR	1D
Moving Averages																		
5 day																		
9 day																		
50 day																		
100 day																		
200 day																		
Bollinger Bands																		
Upper Band																		
Lower Band																		
DMI																		
Bullish																		
Bearish																		
MACD																		
Bullish																		
Bearish																		
RSI																		
Overbought																		
Oversold																		
Stochastic																		
Overbought																		
Oversold																		

Company Ticker	Chart Momentum																
	5 MIN			15 MIN			30 MIN			1 HR			4 HR			1 DAY		

Instrument(s) Traded	Hard Shares		Options		Forex		Crypto		
Trade #	Entry Time	Exit Time	Time Elapsed	Buy/Call Sell/Put	Entry Price	Exit Price	Quantity	Profit/Loss	Total
1									
2									
3									
4									
5									
6									
7									
8									
9									
10									

Total Trades	Winning Trades	Losing Trades	Win Rate %

Notes

DATE:_____ ACCOUNT BALANCE:_____

TRADING POWDER:_____ MAXIMUM RISK AMOUNT PER TRADE:_____

DAILY GOAL: _____

MARKET ANALYSIS

Check the momentum of the market based on Key Indices, Commodities, and ETFs.

Type of Market Day	Key Indices and Commodities					
	S&P 500	Dow 30	Nasdaq	Russell 2000	Crude Oil	Gold
GREEN						
RED						

INDICATORS OVERVIEW

	Ticker Symbol																	
Indicators	5M	15M	30M	1HR	4HR	1D	5M	15M	30M	1HR	4HR	1D	5M	15M	30M	1HR	4HR	1D
Moving Averages																		
5 day																		
9 day																		
50 day																		
100 day																		
200 day																		
Bollinger Bands																		
Upper Band																		
Lower Band																		
DMI																		
Bullish																		
Bearish																		
MACD																		
Bullish																		
Bearish																		
RSI																		
Overbought																		
Oversold																		
Stochastic																		
Overbought																		
Oversold																		

Company Ticker	Chart Momentum																
	5 MIN			15 MIN			30 MIN			1 HR			4 HR			1 DAY		

Instrument(s) Traded	Hard Shares		Options		Forex		Crypto		
Trade #	Entry Time	Exit Time	Time Elapsed	Buy/Call Sell/Put	Entry Price	Exit Price	Quantity	Profit/Loss	Total
1									
2									
3									
4									
5									
6									
7									
8									
9									
10									

Total Trades	Winning Trades	Losing Trades	Win Rate %

Notes

DATE:_____   ACCOUNT BALANCE:_____

TRADING POWDER:_____   MAXIMUM RISK AMOUNT PER TRADE:_____

DAILY GOAL: _____

MARKET ANALYSIS

Check the momentum of the market based on Key Indices, Commodities, and ETFs.

Type of Market Day	Key Indices and Commodities					
	S&P 500	Dow 30	Nasdaq	Russell 2000	Crude Oil	Gold
GREEN						
RED						

INDICATORS OVERVIEW

	Ticker Symbol																	
Indicators	5M	15M	30M	1HR	4HR	1D	5M	15M	30M	1HR	4HR	1D	5M	15M	30M	1HR	4HR	1D
Moving Averages																		
5 day																		
9 day																		
50 day																		
100 day																		
200 day																		
Bollinger Bands																		
Upper Band																		
Lower Band																		
DMI																		
Bullish																		
Bearish																		
MACD																		
Bullish																		
Bearish																		
RSI																		
Overbought																		
Oversold																		
Stochastic																		
Overbought																		
Oversold																		

Company Ticker	Chart Momentum																
	5 MIN			15 MIN			30 MIN			1 HR			4 HR			1 DAY		

Instrument(s) Traded	Hard Shares		Options		Forex		Crypto		
Trade #	Entry Time	Exit TIme	Time Elapsed	Buy/Call Sell/Put	Entry Price	Exit Price	Quantity	Profit/Loss	Total
1									
2									
3									
4									
5									
6									
7									
8									
9									
10									

Total Trades	Winning Trades	Losing Trades	Win Rate %

Notes

DATE:_____   ACCOUNT BALANCE:_____

TRADING POWDER:_____   MAXIMUM RISK AMOUNT PER TRADE:_____

DAILY GOAL: _____

MARKET ANALYSIS

Check the momentum of the market based on Key Indices, Commodities, and ETFs.

Type of Market Day	Key Indices and Commodities					
	S&P 500	Dow 30	Nasdaq	Russell 2000	Crude Oil	Gold
GREEN						
RED						

INDICATORS OVERVIEW

	Ticker Symbol																	
Indicators	5M	15M	30M	1HR	4HR	1D	5M	15M	30M	1HR	4HR	1D	5M	15M	30M	1HR	4HR	1D
Moving Averages																		
5 day																		
9 day																		
50 day																		
100 day																		
200 day																		
Bollinger Bands																		
Upper Band																		
Lower Band																		
DMI																		
Bullish																		
Bearish																		
MACD																		
Bullish																		
Bearish																		
RSI																		
Overbought																		
Oversold																		
Stochastic																		
Overbought																		
Oversold																		

Company Ticker	Chart Momentum																
	5 MIN			15 MIN			30 MIN			1 HR			4 HR			1 DAY		

Instrument(s) Traded	Hard Shares		Options		Forex		Crypto		
Trade #	Entry Time	Exit Time	Time Elapsed	Buy/Call Sell/Put	Entry Price	Exit Price	Quantity	Profit/Loss	Total
1									
2									
3									
4									
5									
6									
7									
8									
9									
10									

Total Trades	Winning Trades	Losing Trades	Win Rate %

Notes

DATE:_____   **ACCOUNT BALANCE:**_____

TRADING POWDER:_____   **MAXIMUM RISK AMOUNT PER TRADE:**_____

DAILY GOAL: _____

MARKET ANALYSIS

Check the momentum of the market based on Key Indices, Commodities, and ETFs.

Type of Market Day	Key Indices and Commodities					
	S&P 500	Dow 30	Nasdaq	Russell 2000	Crude Oil	Gold
GREEN						
RED						

INDICATORS OVERVIEW

	Ticker Symbol																	
Indicators	5M	15M	30M	1HR	4HR	1D	5M	15M	30M	1HR	4HR	1D	5M	15M	30M	1HR	4HR	1D
Moving Averages																		
5 day																		
9 day																		
50 day																		
100 day																		
200 day																		
Bollinger Bands																		
Upper Band																		
Lower Band																		
DMI																		
Bullish																		
Bearish																		
MACD																		
Bullish																		
Bearish																		
RSI																		
Overbought																		
Oversold																		
Stochastic																		
Overbought																		
Oversold																		

Company Ticker	Chart Momentum												
	5 MIN			15 MIN			30 MIN			1 HR		4 HR	1 DAY

Instrument(s) Traded	Hard Shares		Options		Forex		Crypto		
Trade #	Entry Time	Exit Time	Time Elapsed	Buy/Call Sell/Put	Entry Price	Exit Price	Quantity	Profit/Loss	Total
1									
2									
3									
4									
5									
6									
7									
8									
9									
10									

Total Trades	Winning Trades	Losing Trades	Win Rate %

Notes

DATE:_____   ACCOUNT BALANCE:_____

TRADING POWDER:_____   MAXIMUM RISK AMOUNT PER TRADE:_____

DAILY GOAL: _____

MARKET ANALYSIS

Check the momentum of the market based on Key Indices, Commodities, and ETFs.

Type of Market Day	Key Indices and Commodities					
	S&P 500	Dow 30	Nasdaq	Russell 2000	Crude Oil	Gold
GREEN						
RED						

INDICATORS OVERVIEW

	Ticker Symbol																	
Indicators	5M	15M	30M	1HR	4HR	1D	5M	15M	30M	1HR	4HR	1D	5M	15M	30M	1HR	4HR	1D
Moving Averages																		
5 day																		
9 day																		
50 day																		
100 day																		
200 day																		
Bollinger Bands																		
Upper Band																		
Lower Band																		
DMI																		
Bullish																		
Bearish																		
MACD																		
Bullish																		
Bearish																		
RSI																		
Overbought																		
Oversold																		
Stochastic																		
Overbought																		
Oversold																		

Company Ticker	Chart Momentum												
	5 MIN		15 MIN		30 MIN		1 HR		4 HR		1 DAY		

Instrument(s) Traded	Hard Shares		Options		Forex		Crypto			
Trade #	Entry Time	Exit Time	Time Elapsed	Buy/Call Sell/Put	Entry Price	Exit Price	Quantity	Profit/Loss	Total
1									
2									
3									
4									
5									
6									
7									
8									
9									
10									

Total Trades	Winning Trades	Losing Trades	Win Rate %

Notes

DATE:_____   ACCOUNT BALANCE:_____

TRADING POWDER:_____   MAXIMUM RISK AMOUNT PER TRADE:_____

DAILY GOAL: _____

MARKET ANALYSIS

Check the momentum of the market based on Key Indices, Commodities, and ETFs.

Type of Market Day	Key Indices and Commodities					
	S&P 500	Dow 30	Nasdaq	Russell 2000	Crude Oil	Gold
GREEN						
RED						

INDICATORS OVERVIEW

	Ticker Symbol																	
Indicators	5M	15M	30M	1HR	4HR	1D	5M	15M	30M	1HR	4HR	1D	5M	15M	30M	1HR	4HR	1D
Moving Averages																		
5 day																		
9 day																		
50 day																		
100 day																		
200 day																		
Bollinger Bands																		
Upper Band																		
Lower Band																		
DMI																		
Bullish																		
Bearish																		
MACD																		
Bullish																		
Bearish																		
RSI																		
Overbought																		
Oversold																		
Stochastic																		
Overbought																		
Oversold																		

Company Ticker	Chart Momentum											
	5 MIN		15 MIN		30 MIN		1 HR		4 HR		1 DAY	

Instrument(s) Traded	Hard Shares		Options		Forex		Crypto		
Trade #	Entry Time	Exit Time	Time Elapsed	Buy/Call Sell/Put	Entry Price	Exit Price	Quantity	Profit/Loss	Total
1									
2									
3									
4									
5									
6									
7									
8									
9									
10									

Total Trades	Winning Trades	Losing Trades	Win Rate %

Notes

DATE:_____   ACCOUNT BALANCE:_____

TRADING POWDER:_____   MAXIMUM RISK AMOUNT PER TRADE:_____

DAILY GOAL: _____

MARKET ANALYSIS

Check the momentum of the market based on Key Indices, Commodities, and ETFs.

Type of Market Day	Key Indices and Commodities					
	S&P 500	Dow 30	Nasdaq	Russell 2000	Crude Oil	Gold
GREEN						
RED						

INDICATORS OVERVIEW

	Ticker Symbol																	
Indicators	5M	15M	30M	1HR	4HR	1D	5M	15M	30M	1HR	4HR	1D	5M	15M	30M	1HR	4HR	1D
Moving Averages																		
5 day																		
9 day																		
50 day																		
100 day																		
200 day																		
Bollinger Bands																		
Upper Band																		
Lower Band																		
DMI																		
Bullish																		
Bearish																		
MACD																		
Bullish																		
Bearish																		
RSI																		
Overbought																		
Oversold																		
Stochastic																		
Overbought																		
Oversold																		

Company Ticker	Chart Momentum											
	5 MIN		15 MIN		30 MIN		1 HR		4 HR		1 DAY	

Instrument(s) Traded	Hard Shares		Options		Forex		Crypto			
Trade #	Entry Time	Exit Time	Time Elapsed	Buy/Call Sell/Put	Entry Price	Exit Price	Quantity	Profit/Loss	Total
1									
2									
3									
4									
5									
6									
7									
8									
9									
10									

Total Trades	Winning Trades	Losing Trades	Win Rate %

Notes

DATE:_____   ACCOUNT BALANCE:_____

TRADING POWDER:_____   MAXIMUM RISK AMOUNT PER TRADE:_____

DAILY GOAL: _____

MARKET ANALYSIS

Check the momentum of the market based on Key Indices, Commodities, and ETFs.

Type of Market Day	Key Indices and Commodities					
	S&P 500	Dow 30	Nasdaq	Russell 2000	Crude Oil	Gold
GREEN						
RED						

INDICATORS OVERVIEW

	Ticker Symbol																	
Indicators	5M	15M	30M	1HR	4HR	1D	5M	15M	30M	1HR	4HR	1D	5M	15M	30M	1HR	4HR	1D
Moving Averages																		
5 day																		
9 day																		
50 day																		
100 day																		
200 day																		
Bollinger Bands																		
Upper Band																		
Lower Band																		
DMI																		
Bullish																		
Bearish																		
MACD																		
Bullish																		
Bearish																		
RSI																		
Overbought																		
Oversold																		
Stochastic																		
Overbought																		
Oversold																		

Company Ticker	Chart Momentum																
	5 MIN			15 MIN			30 MIN			1 HR			4 HR			1 DAY		

Instrument(s) Traded	Hard Shares		Options		Forex		Crypto		
Trade #	Entry Time	Exit Time	Time Elapsed	Buy/Call Sell/Put	Entry Price	Exit Price	Quantity	Profit/Loss	Total
1									
2									
3									
4									
5									
6									
7									
8									
9									
10									

Total Trades	Winning Trades	Losing Trades	Win Rate %

Notes

DATE:_____   ACCOUNT BALANCE:_____

TRADING POWDER:_____   MAXIMUM RISK AMOUNT PER TRADE:_____

DAILY GOAL: _____

MARKET ANALYSIS

Check the momentum of the market based on Key Indices, Commodities, and ETFs.

Type of Market Day	Key Indices and Commodities					
	S&P 500	Dow 30	Nasdaq	Russell 2000	Crude Oil	Gold
GREEN						
RED						

INDICATORS OVERVIEW

	Ticker Symbol																	
Indicators	5M	15M	30M	1HR	4HR	1D	5M	15M	30M	1HR	4HR	1D	5M	15M	30M	1HR	4HR	1D
Moving Averages																		
5 day																		
9 day																		
50 day																		
100 day																		
200 day																		
Bollinger Bands																		
Upper Band																		
Lower Band																		
DMI																		
Bullish																		
Bearish																		
MACD																		
Bullish																		
Bearish																		
RSI																		
Overbought																		
Oversold																		
Stochastic																		
Overbought																		
Oversold																		

Company Ticker	Chart Momentum												
	5 MIN		15 MIN		30 MIN		1 HR		4 HR		1 DAY		

Instrument(s) Traded	Hard Shares		Options		Forex		Crypto			
Trade #	Entry Time	Exit Time	Time Elapsed	Buy/Call Sell/Put	Entry Price	Exit Price	Quantity	Profit/Loss	Total
1									
2									
3									
4									
5									
6									
7									
8									
9									
10									

Total Trades	Winning Trades	Losing Trades	Win Rate %

Notes

DATE:_____   ACCOUNT BALANCE:_____

TRADING POWDER:_____   MAXIMUM RISK AMOUNT PER TRADE:_____

DAILY GOAL: _____

MARKET ANALYSIS

Check the momentum of the market based on Key Indices, Commodities, and ETFs.

Type of Market Day	Key Indices and Commodities					
	S&P 500	Dow 30	Nasdaq	Russell 2000	Crude Oil	Gold
GREEN						
RED						

INDICATORS OVERVIEW

	Ticker Symbol																	
Indicators	5M	15M	30M	1HR	4HR	1D	5M	15M	30M	1HR	4HR	1D	5M	15M	30M	1HR	4HR	1D
Moving Averages																		
5 day																		
9 day																		
50 day																		
100 day																		
200 day																		
Bollinger Bands																		
Upper Band																		
Lower Band																		
DMI																		
Bullish																		
Bearish																		
MACD																		
Bullish																		
Bearish																		
RSI																		
Overbought																		
Oversold																		
Stochastic																		
Overbought																		
Oversold																		

Company Ticker	Chart Momentum																
	5 MIN			15 MIN			30 MIN			1 HR			4 HR			1 DAY		

Instrument(s) Traded	Hard Shares		Options		Forex		Crypto		
Trade #	Entry Time	Exit Time	Time Elapsed	Buy/Call Sell/Put	Entry Price	Exit Price	Quantity	Profit/Loss	Total
1									
2									
3									
4									
5									
6									
7									
8									
9									
10									

Total Trades	Winning Trades	Losing Trades	Win Rate %

Notes

DATE:_____   ACCOUNT BALANCE:_____

TRADING POWDER:_____   MAXIMUM RISK AMOUNT PER TRADE:_____

DAILY GOAL: _____

MARKET ANALYSIS

Check the momentum of the market based on Key Indices, Commodities, and ETFs.

Type of Market Day	Key Indices and Commodities					
	S&P 500	Dow 30	Nasdaq	Russell 2000	Crude Oil	Gold
GREEN						
RED						

INDICATORS OVERVIEW

	Ticker Symbol																	
Indicators	5M	15M	30M	1HR	4HR	1D	5M	15M	30M	1HR	4HR	1D	5M	15M	30M	1HR	4HR	1D
Moving Averages																		
5 day																		
9 day																		
50 day																		
100 day																		
200 day																		
Bollinger Bands																		
Upper Band																		
Lower Band																		
DMI																		
Bullish																		
Bearish																		
MACD																		
Bullish																		
Bearish																		
RSI																		
Overbought																		
Oversold																		
Stochastic																		
Overbought																		
Oversold																		

Company Ticker	Chart Momentum																
	5 MIN			15 MIN			30 MIN			1 HR			4 HR			1 DAY		

Instrument(s) Traded	Hard Shares		Options		Forex		Crypto		
Trade #	Entry Time	Exit Time	Time Elapsed	Buy/Call Sell/Put	Entry Price	Exit Price	Quantity	Profit/Loss	Total
1									
2									
3									
4									
5									
6									
7									
8									
9									
10									

Total Trades	Winning Trades	Losing Trades	Win Rate %

Notes

DATE:_____   ACCOUNT BALANCE:_____

TRADING POWDER:_____   MAXIMUM RISK AMOUNT PER TRADE:_____

DAILY GOAL: _____

MARKET ANALYSIS

Check the momentum of the market based on Key Indices, Commodities, and ETFs.

Type of Market Day	Key Indices and Commodities					
	S&P 500	Dow 30	Nasdaq	Russell 2000	Crude Oil	Gold
GREEN						
RED						

INDICATORS OVERVIEW

	Ticker Symbol																	
Indicators	5M	15M	30M	1HR	4HR	1D	5M	15M	30M	1HR	4HR	1D	5M	15M	30M	1HR	4HR	1D
Moving Averages																		
5 day																		
9 day																		
50 day																		
100 day																		
200 day																		
Bollinger Bands																		
Upper Band																		
Lower Band																		
DMI																		
Bullish																		
Bearish																		
MACD																		
Bullish																		
Bearish																		
RSI																		
Overbought																		
Oversold																		
Stochastic																		
Overbought																		
Oversold																		

Company Ticker	Chart Momentum																
	5 MIN			15 MIN			30 MIN			1 HR			4 HR			1 DAY		

Instrument(s) Traded	Hard Shares		Options		Forex		Crypto		
Trade #	Entry Time	Exit Time	Time Elapsed	Buy/Call Sell/Put	Entry Price	Exit Price	Quantity	Profit/Loss	Total
1									
2									
3									
4									
5									
6									
7									
8									
9									
10									

Total Trades	Winning Trades	Losing Trades	Win Rate %

Notes

DATE:_____   ACCOUNT BALANCE:_____

TRADING POWDER:_____   MAXIMUM RISK AMOUNT PER TRADE:_____

DAILY GOAL: _____

MARKET ANALYSIS

Check the momentum of the market based on Key Indices, Commodities, and ETFs.

Type of Market Day	Key Indices and Commodities					
	S&P 500	Dow 30	Nasdaq	Russell 2000	Crude Oil	Gold
GREEN						
RED						

INDICATORS OVERVIEW

	Ticker Symbol																	
Indicators	5M	15M	30M	1HR	4HR	1D	5M	15M	30M	1HR	4HR	1D	5M	15M	30M	1HR	4HR	1D
Moving Averages																		
5 day																		
9 day																		
50 day																		
100 day																		
200 day																		
Bollinger Bands																		
Upper Band																		
Lower Band																		
DMI																		
Bullish																		
Bearish																		
MACD																		
Bullish																		
Bearish																		
RSI																		
Overbought																		
Oversold																		
Stochastic																		
Overbought																		
Oversold																		

Company Ticker	Chart Momentum											
	5 MIN		15 MIN		30 MIN		1 HR		4 HR		1 DAY	

Instrument(s) Traded	Hard Shares		Options		Forex		Crypto		
Trade #	Entry Time	Exit Time	Time Elapsed	Buy/Call Sell/Put	Entry Price	Exit Price	Quantity	Profit/Loss	Total
1									
2									
3									
4									
5									
6									
7									
8									
9									
10									

Total Trades	Winning Trades	Losing Trades	Win Rate %

Notes

DATE:_____   ACCOUNT BALANCE:_____

TRADING POWDER:_____   MAXIMUM RISK AMOUNT PER TRADE:_____

DAILY GOAL: _____

MARKET ANALYSIS

Check the momentum of the market based on Key Indices, Commodities, and ETFs.

Type of Market Day	Key Indices and Commodities					
	S&P 500	Dow 30	Nasdaq	Russell 2000	Crude Oil	Gold
GREEN						
RED						

INDICATORS OVERVIEW

	Ticker Symbol																	
Indicators	5M	15M	30M	1HR	4HR	1D	5M	15M	30M	1HR	4HR	1D	5M	15M	30M	1HR	4HR	1D
Moving Averages																		
5 day																		
9 day																		
50 day																		
100 day																		
200 day																		
Bollinger Bands																		
Upper Band																		
Lower Band																		
DMI																		
Bullish																		
Bearish																		
MACD																		
Bullish																		
Bearish																		
RSI																		
Overbought																		
Oversold																		
Stochastic																		
Overbought																		
Oversold																		

Company Ticker	Chart Momentum											
	5 MIN			15 MIN			30 MIN		1 HR		4 HR	1 DAY

Instrument(s) Traded	Hard Shares		Options		Forex		Crypto			
Trade #	Entry Time	Exit Time	Time Elapsed	Buy/Call Sell/Put	Entry Price	Exit Price	Quantity	Profit/Loss	Total
1									
2									
3									
4									
5									
6									
7									
8									
9									
10									

Total Trades	Winning Trades	Losing Trades	Win Rate %

Notes

DATE:_____   **ACCOUNT BALANCE:**_____

TRADING POWDER:_____   **MAXIMUM RISK AMOUNT PER TRADE:**_____

DAILY GOAL: _____

MARKET ANALYSIS

Check the momentum of the market based on Key Indices, Commodities, and ETFs.

Type of Market Day	Key Indices and Commodities					
	S&P 500	Dow 30	Nasdaq	Russell 2000	Crude Oil	Gold
GREEN						
RED						

INDICATORS OVERVIEW

	Ticker Symbol																	
Indicators	5M	15M	30M	1HR	4HR	1D	5M	15M	30M	1HR	4HR	1D	5M	15M	30M	1HR	4HR	1D
Moving Averages																		
5 day																		
9 day																		
50 day																		
100 day																		
200 day																		
Bollinger Bands																		
Upper Band																		
Lower Band																		
DMI																		
Bullish																		
Bearish																		
MACD																		
Bullish																		
Bearish																		
RSI																		
Overbought																		
Oversold																		
Stochastic																		
Overbought																		
Oversold																		

Company Ticker	Chart Momentum																
	5 MIN			15 MIN			30 MIN			1 HR			4 HR			1 DAY		

Instrument(s) Traded	Hard Shares		Options		Forex		Crypto		
Trade #	Entry Time	Exit Time	Time Elapsed	Buy/Call Sell/Put	Entry Price	Exit Price	Quantity	Profit/Loss	Total
1									
2									
3									
4									
5									
6									
7									
8									
9									
10									

Total Trades	Winning Trades	Losing Trades	Win Rate %

Notes

DATE:_____   ACCOUNT BALANCE:_____

TRADING POWDER:_____   MAXIMUM RISK AMOUNT PER TRADE:_____

DAILY GOAL: _____

MARKET ANALYSIS

Check the momentum of the market based on Key Indices, Commodities, and ETFs.

Type of Market Day	Key Indices and Commodities					
	S&P 500	Dow 30	Nasdaq	Russell 2000	Crude Oil	Gold
GREEN						
RED						

INDICATORS OVERVIEW

	Ticker Symbol																	
Indicators	5M	15M	30M	1HR	4HR	1D	5M	15M	30M	1HR	4HR	1D	5M	15M	30M	1HR	4HR	1D
Moving Averages																		
5 day																		
9 day																		
50 day																		
100 day																		
200 day																		
Bollinger Bands																		
Upper Band																		
Lower Band																		
DMI																		
Bullish																		
Bearish																		
MACD																		
Bullish																		
Bearish																		
RSI																		
Overbought																		
Oversold																		
Stochastic																		
Overbought																		
Oversold																		

Company Ticker	Chart Momentum											
	5 MIN			15 MIN			30 MIN			1 HR		4 HR	1 DAY

Instrument(s) Traded	Hard Shares		Options		Forex		Crypto		
Trade #	Entry Time	Exit Time	Time Elapsed	Buy/Call Sell/Put	Entry Price	Exit Price	Quantity	Profit/Loss	Total
1									
2									
3									
4									
5									
6									
7									
8									
9									
10									

Total Trades	Winning Trades	Losing Trades	Win Rate %

Notes

DATE:_____   ACCOUNT BALANCE:_____

TRADING POWDER:_____   MAXIMUM RISK AMOUNT PER TRADE:_____

DAILY GOAL: _____

MARKET ANALYSIS

Check the momentum of the market based on Key Indices, Commodities, and ETFs.

Type of Market Day	Key Indices and Commodities					
	S&P 500	Dow 30	Nasdaq	Russell 2000	Crude Oil	Gold
GREEN						
RED						

INDICATORS OVERVIEW

	Ticker Symbol																	
Indicators	5M	15M	30M	1HR	4HR	1D	5M	15M	30M	1HR	4HR	1D	5M	15M	30M	1HR	4HR	1D
Moving Averages																		
5 day																		
9 day																		
50 day																		
100 day																		
200 day																		
Bollinger Bands																		
Upper Band																		
Lower Band																		
DMI																		
Bullish																		
Bearish																		
MACD																		
Bullish																		
Bearish																		
RSI																		
Overbought																		
Oversold																		
Stochastic																		
Overbought																		
Oversold																		

Company Ticker	Chart Momentum																
	5 MIN			15 MIN			30 MIN			1 HR			4 HR			1 DAY		

Instrument(s) Traded	Hard Shares		Options		Forex		Crypto		
Trade #	Entry Time	Exit Time	Time Elapsed	Buy/Call Sell/Put	Entry Price	Exit Price	Quantity	Profit/Loss	Total
1									
2									
3									
4									
5									
6									
7									
8									
9									
10									

Total Trades	Winning Trades	Losing Trades	Win Rate %

Notes

DATE:_____

ACCOUNT BALANCE:_____

TRADING POWDER:_____

MAXIMUM RISK AMOUNT PER TRADE:_____

DAILY GOAL: _____

MARKET ANALYSIS

Check the momentum of the market based on Key Indices, Commodities, and ETFs.

Type of Market Day	Key Indices and Commodities					
	S&P 500	Dow 30	Nasdaq	Russell 2000	Crude Oil	Gold
GREEN						
RED						

INDICATORS OVERVIEW

	Ticker Symbol																	
Indicators	5M	15M	30M	1HR	4HR	1D	5M	15M	30M	1HR	4HR	1D	5M	15M	30M	1HR	4HR	1D
Moving Averages																		
5 day																		
9 day																		
50 day																		
100 day																		
200 day																		
Bollinger Bands																		
Upper Band																		
Lower Band																		
DMI																		
Bullish																		
Bearish																		
MACD																		
Bullish																		
Bearish																		
RSI																		
Overbought																		
Oversold																		
Stochastic																		
Overbought																		
Oversold																		

Company Ticker	Chart Momentum												
	5 MIN		15 MIN		30 MIN		1 HR		4 HR		1 DAY		

Instrument(s) Traded	Hard Shares		Options		Forex		Crypto			
Trade #	Entry Time	Exit Time	Time Elapsed	Buy/Call Sell/Put	Entry Price	Exit Price	Quantity	Profit/Loss	Total	
1										
2										
3										
4										
5										
6										
7										
8										
9										
10										

Total Trades	Winning Trades	Losing Trades	Win Rate %

Notes

DATE:_____   ACCOUNT BALANCE:_____

TRADING POWDER:_____   MAXIMUM RISK AMOUNT PER TRADE:_____

DAILY GOAL: _____

MARKET ANALYSIS

Check the momentum of the market based on Key Indices, Commodities, and ETFs.

Type of Market Day	Key Indices and Commodities					
	S&P 500	Dow 30	Nasdaq	Russell 2000	Crude Oil	Gold
GREEN						
RED						

INDICATORS OVERVIEW

	Ticker Symbol																
Indicators	5M	15M	30M	1HR	4HR	1D	5M	15M	30M	1HR	4HR	1D	5M	15M	30M	1HR	4HR	1D
Moving Averages																		
5 day																		
9 day																		
50 day																		
100 day																		
200 day																		
Bollinger Bands																		
Upper Band																		
Lower Band																		
DMI																		
Bullish																		
Bearish																		
MACD																		
Bullish																		
Bearish																		
RSI																		
Overbought																		
Oversold																		
Stochastic																		
Overbought																		
Oversold																		

Company Ticker	Chart Momentum																
	5 MIN			15 MIN			30 MIN			1 HR			4 HR			1 DAY		

Instrument(s) Traded	Hard Shares		Options		Forex		Crypto		
Trade #	Entry Time	Exit Time	Time Elapsed	Buy/Call Sell/Put	Entry Price	Exit Price	Quantity	Profit/Loss	Total
1									
2									
3									
4									
5									
6									
7									
8									
9									
10									

Total Trades	Winning Trades	Losing Trades	Win Rate %

Notes

DATE:_____ ACCOUNT BALANCE:_____

TRADING POWDER:_____ MAXIMUM RISK AMOUNT PER TRADE:_____

DAILY GOAL: _____

MARKET ANALYSIS

Check the momentum of the market based on Key Indices, Commodities, and ETFs.

Type of Market Day	Key Indices and Commodities					
	S&P 500	Dow 30	Nasdaq	Russell 2000	Crude Oil	Gold
GREEN						
RED						

INDICATORS OVERVIEW

	Ticker Symbol																	
Indicators	5M	15M	30M	1HR	4HR	1D	5M	15M	30M	1HR	4HR	1D	5M	15M	30M	1HR	4HR	1D
Moving Averages																		
5 day																		
9 day																		
50 day																		
100 day																		
200 day																		
Bollinger Bands																		
Upper Band																		
Lower Band																		
DMI																		
Bullish																		
Bearish																		
MACD																		
Bullish																		
Bearish																		
RSI																		
Overbought																		
Oversold																		
Stochastic																		
Overbought																		
Oversold																		

Company Ticker	Chart Momentum																
	5 MIN			15 MIN			30 MIN			1 HR			4 HR			1 DAY		

Instrument(s) Traded	Hard Shares		Options		Forex		Crypto		
Trade #	Entry Time	Exit Time	Time Elapsed	Buy/Call Sell/Put	Entry Price	Exit Price	Quantity	Profit/Loss	Total
1									
2									
3									
4									
5									
6									
7									
8									
9									
10									

Total Trades	Winning Trades	Losing Trades	Win Rate %

Notes

DATE:_____

ACCOUNT BALANCE:_____

TRADING POWDER:_____

MAXIMUM RISK AMOUNT PER TRADE:_____

DAILY GOAL: _____

MARKET ANALYSIS

Check the momentum of the market based on Key Indices, Commodities, and ETFs.

Type of Market Day	Key Indices and Commodities					
	S&P 500	Dow 30	Nasdaq	Russell 2000	Crude Oil	Gold
GREEN						
RED						

INDICATORS OVERVIEW

	Ticker Symbol																	
Indicators	5M	15M	30M	1HR	4HR	1D	5M	15M	30M	1HR	4HR	1D	5M	15M	30M	1HR	4HR	1D
Moving Averages																		
5 day																		
9 day																		
50 day																		
100 day																		
200 day																		
Bollinger Bands																		
Upper Band																		
Lower Band																		
DMI																		
Bullish																		
Bearish																		
MACD																		
Bullish																		
Bearish																		
RSI																		
Overbought																		
Oversold																		
Stochastic																		
Overbought																		
Oversold																		

Company Ticker	Chart Momentum																
	5 MIN			15 MIN			30 MIN			1 HR			4 HR			1 DAY		

Instrument(s) Traded	Hard Shares		Options		Forex		Crypto		
Trade #	Entry Time	Exit Time	Time Elapsed	Buy/Call Sell/Put	Entry Price	Exit Price	Quantity	Profit/Loss	Total
1									
2									
3									
4									
5									
6									
7									
8									
9									
10									

Total Trades	Winning Trades	Losing Trades	Win Rate %

Notes

DATE:_____   **ACCOUNT BALANCE:**_____

TRADING POWDER:_____   **MAXIMUM RISK AMOUNT PER TRADE:**_____

DAILY GOAL:_____

MARKET ANALYSIS

Check the momentum of the market based on Key Indices, Commodities, and ETFs.

Type of Market Day	Key Indices and Commodities					
	S&P 500	Dow 30	Nasdaq	Russell 2000	Crude Oil	Gold
GREEN						
RED						

INDICATORS OVERVIEW

	Ticker Symbol																	
Indicators	5M	15M	30M	1HR	4HR	1D	5M	15M	30M	1HR	4HR	1D	5M	15M	30M	1HR	4HR	1D
Moving Averages																		
5 day																		
9 day																		
50 day																		
100 day																		
200 day																		
Bollinger Bands																		
Upper Band																		
Lower Band																		
DMI																		
Bullish																		
Bearish																		
MACD																		
Bullish																		
Bearish																		
RSI																		
Overbought																		
Oversold																		
Stochastic																		
Overbought																		
Oversold																		

Company Ticker	Chart Momentum																	
	5 MIN			15 MIN			30 MIN			1 HR			4 HR			1 DAY		

Instrument(s) Traded	Hard Shares		Options		Forex		Crypto		
Trade #	Entry Time	Exit Time	Time Elapsed	Buy/Call Sell/Put	Entry Price	Exit Price	Quantity	Profit/Loss	Total
1									
2									
3									
4									
5									
6									
7									
8									
9									
10									

Total Trades	Winning Trades	Losing Trades	Win Rate %

Notes

DATE:_____   ACCOUNT BALANCE:_____

TRADING POWDER:_____   MAXIMUM RISK AMOUNT PER TRADE:_____

DAILY GOAL:_____

MARKET ANALYSIS

Check the momentum of the market based on Key Indices, Commodities, and ETFs.

Type of Market Day	Key Indices and Commodities					
	S&P 500	Dow 30	Nasdaq	Russell 2000	Crude Oil	Gold
GREEN						
RED						

INDICATORS OVERVIEW

	Ticker Symbol																	
Indicators	5M	15M	30M	1HR	4HR	1D	5M	15M	30M	1HR	4HR	1D	5M	15M	30M	1HR	4HR	1D
Moving Averages																		
5 day																		
9 day																		
50 day																		
100 day																		
200 day																		
Bollinger Bands																		
Upper Band																		
Lower Band																		
DMI																		
Bullish																		
Bearish																		
MACD																		
Bullish																		
Bearish																		
RSI																		
Overbought																		
Oversold																		
Stochastic																		
Overbought																		
Oversold																		

Company Ticker	Chart Momentum												
	5 MIN		15 MIN		30 MIN		1 HR		4 HR		1 DAY		

Instrument(s) Traded	Hard Shares		Options		Forex		Crypto		
Trade #	Entry Time	Exit Time	Time Elapsed	Buy/Call Sell/Put	Entry Price	Exit Price	Quantity	Profit/Loss	Total
1									
2									
3									
4									
5									
6									
7									
8									
9									
10									

Total Trades	Winning Trades	Losing Trades	Win Rate %

Notes

DATE:_____

ACCOUNT BALANCE:_____

TRADING POWDER:_____

MAXIMUM RISK AMOUNT PER TRADE:_____

DAILY GOAL:_____

MARKET ANALYSIS

Check the momentum of the market based on Key Indices, Commodities, and ETFs.

Type of Market Day	Key Indices and Commodities					
	S&P 500	Dow 30	Nasdaq	Russell 2000	Crude Oil	Gold
GREEN						
RED						

INDICATORS OVERVIEW

	Ticker Symbol																	
Indicators	5M	15M	30M	1HR	4HR	1D	5M	15M	30M	1HR	4HR	1D	5M	15M	30M	1HR	4HR	1D
Moving Averages																		
5 day																		
9 day																		
50 day																		
100 day																		
200 day																		
Bollinger Bands																		
Upper Band																		
Lower Band																		
DMI																		
Bullish																		
Bearish																		
MACD																		
Bullish																		
Bearish																		
RSI																		
Overbought																		
Oversold																		
Stochastic																		
Overbought																		
Oversold																		

Company Ticker	Chart Momentum																
	5 MIN			15 MIN			30 MIN			1 HR			4 HR			1 DAY		

Instrument(s) Traded	Hard Shares		Options		Forex		Crypto		
Trade #	Entry Time	Exit Time	Time Elapsed	Buy/Call Sell/Put	Entry Price	Exit Price	Quantity	Profit/Loss	Total
1									
2									
3									
4									
5									
6									
7									
8									
9									
10									

Total Trades	Winning Trades	Losing Trades	Win Rate %

Notes

DATE:_____   **ACCOUNT BALANCE:**_____

TRADING POWDER:_____   **MAXIMUM RISK AMOUNT PER TRADE:**_____

DAILY GOAL: _____

MARKET ANALYSIS

Check the momentum of the market based on Key Indices, Commodities, and ETFs.

Type of Market Day	Key Indices and Commodities					
	S&P 500	Dow 30	Nasdaq	Russell 2000	Crude Oil	Gold
GREEN						
RED						

INDICATORS OVERVIEW

	Ticker Symbol																	
Indicators	5M	15M	30M	1HR	4HR	1D	5M	15M	30M	1HR	4HR	1D	5M	15M	30M	1HR	4HR	1D
Moving Averages																		
5 day																		
9 day																		
50 day																		
100 day																		
200 day																		
Bollinger Bands																		
Upper Band																		
Lower Band																		
DMI																		
Bullish																		
Bearish																		
MACD																		
Bullish																		
Bearish																		
RSI																		
Overbought																		
Oversold																		
Stochastic																		
Overbought																		
Oversold																		

Company Ticker	Chart Momentum											
	5 MIN		15 MIN		30 MIN		1 HR		4 HR		1 DAY	

Instrument(s) Traded	Hard Shares		Options		Forex		Crypto			
Trade #	Entry Time	Exit Time	Time Elapsed	Buy/Call Sell/Put	Entry Price	Exit Price	Quantity	Profit/Loss	Total	
1										
2										
3										
4										
5										
6										
7										
8										
9										
10										

Total Trades	Winning Trades	Losing Trades	Win Rate %

Notes

DATE:_____   ACCOUNT BALANCE:_____

TRADING POWDER:_____   MAXIMUM RISK AMOUNT PER TRADE:_____

DAILY GOAL: _____

MARKET ANALYSIS

Check the momentum of the market based on Key Indices, Commodities, and ETFs.

Type of Market Day	Key Indices and Commodities					
	S&P 500	Dow 30	Nasdaq	Russell 2000	Crude Oil	Gold
GREEN						
RED						

INDICATORS OVERVIEW

	Ticker Symbol																	
Indicators	5M	15M	30M	1HR	4HR	1D	5M	15M	30M	1HR	4HR	1D	5M	15M	30M	1HR	4HR	1D
Moving Averages																		
5 day																		
9 day																		
50 day																		
100 day																		
200 day																		
Bollinger Bands																		
Upper Band																		
Lower Band																		
DMI																		
Bullish																		
Bearish																		
MACD																		
Bullish																		
Bearish																		
RSI																		
Overbought																		
Oversold																		
Stochastic																		
Overbought																		
Oversold																		

Company Ticker	Chart Momentum																
	5 MIN			15 MIN			30 MIN			1 HR			4 HR			1 DAY		

Instrument(s) Traded	Hard Shares		Options		Forex		Crypto		
Trade #	Entry Time	Exit Time	Time Elapsed	Buy/Call Sell/Put	Entry Price	Exit Price	Quantity	Profit/Loss	Total
1									
2									
3									
4									
5									
6									
7									
8									
9									
10									

Total Trades	Winning Trades	Losing Trades	Win Rate %

Notes

DATE:_____   ACCOUNT BALANCE:_____

TRADING POWDER:_____   MAXIMUM RISK AMOUNT PER TRADE:_____

DAILY GOAL: _____

MARKET ANALYSIS

Check the momentum of the market based on Key Indices, Commodities, and ETFs.

Type of Market Day	Key Indices and Commodities					
	S&P 500	Dow 30	Nasdaq	Russell 2000	Crude Oil	Gold
GREEN						
RED						

INDICATORS OVERVIEW

	Ticker Symbol																	
Indicators	5M	15M	30M	1HR	4HR	1D	5M	15M	30M	1HR	4HR	1D	5M	15M	30M	1HR	4HR	1D
Moving Averages																		
5 day																		
9 day																		
50 day																		
100 day																		
200 day																		
Bollinger Bands																		
Upper Band																		
Lower Band																		
DMI																		
Bullish																		
Bearish																		
MACD																		
Bullish																		
Bearish																		
RSI																		
Overbought																		
Oversold																		
Stochastic																		
Overbought																		
Oversold																		

Company Ticker	Chart Momentum					
	5 MIN	15 MIN	30 MIN	1 HR	4 HR	1 DAY

Instrument(s) Traded	Hard Shares		Options		Forex		Crypto		
Trade #	Entry Time	Exit Time	Time Elapsed	Buy/Call Sell/Put	Entry Price	Exit Price	Quantity	Profit/Loss	Total
1									
2									
3									
4									
5									
6									
7									
8									
9									
10									

Total Trades	Winning Trades	Losing Trades	Win Rate %

Notes

DATE:_____   ACCOUNT BALANCE:_____

TRADING POWDER:_____   MAXIMUM RISK AMOUNT PER TRADE:_____

DAILY GOAL: _____

MARKET ANALYSIS

Check the momentum of the market based on Key Indices, Commodities, and ETFs.

Type of Market Day	Key Indices and Commodities					
	S&P 500	Dow 30	Nasdaq	Russell 2000	Crude Oil	Gold
GREEN						
RED						

INDICATORS OVERVIEW

	Ticker Symbol																	
Indicators	5M	15M	30M	1HR	4HR	1D	5M	15M	30M	1HR	4HR	1D	5M	15M	30M	1HR	4HR	1D
Moving Averages																		
5 day																		
9 day																		
50 day																		
100 day																		
200 day																		
Bollinger Bands																		
Upper Band																		
Lower Band																		
DMI																		
Bullish																		
Bearish																		
MACD																		
Bullish																		
Bearish																		
RSI																		
Overbought																		
Oversold																		
Stochastic																		
Overbought																		
Oversold																		

Company Ticker	Chart Momentum																
	5 MIN			15 MIN			30 MIN			1 HR			4 HR			1 DAY		

Instrument(s) Traded	Hard Shares		Options		Forex		Crypto		
Trade #	Entry Time	Exit Time	Time Elapsed	Buy/Call Sell/Put	Entry Price	Exit Price	Quantity	Profit/Loss	Total
1									
2									
3									
4									
5									
6									
7									
8									
9									
10									

Total Trades	Winning Trades	Losing Trades	Win Rate %

Notes

DATE:_____   ACCOUNT BALANCE:_____

TRADING POWDER:_____   MAXIMUM RISK AMOUNT PER TRADE:_____

DAILY GOAL: _____

MARKET ANALYSIS

Check the momentum of the market based on Key Indices, Commodities, and ETFs.

Type of Market Day	Key Indices and Commodities					
	S&P 500	Dow 30	Nasdaq	Russell 2000	Crude Oil	Gold
GREEN						
RED						

INDICATORS OVERVIEW

	Ticker Symbol																	
Indicators	5M	15M	30M	1HR	4HR	1D	5M	15M	30M	1HR	4HR	1D	5M	15M	30M	1HR	4HR	1D
Moving Averages																		
5 day																		
9 day																		
50 day																		
100 day																		
200 day																		
Bollinger Bands																		
Upper Band																		
Lower Band																		
DMI																		
Bullish																		
Bearish																		
MACD																		
Bullish																		
Bearish																		
RSI																		
Overbought																		
Oversold																		
Stochastic																		
Overbought																		
Oversold																		

Company Ticker	Chart Momentum																
	5 MIN			15 MIN			30 MIN			1 HR			4 HR			1 DAY		

Instrument(s) Traded	Hard Shares		Options		Forex		Crypto		
Trade #	Entry Time	Exit Time	Time Elapsed	Buy/Call Sell/Put	Entry Price	Exit Price	Quantity	Profit/Loss	Total
1									
2									
3									
4									
5									
6									
7									
8									
9									
10									

Total Trades	Winning Trades	Losing Trades	Win Rate %

Notes

DATE:_____   ACCOUNT BALANCE:_____

TRADING POWDER:_____   MAXIMUM RISK AMOUNT PER TRADE:_____

DAILY GOAL: _____

MARKET ANALYSIS

Check the momentum of the market based on Key Indices, Commodities, and ETFs.

Type of Market Day	Key Indices and Commodities					
	S&P 500	Dow 30	Nasdaq	Russell 2000	Crude Oil	Gold
GREEN						
RED						

INDICATORS OVERVIEW

| | Ticker Symbol | | | | | | | | | | | | | | | | | |
| | | | | | | | | | | | | | | | | | |
Indicators	5M	15M	30M	1HR	4HR	1D	5M	15M	30M	1HR	4HR	1D	5M	15M	30M	1HR	4HR	1D
Moving Averages																		
5 day																		
9 day																		
50 day																		
100 day																		
200 day																		
Bollinger Bands																		
Upper Band																		
Lower Band																		
DMI																		
Bullish																		
Bearish																		
MACD																		
Bullish																		
Bearish																		
RSI																		
Overbought																		
Oversold																		
Stochastic																		
Overbought																		
Oversold																		

Company Ticker	Chart Momentum																
	5 MIN			15 MIN			30 MIN			1 HR			4 HR			1 DAY		

Instrument(s) Traded	Hard Shares		Options		Forex		Crypto		
Trade #	Entry Time	Exit Time	Time Elapsed	Buy/Call Sell/Put	Entry Price	Exit Price	Quantity	Profit/Loss	Total
1									
2									
3									
4									
5									
6									
7									
8									
9									
10									

Total Trades	Winning Trades	Losing Trades	Win Rate %

Notes

DATE:_____ ACCOUNT BALANCE:_____

TRADING POWDER:_____ MAXIMUM RISK AMOUNT PER TRADE:_____

DAILY GOAL: _____

MARKET ANALYSIS

Check the momentum of the market based on Key Indices, Commodities, and ETFs.

Type of Market Day	Key Indices and Commodities					
	S&P 500	Dow 30	Nasdaq	Russell 2000	Crude Oil	Gold
GREEN						
RED						

INDICATORS OVERVIEW

	Ticker Symbol																	
Indicators	5M	15M	30M	1HR	4HR	1D	5M	15M	30M	1HR	4HR	1D	5M	15M	30M	1HR	4HR	1D
Moving Averages																		
5 day																		
9 day																		
50 day																		
100 day																		
200 day																		
Bollinger Bands																		
Upper Band																		
Lower Band																		
DMI																		
Bullish																		
Bearish																		
MACD																		
Bullish																		
Bearish																		
RSI																		
Overbought																		
Oversold																		
Stochastic																		
Overbought																		
Oversold																		

Company Ticker	Chart Momentum																
	5 MIN			15 MIN			30 MIN			1 HR			4 HR			1 DAY		

Instrument(s) Traded	Hard Shares		Options		Forex		Crypto		
Trade #	Entry Time	Exit Time	Time Elapsed	Buy/Call Sell/Put	Entry Price	Exit Price	Quantity	Profit/Loss	Total
1									
2									
3									
4									
5									
6									
7									
8									
9									
10									

Total Trades	Winning Trades	Losing Trades	Win Rate %

Notes

WEEKLY CALENDAR

Week	Start Date	End Date	Total Trades	Winning Trades	Losing Trades	Win Rate %	Start Balance	End Balance	Net Gain
1.									
2.									
3.									
4.									
5.									
6.									
7.									
8.									
9.									
10.									
11.									
12.									
13.									
14.									
15.									
16.									
17.									
18.									
19.									
20.									
21.									
22.									
23.									
24.									
25.									
26.									

WEEKLY CALENDAR

Week	Start Date	End Date	Total Trades	Winning Trades	Losing Trades	Win Rate %	Start Balance	End Balance	Net Gain
27.									
28.									
29.									
30.									
31.									
32.									
33.									
34.									
35.									
36.									
37.									
38.									
39.									
40.									
41.									
42.									
43.									
44.									
45.									
46.									
47.									
48.									
49.									
50.									
51.									
52.									

MONTHLY CALENDAR

Month	Start Date	End Date	Total Trades	Winning Trades	Losing Trades	Win Rate %	Start Balance	End Balance	Net Gain
1.									
2.									
3.									
4.									
5.									
6.									
7.									
8.									
9.									
10.									
11.									
12.									